Guide to Economic Indicators

Guide to Economic Indicators

4TH EDITION

Norman Frumkin

M.E.Sharpe
Armonk, New York
London, England

Library of Congress Cataloging-in-Publication Data

Frumkin, Norman.
    Guide to economic indicators / Norman Frumkin.—4th ed.
        p. cm.
    Includes bibliographical references and indexes.
    ISBN 0-7656-1646-7 (hardcover : alk. paper); 0-7656-1647-5 (pbk.: alk. paper)
    1. Economic indicators—United States. 2. Business cycles—United States—Statistics.
3. United States—Ecomomic conditions—Statistics. I. Title.

HC103.F9 2006
330.973'0021—dc22   2005013951

Printed in the United States of America

To Sarah, Jacob, Samuel, Susan, Isaac, Ann, Jonah

In memory of

Anne Frances Feldman Frumkin and Joseph Harry Frumkin

Contents

Tables, Formulas, and Figure

Tables

Formulas

Figure

Preface

Guide to Economic Indicators is a reference book that gives concise explanations of the meanings and uses of various macroeconomic indicators. The selected indicators reflect the overall domestic and international conditions of the American economy, as well as particular segments of it. They are prepared primarily by U.S. government agencies, with a small number prepared by private organizations.

The book explains the basic features of more than sixty statistical measures of the U.S. economy. It is meant for economists, students, investors, journalists, executives, and citizens interested in economic affairs. Readers who are interested in an overall perspective on economic indicators may find Chapter 1, "Attributes of Economic Indicators," in *Tracking America's Economy* helpful.[1]

This fourth edition updates the explanations of the indicators to include their characteristics as of mid-2005 and the historical data through 2004. It also expands the coverage by adding the following new indicators:

- Insured Unemployment
- Job Gains and Losses
- Job Openings and Labor Turnover
- House Prices: New and Existing Houses
- Housing Vacancy Rates
- Mortgage Loan Applications
- Selected Services Revenue

Other new topics are data sharing among U.S. government statistical agencies that prepare economic indicators (see below), the impact of labor force participation on unemployment (see Chapter 47, "Unemployment"), and the Appendix on sampling and nonsampling errors in statistical surveys.

The following indicators that were in the third edition are no longer provided by the source organizations and so are not included in this edition:

- Business Failures
- Business Starts
- Business Optimism Indexes
- Job Quality Index
- Experimental Recession Indexes (no longer provided on a real-time basis)
- Growth Cycles (provided in occasional papers, but not on a regular periodic schedule)

In addition, I have discontinued the Money Supply and the CRB Futures Price Index as economic indicators. In 2000, the Federal Reserve ended its inclusion of annual money supply growth targets in its Monetary Policy Report to Congress each February. The requirement by the Full Employment and Balanced Growth Act of 1978 that money supply targets be included in the Federal Reserve's reports to Congress expired in 2000, and the Federal Reserve concluded that the relationship between the money supply on the one hand, and economic growth and price movements on the other, had become increasingly tenuous. I also consider the money supply conceptually to have been a passive reflection of changes in financial assets rather than an active monetary policy tool for influencing the economy.[2] With respect to the CRB Futures Price Index, I consider the index to primarily be a financial instrument for traders in commodity futures index contracts; what the index measures has little effect on overall economic growth or price movements.

The indicators appear in alphabetical order. The format of topics is the same for all indicators: capsule explanation, where and when available (including website), content, methodology, accuracy (sampling/revision error), relevance, recent trends, and the reference to the primary data source. To facilitate cross-referencing, indicators covered in the book are italicized when they are mentioned in chapters other than those in which they are the primary focus.

Economic indicators are often based on survey estimates obtained from samples of households, businesses, and governments. Such survey estimates are subject to sampling error, as noted in the above paragraph under "accuracy." Indicators, whether based on sample data or not, are also subject to various kinds of nonsampling error. For the effects of sampling and nonsampling errors, see the Appendix: Note on Sampling and Nonsampling Errors in Statistical Surveys.

I thank Lynn Taylor, economics editor of M.E. Sharpe, for initiating this fourth edition and for facilitating the completion of the book. And I thank Myron Sharpe for his continued confidence in my work.

Edward Steinberg, on the economics faculties of New York University and Shippensburg University, reviewed the entire manuscript. He contributed immeasurably to the substance and clarity of the book. Others who reviewed particular indicators are: Charles Anderson, Christopher Bach, Bruce Baker, Steven Berman, Robert Callis, Brian Catron, Richard Curtin, Dennis Duke, Lynn Franco, Jacob Frumkin, Samuel Frumkin, Sarah Frumkin, Kenneth Goldstein, John Golmant, Kevin Hintzman, Thomas Jabine, Mickey Kalavsky, Ralph Kauffman, Pamela Kelly, Kurt Kunze, David Lassman, Patrick Lawler, Virginia Lewis, Mico Loretan, David Mead, Charlotte Mueller, Ataman Ozyildirim, Karen Pence, David Roderer, Brooks Robinson, Harry Rosenberg, Chris Savage, Scott Scheleur, Shelly Smith, Tony Sznoluch, Kevin Thorpe, Katherine Wallman, and Tiffany Yanosky. I had helpful discussions with Mary Bowler, Angie Clinton, Carmen DeNavas-Walt, Gerhard Fries, Charles Gilbert, Daniel Ginsburg, Bruce Grimm, Ryan Helwig, Paul Hanezaryk, James Herbert, David Hirschberg, Patrick Jackman, Mila Kareva, Kim Kowalewski, Nellie Liang, Wayne Lee, Peter Miller, Charles Nelson, William Nelson, Robert Parker, Al Schwenk, Howard Silverblatt, Kenneth Stewart, Kathleen Short, and Daniel Weinberg. Sylvia Elan assisted in proofreading the prepublication pages. The editorial staff of M.E. Sharpe ensured the high quality of the publication: Amanda Allensworth prepared the manuscript for production; Angela Piliouras was the production editor; Susanna Sharpe was the copyeditor; Zeph Ernest was the typesetter; Denise Carlson prepared the index.

I thank all of the above for their help, which was essential, though they may not agree with various aspects of the book. I am responsible for everything in the book.

Data Sharing and Confidentiality of Federal Government Statistical Data

A recent change affecting the production of federal government business statistics promises to have long-run benefits for the quality of the data used in preparing economic indicators and for the efficiency of the federal agencies in producing the statistics. This is the new legislation in 2002 that allows the sharing of statistical business data among the U.S. Bureau of the Census, U.S. Bureau of Labor Statistics (BLS), and U.S. Bureau of Economic Analysis (BEA) under prescribed procedures to protect the confidentiality of the data provided by individual respondents.[3] The legislation limits the definition of the "data" to the description, estimation, and analysis of groups, while not permitting the identification of individuals or organizations that make up the groups.

An ongoing business-data sharing activity under the new legislation is the matching of BEA's surveys of foreign direct investment in the United States and abroad with the Census Bureau's survey of industrial research and development. This has led to (a) improved coverage of companies in the Census Bureau's survey that previously were not identified as having research-and-development activities, and (b) the capability for the BEA to augment its research-and-development data with information from the Census Bureau's survey, to identify quality issues arising from reporting differences in the respective surveys, and to improve its survey sample frames. Examples of planned data sharing in the future are the matching of various elements of the business establishment lists of the Census Bureau and BLS that will identify differences in the lists, particularly for industry codes, which has long been considered an important problem; and the sharing of selected company and revenue data from the BEA's international surveys with the international price index program of the BLS, which will enable the BLS to study the feasibility of developing a new international price index for royalties and license fees, and subsequently, allow the BEA to compare selected elements from its sample frame with the BLS sample frame to find omissions in both lists. Other potential data-sharing areas include the use of Census Bureau records to facilitate a more efficient sampling for the BLS producer price index program, and the exchange by the BEA and BLS of local area data within the United States to develop experimental inter-area price indexes to permit comparisons of price *levels* between local areas.

This business data sharing is grounded in several requirements of the new legislation that strengthen the confidentiality of data provided by respondents to federal government surveys. For planned data sharing of mandatory surveys in which survey respondents are required by law to report, as distinct from voluntary surveys in which survey respondents are not required by law to report, in those instances when the respondents on mandatory surveys were not informed that the data could be shared, the agencies must publish a notice of the proposed data sharing in the *Federal Register,* specifying the data to be shared and the statistical purposes for which the data are to be used, and allowing a minimum of sixty days for public comment. Also, before sharing any business data the agencies must enter into a written agreement that specifies the data to be shared and the statistical purposes for which the data are to be used; the officers, employees, and agents authorized to examine the data to be shared; and the appropriate security procedures to safeguard the confidentiality of the data provided by individual respondents.

Using This Book

The more than sixty indicators in this book are classified in forty-nine generic categories in alphabetic order. To help those with an interest in particular aspects of the economy, the indicators are grouped below under broad topics. The broad groupings are: economic growth, household income and expenditure, business profits and investment, labor, inflation and deflation, production, housing, finance, government, international, cyclical indicators and forecasting, economic well-being, and psychology. Obviously, several indicators appear in multiple groupings.

ECONOMIC GROWTH

Gross Domestic Product
Industrial Production Index

HOUSEHOLD INCOME AND EXPENDITURE

Personal Income and Saving
Retail Sales
Consumer Credit
Consumer Credit Delinquency
Bankruptcies: Personal
Consumer Attitude Indexes

Manufacturing Business Activity Index
Non-Manufacturing Business Activity Index

ECONOMIC WELL-BEING

Distribution of Income
Distribution of Wealth
Poverty
Farm Parity Ratio
Consumer Credit Delinquency
Mortgage Delinquency and Foreclosure
Bankruptcies: Personal

PSYCHOLOGY

Consumer Attitude Indexes

Notes

1. Norman Frumkin, *Tracking America's Economy*, 4th ed. (Armonk, NY: M.E. Sharpe, 2004), ch. 1.

2. Frumkin, *Tracking America's Economy*, pp. 303–304.

3. Confidential Information Protection and Statistical Efficiency Act of 2002 (CIPSEA) as Title V of the E-Government Act of 2002 (Public Law 107–347). For an overall description of CIPSEA, see Executive Office of the President, Office of Management and Budget, *Statistical Programs of the United States Government: Fiscal Year 2005*. Washington, DC, 2004, pp. 43–45. The Bureau of the Census and the Bureau of Economic Analysis are in the U.S. Department of Commerce, and the Bureau of Labor Statistics is in the U.S. Department of Labor.

Guide to Economic Indicators

1
Average Weekly Earnings

Average weekly earnings represent the money wages and salaries of workers in private nonagricultural industries. Noncash fringe benefits are excluded. Because wages and salaries reflect movements in employment between high-paying and low-paying industries and occupations, the data are affected by changes in the composition of the industrial and occupational job structure.

Where and When Available

Data on average weekly earnings of workers are prepared monthly by the Bureau of Labor Statistics (BLS) in the U.S. Department of Labor. The data are published in a news release and in two monthly BLS journals, *Monthly Labor Review* and *Employment and Earnings* (www.bls.gov).

The data are available on the third Friday after the week containing the twelfth of the month. Thus, the information is released on the first or second Friday of the month following the month in question. On the day the monthly numbers are published, the commissioner of labor statistics reports on recent employment and unemployment trends to the Joint Economic Committee of Congress. Preliminary data are provided for the immediately preceding month; these are revised in the subsequent two months. Annual revisions are made in February of the following year.

Content

Average weekly earnings data cover the wages and salaries of production workers in manufacturing industries, as well as the wages, salaries, and commissions of nonsupervisory workers in other private nonagricultural industries before the payment of income and Social Security taxes. Earnings are excluded for office and sales workers in manufacturing, for supervisors and executives in all industries, and for government workers. The data reflect the effect of changes in the distribution of jobs among industries and occupations. By contrast, the *employment cost index,* which measures changes in labor costs to employers, maintains a fixed composition of industries and occupations.

Earnings include wages for time at work and for paid vacations, sick leave, holidays, and overtime (whether or not a premium is paid for overtime). The data exclude health, retirement, and other non-cash fringe benefits, the employer share of Social Security taxes, bonuses, retroactive payments, tips, and in-kind payments such as free rent and meals. The data are provided in current dollars and in constant (1982) dollars.

The average weekly earnings data are seasonally adjusted.

Methodology

The data for weekly earnings are obtained from the establishment survey used to measure *employment.* The methodology of the survey is described under that indicator. There is no independent benchmark figure for weekly earnings; the data are revised every February with the annual employment benchmark to reflect revisions in the distribution of employment among industries. Average weekly earnings are derived by multiplying *average weekly hours* by average hourly earnings. Average hourly earnings are estimated by dividing total wages and salaries by the number of hours of production and nonsupervisory employees during the pay period. The constant dollar data are calculated by dividing actual earnings by the consumer price index for urban wage earners and clerical workers.

Accuracy

There are no sampling error estimates for the average weekly earnings data. However, there are sampling error estimates for average hourly earnings and average weekly hours, the components that are multiplied together to obtain average weekly earnings (see Methodology above). The sampling error (for one standard error) for both average hourly earning and average weekly hours is 0.2 percent, which is indicative of what the error for average

Table 1.1

Average Weekly Earnings in Private Nonagricultural Industries

			Annual percentage change	
	Current dollars	1982 dollars	Current dollars	1982 dollars
1995	399.53	258.43	2.3	−0.6
1996	412.74	259.58	3.3	0.4
1997	431.25	265.22	4.5	2.2
1998	448.04	271.87	3.9	2.5
1999	462.49	274.64	3.2	1.0
2000	480.41	275.62	3.9	0.4
2001	493.20	275.38	2.7	−0.1
2002	506.07	278.83	2.6	1.3
2003	517.30	278.72	2.2	−0.0
2004	528.56	277.61	2.2	−0.4
		1995–2004 (annual average)	3.2	0.8

weekly earnings would be if it were available. For further information on the interpretation of sampling and nonsampling errors, see the Appendix.

Relevance

Average weekly earnings data are based on job-related earnings of workers of modest income in private nonfarm industies. This working population of civilian family households and unrelated individuals accounts for approximately 40 percent of the noninstitutional population who are sixteen years of age and older (people outside of jails, old-age homes, long-term medical care, and other sheltered housing). The earnings data are relevant for several reasons. First, they provide a measure of consumer purchasing power as indicated by changes in wage earnings for an important segment of the spending public. Second, because they gauge the economic well-being of ordinary workers, their trends may suggest the direction of future wage demands. Third, comparisons of wages and salaries in different industries indicate that shifts of jobs among industries may affect wage earnings.

Recent Trends

From 1995 to 2004, average weekly earnings in current dollars increased continuously, while earnings in price-adjusted (1982) dollars declined in four of the ten years (Table 1.1). The largest increases in price-adjusted dollars occurred in 1997 and 1998, and the second largest increases were in 1999 and 2002. Price-adjusted dollars declined in 1995, 2001, and 2004, and showed no change in 2003.

Over the entire nine-year period, the annual increases in current-dollar earnings averaged 3.2 percent, and the annual increases and decreases in price-adjusted 1982 dollar earnings increased at an average annual rate of 0.8 percent.

References from Primary Data Source

Bureau of Labor Statistics, U.S. Department of Labor. *Monthly Labor Review* and *Employment and Earnings*. Monthly.

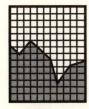

2
Average Weekly Hours

Average weekly hours represent the length of the workweek in private nonagricultural industries. The data are affected by changes in both the industrial and occupational composition of employment.

Where and When Available

Data on average weekly hours in the workplace are prepared monthly by the Bureau of Labor Statistics (BLS) in the U.S. Department of Labor. The data are published in a news release and two monthly BLS journals, *Monthly Labor Review* and *Employment and Earnings* (www.bls.gov).

The data are available on the third Friday after the week containing the twelfth of the month. Thus, the information is released on the first or second Friday of the month following the month in question. On the day the monthly numbers are released, the commissioner of labor statistics reports on recent employment and unemployment trends to the Joint Economic Committee of Congress. Preliminary data are provided for the immediately preceding month; these are revised in the subsequent two months. Annual revisions are made in February of the following year.

Content

Average weekly hours measure time on the job, including straight-time and overtime hours (whether or not a premium is paid for overtime), for

the average of full-time and part-time workers in private nonagricultural industries. The inclusion of paid absences from work means that
hours are counted on the basis of "hours paid for" rather than "hours
worked." The hours information covers production workers in manufacturing industries and nonsupervisory workers in other industries. Hours
for office and sales workers in manufacturing, for executives in all industries, and for government workers are excluded.

Separate data on *overtime* hours are provided for manufacturing industries. These are defined to include work time for which premium pay
is received beyond the straight-time workday or workweek. Holiday hours
are included only if premium wages are paid. Hours associated with
incentive pay for shift differentials such as night or weekend work, hazardous conditions, or similar situations are excluded. Because these separate data on overtime are limited to work for premium pay, they differ
from the overtime included in average weekly hours, which includes all
overtime even if no premium pay is involved.

The average weekly hours data are seasonally adjusted.

Methodology

The data for weekly hours are obtained from the establishment survey
used to measure *employment*. The methodology of the survey is described
under that indicator. There are no independent benchmark data for weekly
hours; they are revised every February with the annual employment
benchmark because of revisions in the composition of employment
among industries. Weekly hours are derived by dividing total hours paid
for by the number of employees during the pay period. These are adjusted for pay periods that are longer than one week so that they represent a seven-day period. Separate data are collected on the survey form
for overtime hours.

Accuracy

The sampling error (for one standard error) for the average weekly hours
data in private industries is 0.2 percent. For example, if the estimated
average weekly hours for private industries were 35 hours, in two of
three cases the "true" level would be somewhere between 34.93 and
35.07 hours. For further information on the interpretation of sampling
and nonsampling errors, see the Appendix.

Table 2.1

Average Weekly Hours in Private Nonagricultural Industries

	All private nonagricultural industries	Manufacturing industries	Overtime in manufacturing
1995	34.3	41.3	4.7
1996	34.3	41.3	4.8
1997	34.5	41.7	5.1
1998	34.5	41.4	4.8
1999	34.3	41.4	4.8
2000	34.3	41.3	4.7
2001	34.0	40.3	4.0
2002	33.9	40.5	4.2
2003	33.7	40.4	4.2
2004	33.7	40.8	4.6

Relevance

Average weekly hours is a sensitive barometer of labor demand. Employers generally prefer to increase or decrease hours worked before hiring or laying off workers in response to movements in *retail sales, corporate profits, manufacturers' orders, inventory–sales ratios,* or planned production schedules. This is particularly true when the changes in the demand for labor are small or are expected to be temporary.

Weekly hours in manufacturing is a component of the leading index of *leading, coincident, and lagging indexes.* The monthly volatility of weekly hours makes discerning a short-term trend difficult. Movements over several months should be assessed when analyzing trends.

Recent Trends

From 1995 to 2004, average weekly hours in all private nonagricultural industries peaked at 34.5 hours in 1997–98, and then declined to 33.7 hours in 2003–04 (Table 2.1). Weekly hours in manufacturing industries were 6 to 7 hours higher than those in all nonagricultural industries from 1995 to 2004. Manufacturing hours peaked at 41.7 hours in 1997, declined to an average of 40.4 hours during 2001–03, and rose to 40.8 hours in 2004. Overtime in manufacturing industries peaked at 5.1 hours in 1997, declined to 4.0 hours in 2001, and then rose to 4.6 hours in 2004.

References from Primary Data Source

Bureau of Labor Statistics, U.S. Department of Labor. *Monthly Labor Review* and
   Employment and Earnings. Monthly.

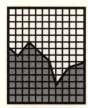

3
Balance of Payments

The balance-of-payments accounts are the most comprehensive measure of U.S. international economic transactions with other countries. The transactions include exports and imports of goods and services, income receipts and payments on foreign investments, transfer payments such as pensions and government grants, and changes in U.S. and foreign holdings of financial assets and liabilities associated with international monetary reserves, direct investment transactions, banking and nonbanking transctions, and securities transactions. The various balances focus on the difference between exports and imports and international flows of transfer payments, but exclude changes in financial assets and liabilities. When exports exceed imports, the balance is in surplus, and when imports exceed exports, the balance is in deficit. A surplus balance is sometimes referred to as "favorable" and a deficit as "unfavorable."

Where and When Available

The Bureau of Economic Analysis (BEA) in the U.S. Department of Commerce provides quarterly measures of the balance of payments. They are published in a news release and in the BEA monthly journal, *Survey of Current Business* (www.bea.gov).

The data are available seventy to seventy-five days after the end of the quarter to which they refer. They are initially revised in the succeeding quarter and then subsequently in June of the following year as part of the annual revisions. The annual revisions also change the data for several of the preceding years.

Content

The balance of payments has two broad components. One is foreign trade in goods, services, investment income, and unilateral transfers. The other is the money and capital flows necessary to finance trade, transfers, and grants. The two components are definitionally equivalent but do not match statistically because of inadequacies in the data. The difference caused by these data problems is noted as the statistical discrepancy.

Balance-of-payments data are provided for total U.S. transactions with all nations and separate transactions with particular nations and regions of the world. The United States includes the fifty states and the District of Columbia, Puerto Rico (except transactions between the states and Puerto Rico), and the Virgin Islands.

The balance-of-payments data are in current dollars. They are converted to constant dollars for the *gross domestic product.*

Several elements make up the foreign trade, transfer, and grant categories of the balance of payments. Exports and imports of goods, services, and income encompass merchandise trade in the balance of trade plus the following services and income: transfers under the foreign military sales program; defense purchases; travel, passenger, and freight transportation between the United States and other countries provided by American and foreign companies; other services provided by Americans and foreigners, such as insurance, telecommunications, construction, and engineering; royalties and license fees; and dividend and interest income paid by Americans and foreigners on foreign investments.

Unilateral transfers are transactions between U.S. residents and residents of foreign countries in which goods, services, or financial assets are transferred and nothing of economic value is received in return. Examples include U.S. government military and nonmilitary grants for which no payment is expected or where the payment terms are agreed to at a future time after the transfer occurs; private and government pension payments to American workers living in foreign countries and by other nations to foreign workers living in the United States; and gifts sent abroad by individuals and nonprofit organizations.

Increases or decreases in U.S. assets abroad and foreign assets in the United States measure the means of financing mentioned above foreign trade in goods and services, unilateral transfers, and military grants. The main elements of U.S. assets abroad are as follows. U.S. government official reserve assets include the U.S. gold stock, special drawing rights and the reserve position in the International Monetary Fund (IMF), and U.S. Treasury and Federal Reserve holdings of foreign currencies. Other government assets include loans to foreign nations and to U.S. private parties for investment abroad, capital contributions to international organizations except the IMF, and U.S. holdings of foreign currencies and other short-term assets associated with foreign-aid programs and financial operations such as guarantee programs of the Export-Import Bank. U.S. private assets include direct investment abroad (ownership of at least 10 percent of foreign companies) by U.S. private parties, U.S. private holdings of foreign bonds and stocks, and U.S. bank and nonbank loans to foreigners.

The main elements of foreign assets in the United States are as follows. Foreign official assets are investments by foreign governments in U.S. government securities, U.S. government liabilities for foreign deposits in advance of delivery of foreign military sales items, and foreign government holdings of U.S. corporate debt and equity securities and of state and local government securities. Other foreign assets are direct investment in the United States (ownership of at least 10 percent of American companies) by foreign private parties; private foreign holdings of U.S. Treasury securities, state and local government securities, and corporate debt and equity securities, and loans to Americans by foreign banks and nonbanks.

The indicator provides four separate balances of exports minus imports: (1) goods trade; (2) goods and services; (3) investment income; and (4) balance on current account (goods, services, income, and all unilateral current transfers). Balances are not calculated for changes in financial assets and liabilities because meaningful distinctions are difficult to make for such categories as short-term and long-term capital.

The balance-of-payments data are seasonally adjusted when seasonal patterns are present.

Methodology

The database used in preparing the balance of payments comes from several sources. Data for goods exports and imports are based mainly on Census Bureau surveys (see *balance of trade*). The main sources for other components are: U.S. International Trade Administration surveys of average international traveler expenditures and U.S. Department of Homeland Security data on the number of travelers; BEA surveys of international operations of U.S. and foreign ship operators and airlines; Census Bureau data on the tonnage of merchandise exports and imports; reports by the Department of Defense on foreign military sales and the Department of Agriculture on foreign-aid shipments of food; BEA surveys of incoming and outgoing foreign direct investment, and Treasury Department surveys (conducted by the Federal Reserve Bank of New York) of international assets and liabilities of U.S. banks and nonbank companies.

The quarterly measures are based on reported data for most items, and estimates for those for which reported data are available either annually or less frequently. They are revised every June when more complete information is available. These revisions change some of the components for the past three to five years.

The statistical discrepancy is defined as the accounting difference between the sums of credits and debits in the balance of payments. Credits are exports of goods, services, and income; unilateral transfers to the United States; capital inflows or a decrease in U.S. assets; a decrease in U.S. official assets, and an increase in foreign official assets in the United States. Debits are imports of goods, services, and income; unilateral transfers to foreigners; capital outflows or an increase in U.S. assets; an increase in U.S. official reserve assets, and a decrease in foreign official assets in the United States. A discrepancy results from the fact that data for the various components are developed independently and, consequently, are not fully consistent in coverage, definition, timing, and accuracy. The discrepancy is a net figure in which overstatement of one data element is offset by understatement of another data element. When the discrepancy is positive, it signifies unrecorded funds entering the United States; a negative discrepancy indicates unrecorded funds leaving the United States.

Accuracy

There are no estimates of sampling or revision error in the balance-of-payments data. Since offsetting errors among the data elements may reduce the statistical discrepancy, that figure provides an overall minimum magnitude of the net inconsistencies in the various data sources.

Relevance

The balance of payments reflects U.S. participation in world markets overall. It points up the relative importance of international product

Table 3.1

U.S. Balance of Payments (billions of dollars)

	Balance on goods, services, and income	Statistical discrepancy
1995	−75.5	28.3
1996	−81.7	−12.2
1997	−95.7	−79.4
1998	−160.7	145.0
1999	−249.5	68.8
2000	−357.2	−69.4
2001	−337.5	−9.6
2002	−411.2	−23.7
2003	−448.5	−37.8
2004	−587.1	85.1

	Balance on goods	Balance on services	Balance on income
2000	−452.4	74.1	21.1
2001	−427.2	64.5	25.2
2002	−482.3	61.1	10.0
2003	−547.3	52.5	46.3
2004	−665.4	47.8	30.4

markets to the American economy and indicates those markets that are gaining or losing ground. It also highlights shifts in international investment, including the effect on interest flows and dividend flows entering and leaving the United States. The extent to which the U.S. consumes and produces for world markets affects the *gross domestic product.*

The impact of international transactions, including their financing, affects the *value of the dollar* and American competitiveness. When Americans spend and invest more money abroad than foreigners spend and invest in the United States, the value of the dollar tends to decrease; greater spending and investment by foreigners in the United States tends to raise the dollar.

A large balance-of-payments deficit limits the flexibility of the Federal Reserve in conducting monetary policy (see *balance of trade*). Large deficits also create a growing foreign debt that raises interest payments to foreigners and thereby reduces the standard of living for Americans.

Recent Trends

From 1995 to 2004, the balance on goods, services, and income was consistently negative, in which imports exceeded exports (Table 3.1).

This general pattern was accompanied by continuously increasing negative movements during the period, with the negative balance rising from $75.5 billion in 1995 to $587.1 billion in 2004.

For the goods, services, and income components from 2000 to 2004, goods continuously accounted for the entire increasing overall negative balance noted above, amounting to $665.4 billion in 2004. Services had a positive balance of $47.8 billion in 2004, though the positive balance declined continuously from 2000. Income had a positive balance of $30.4 billion in 2004, with a fluctuating positive balance during 2000–04.

The statistical discrepancy fluctuated between a positive and negative position during 1995–2004, ranging from a positive $134.6 billion in 1998 to a negative $95.0 billion in 2002. The statistical discrepancy was a positive $51.9 billion in 2004.

Reference from Primary Data Source

Bureau of Economic Analysis, U.S. Department of Commerce. *Survey of Current Business.* Monthly.

4
Balance of Trade

The balance of trade represents U.S. foreign trade in merchandise. Merchandise is goods, as distinct from services. The "balance" is the difference between exports and imports. When exports exceed imports, the balance is in surplus, and when imports exceed exports, the balance is in deficit. A surplus is sometimes referred to as a "favorable" balance and a deficit as an "unfavorable" balance (see *balance of payments*).

Where and When Available

Two agencies provide balance-of-trade figures. The Bureau of the Census in the U.S. Department of Commerce provides monthly data, and the Bureau of Economic Analysis (BEA) in the U.S. Department of Commerce provides monthly and quarterly data. The data from the two agencies are published in a joint news release. The BEA data are published in more detail in the BEA monthly journal, *Survey of Current Business* (www.bea.gov). The Census Bureau data are published in more detail in the *FT 900 Supplement* (www.census.gov).

The balance-of-trade data are available 45 to 50 days after the month to which they refer. They are initially revised the following month and subsequently in quarterly and annual data as part of the *balance of payments*.

Content

Merchandise export and import data are provided for U.S. total foreign trade with all nations, plus detail for trade with particular nations and regions of the world, as well as for individual commodities. U.S. trade includes that of the fifty states and the District of Columbia, Puerto Rico, and the Virgin Islands. The trade data exclude shipments between the United States and the commonwealth of Puerto Rico, the Virgin Islands, and other U.S. possessions; however, supplementary data are provided on U.S. export and import trade with Puerto Rico, U.S. exports to the Virgin Islands, and imports from Guam, American Samoa, and the Northern Mariana Islands.

Constant-dollar inflation-adjusted measures of exports and imports are also prepared.

Exports cover domestically produced goods plus imported items that subsequently are exported without substantial physical change to the imported item (referred to as a re-export). Exports are valued at the dollar price at the U.S. port of export. This includes inland transportation, insurance, and other costs to deliver the merchandise alongside the ship or plane, but it excludes overseas transportation, insurance, and other charges beyond the U.S. port (referred to as f.a.s., free alongside ship). The month of exportation is the month in which the shipment leaves the United States.

Imports cover goods for immediate consumption plus those stored in Customs bonded warehouses and in U.S. Foreign Trade Zones. They are valued at the f.a.s. price at the foreign port of export (see exports in the above paragraph). The month of importation is within approximately ten days after the merchandise enters a Customs warehouse.

The distinction between the Census Bureau and the BEA data is that BEA adjusts the Census measures to conform to the *balance- of- payments* definitions. This results in three primary differences: (1) foreign military sales and U.S. military agencies' purchases from abroad identified in the Census Bureau documents are excluded by BEA but included elsewhere in the balance-of-payments accounts; (2) for imports from Canada, inland freight costs for transporting goods from the point of origin in Canada to the Canadian border are excluded in the Census data and included in the BEA data; (3) Census Bureau data include only nonmonetary gold that is shipped across international borders, while BEA data also include nonmonetary gold that changes ownership through book entries without being shipped across international borders. Nonmonetary gold represents all trade in gold in which at least one of the parties to the transaction is a private party; it excludes gold movements between governments, central banks, and international monetary institutions. Monetary gold represents gold movements between the U.S. Treasury or the Federal Reserve Board acting for the Treasury and foreign governments or their central banks and the International Monetary Fund.

The balance-of-trade data are seasonally adjusted.

Methodology

The basic data on merchandise exports and imports are developed from surveys conducted by the Census Bureau. They are adjusted by the BEA to reflect the *balance-of-payments* definitions.

Bureau of the Census

The export statistics are derived mainly from mandatory information supplied by commercial exporters to the Customs Bureau, which provides the data to the Census Bureau. The Customs Bureau checks exports requiring licenses from the State Department for military items and from the Commerce Department for nonmilitary strategic materials. These data are supplemented by data from some exporters who report their shipments directly to the Census Bureau. In addition, the Department of Defense reports military aid shipments data to the Census Bureau. Export data for shipments over $2,500 are compiled from the universe (100 percent sample) of all such reports. Low-valued exports of $2,500 and under accounted for 2.2 percent of all exports in 1997. Shipments of $2,500 and under are estimated from factors based on ratios of low-valued exports to total exports in past periods. The threshold dollar exemption for low-valued exports from reporting requirements is raised from time to time, most recently in October 1989.

The import statistics are derived from mandatory information supplied by importers to the Customs Bureau, which reviews the documents for accuracy and provides the corrected data to Census. Import data for shipments over $2,000, or over $250 for certain goods entering under quota, are compiled from the universe (100 percent sample) of all such reports. Low-valued imports of $2,000 and under, and under $250 for certain imports under quotas, accounted for 0.7 percent of all imports in 1997. Shipments of $2,000 and under are estimated from factors based on ratios of low-valued imports to total imports for past periods. The threshold dollar exemption, exempting low-valued imports from reporting requirements, is raised from time to time, most recently in July 1998.

The constant-dollar measures are derived mainly by deflating the current-dollar data by the *producer price indexes.*

Bureau of Economic Analysis

The statistical adjustments made to conform the Census Bureau data to the *balance-of-payments* definitions are based on separate information obtained from a variety of sources such as the Department of Defense for military exports, the Census Bureau data for U.S. inland freight, the BEA reconciliations with Statistics Canada for inland freight costs for Canadian foreign trade, and the Federal Reserve Board for nonmonetary gold trade.

Accuracy

There are no estimates of sampling or revision error for the balance-of-trade data. Practically all of the Census data are based on surveys of the universe of exporters and importers.

Relevance

The balance of trade impacts the *gross domestic product, employment,* and the *value of the dollar.* Export and import levels are influenced by economic growth at home and abroad and by the competitive position of American products in international markets and foreign goods in U.S. markets.

A surplus in the trade balance or a reduction in the trade deficit reflects increased economic growth and job expansion, while a deficit or reduction in the surplus reflects decreased economic growth and employment. This occurs because exports are produced in the United States and thus generate American production and employment, while American spending for imports stimulates production and employment abroad.

Over the long run, imports tend to hold down inflation because imports compete with American goods. Imports also moderate inflation during temporary shortages of domestic goods by providing a supplementary supply. Shortages may occur when drought or frost reduces food harvests; when an unexpected surge occurs in consumption; or when sudden bottlenecks appear in the production of lum-

Table 4.1

U.S. Balance of Trade (billions of dollars)

	BEA definition	Census Bureau definition
1995	−174.2	−158.8
1996	−191.0	−170.2
1997	−198.1	−180.5
1998	−246.7	−229.8
1999	−346.0	−328.8
2000	−452.4	−436.1
2001	−427.2	−411.9
2002	−482.3	−468.3
2003	−547.3	−532.4
2004	−665.4	−650.8

ber, paper, or other products for which domestic supply cannot be expanded readily.

The balance of trade also affects the conduct of U.S. economic policy. Thus, a large trade deficit limits the flexibility of the Federal Reserve in conducting monetary policy for influencing the economy. The trade deficit is financed by borrowing from domestic lenders or from abroad. Borrowing from domestic lenders to finance the deficit could lead to higher *interest rates,* unless accommodated by an increase in bank credit, which in turn may lead to higher inflation. Borrowing from abroad can lead to a rise in the *value of the dollar:* the influx of foreign funds into the United States bids up the dollar compared with other currencies, which worsens the deficit by making exports more expensive and imports cheaper.

The balance of trade also may affect U.S. living conditions. A continuing large deficit financed from abroad creates growing foreign debt. Over the long run, this results in greater amounts of money paid in interest as payments to foreigners. Consequently, U.S. incomes and living conditions are reduced.

Recent Trends

From 1995 to 2004, the balance of trade under both the BEA and Census Bureau definitions showed continuous increased negative balances, that is, increasing deficits (Table 4.1). The trade deficit under the BEA definition exceeded that under the Census Bureau definition by $15 to $20 billion in all years. The BEA deficit was $665.4 billion and the Census Bureau deficit was $650.8 billion in 2004.

References from Primary Data Sources

Bureau of the Census, U.S. Department of Commerce. *FT 900 Supplement*. Monthly.
Bureau of Economic Analysis and Bureau of the Census, U.S. Department of Commerce. *U.S. International Trade in Goods and Services*. Monthly.
Bureau of Economic Analysis, U.S. Department of Commerce. *Survey of Current Business*. Monthly.

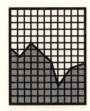

5
Bank Loans: Commercial and Industrial

Commercial and industrial bank loans are loans made by commercial banks to individuals, partnerships, and corporations for nonfarm business use. They also include bank loans made to investors for financial acquisitions such as company takeovers. The indicator thus focuses on loans made to income-generating business activity, as distinct from household consumer use.

Where and When Available

Commercial and industrial bank loan data are provided weekly and monthly by the Federal Reserve Board (FRB). They are published in a statistical release (H.8) and in the monthly statistical supplement to the FRB quarterly journal, *Federal Reserve Bulletin* (www.federalreserve.gov).

The weekly data are available every Friday for the week ending Wednesday of the previous week. The monthly data are available on the second Friday of the month after the month to which they refer. The measures are revised on a continuing basis with the receipt of more accurate data.

Content

Commercial and industrial bank loans represent loans outstanding. They cover existing loans from the previous period and new loans, minus those repaid, sold, or securitized outside the system (e.g., collateralized loan obligations) during the period. Secured and unsecured loans are included. In addition to traditional loans extended to borrowers, the data include banks' own acceptances (bills for which banks pledge their credit on behalf of their customers).

The data exclude loans to farmers, securities and real estate firms, other banks, and companies that mainly extend business or personal credit; commercial paper of financial institutions bought by banks; and loans secured by real estate. No data are available on the distribution of short-term and long-term loans.

The bank loan data are seasonally adjusted.

Methodology

The bank loan data are obtained from weekly reports of a nonprobability sample of Federal Reserve member and nonmember banks, both large and small, and from quarterly reports for banks not reporting weekly. The weekly and monthly data for all commercial banks include estimates for banks not reporting weekly. Estimates for the nonweekly reporting banks are based on relationships developed from the quarterly reports of all banks, those reporting weekly and those reporting quarterly. The bank loan data are benchmarked to the quarterly reports four times a year.

Accuracy

Estimates of revisions to the bank loan figures are encompassed within a larger statistical category of "bank credit," which includes commercial and industrial and other bank loans plus U.S. government and other securities owned by banks. Revisions for this much broader category are within plus or minus 0.5 percentage point of the annual growth rate of bank credit. The commercial and industrial bank loan component probably has a larger revision error, although the actual range is not known.

Relevance

The bank loan data provide a clue to business's willingness to go into debt. For analytical purposes, the monthly movement and the monthly level are viewed differently. A rapid increase in bank loans suggests an optimistic outlook for business prospects, a slow rate of loan expansion indicates a cautious business outlook, while a decrease suggests a greater business emphasis on paying off existing loans.

Table 5.1

Bank Loans: Commercial and Industrial

	Loans outstanding (billions of dollars) December	Annual percentage change December to December
1995	723.8	11.3
1996	784.7	8.4
1997	854.1	8.8
1998	947.4	10.9
1999	998.8	5.4
2000	1,087.0	8.8
2001	1,027.2	−5.5
2002	963.1	−6.2
2003	891.6	−7.4
2004	911.4	1.9

By contrast, the simple existence of debt is a burden to business because of the principal and interest payments. Thus, existing debt becomes a depressant to further borrowing. The monthly level of existing commercial and industrial loans (in constant dollars) is a component of the lagging index of the *leading, coincident, and lagging indexes.*

Recent Trends

From 1995 to 2004, bank loans to commercial and industrial borrowers showed diverse movements over the nine-year period (Table 5.1). Bank loans had fluctuating increases of 5 to 11 percent from 1995 to 2000, and after falling by a pace that accelerated from 5.5 percent in 2001 to 7.4 percent in 2003, rose by 2.2 percent in 2004. Bank loans ranged from a low of $724 billion in 1995 to a high of $1,087 billion in 2000.

Reference from Primary Data Source

Board of Governors of the Federal Reserve System. *Statistical Supplement to the Federal Reserve Bulletin,* the *Statistical Supplement* is monthly, and the *Federal Reserve Bulletin,* is quarterly.

6
Bankruptcies: Personal

Personal bankruptcy data highlight requests that household debtors be declared in bankruptcy and that arrangements be made for a resolution of creditor claims for monetary resolution. The requests, which are termed "filings," may be made by the debtors themselves ("voluntary filings") or by their creditors ("involuntary filings").

Where and When Available

The personal bankruptcy data are provided quarterly by the Administrative Office of the United States Courts, Statistics Division. They are published in *Statistical Tables for the Federal Judiciary* (www.uscourts. gov.bnkrptcystats/bankruptcystats.htm).

The data are available approximately seven weeks after the calendar quarter to which they refer. They represent the total for the quarter and the cumulated annual total of the most recent four quarters. For example, the January 1 to December 31 data combine the four calendar quarters from January to December, and the April 1 to March 31 data combine the four calendar quarters from April to March. Revised data are incorporated as they become available.

Content

The purpose of declaring bankruptcy is to obtain a fair resolution of overdue debts owed creditors based on the debtor's financial assets and needs, and to give the debtor a financial fresh start in life. A personal bankruptcy occurs when a U.S. court declares an individual who has overdue personal debts to be financially incapable of paying some or all of the debts, and thus discharges those debts. The bankruptcy protects the debtor's assets from the claims of creditors in whole or in part, depending on the terms of the bankruptcy.

The personal bankruptcy data (officially referred to as "nonbusiness bankruptcy filings") focus on the number of filings to the U.S. courts by household debtors or their creditors requesting that the debtors be declared in bankruptcy. The court completes its work when it acts to dismiss the request or refers it to the Office of the U.S Trustee of the U.S. Department of Justice. The Office of the U.S. Trustee is responsible for the specific resolution of how the debts will be satisfied. This indicator is confined to filings; it does not include the later resolution of cases by the Trustee Office.

The federal bankruptcy statute provides for different categories of liability.[1] These vary by the type and amount of a debtor's assets that are protected from being distributed to creditors. The two major variants of the statute for households are Chapters 7 and 13 (these chapters include business bankruptcies, but the data here are confined to personal bankruptcies). Chapter 7 bankruptcies absolve household debtors from part or all debt by discharging them from the liability of the debt that is discharged. Chapter 7 may include the sale of the debtor's properties (liquidation) that are not exempt from the claims of creditors, with the proceeds of the sale used to pay certain creditor claims. Chapter 13 gives household debtors a temporary respite in paying creditors in order to develop a financial plan such as budgeting part of the debtor's future earnings to pay part or all of the debt. Chapter 13 protection is limited to debtors with liabilities below certain levels for secured and unsecured debt.[2] Debtors having liabilities above these thresholds must use Chapter 11. Chapter 11 contains financial reorganization plans associated with secured and unsecured debt for both personal and business bankruptcies; only the personal component is included in the data here. Chapter 12 gives bankruptcy protection to a family farmer with a regular income; it is a business bankruptcy and is not included here.

Some persons who can pay part or all of their debts without suffering undue hardship might declare bankruptcy to avoid paying their debts. There are no comprehensive data on the extent of such abuse of the bankruptcy system.

The personal bankruptcy data are not seasonally adjusted. However, users of the data have estimated seasonal patterns.

Methodology

The personal bankruptcy data are prepared by the Administrative Office of the United States Courts, Statistics Division. The data are obtained electronically from the ninety-four U.S. bankruptcy courts around the country. The data are obtained from the universe of all bankruptcy filings. Revised data are incorporated in each quarterly tabulation as more complete or accurate data are received from the district courts. There is no formal schedule for revisions.

Accuracy

There are no estimates of revision error for the personal bankruptcy data.

Relevance

Personal bankruptcies result from many factors, such as excessive household debt in relation to income, issuance of credit cards to noncreditworthy households, and a lessening social stigma associated with bankruptcy.[3] (Estimates of the "stigma" effect are based on indirect statistical analysis, because direct measures of stigma are not available.[4]) Bankruptcy typically becomes a possibility when household debt loads (consumer and mortgage scheduled debt-service payments in relation to disposable personal income (see *personal income and saving*)—are high, and persons suffer a disruption of income due to *unemployment,* business losses, accidents, sickness, divorce, or other unexpected events that significantly diminish income or increase expenses.

What is the impact of bankruptcy on the economy? First, it is important to recognize that bankruptcy is a culmination of many problems associated with households' being overextended in debt, such as those noted above. Thus, bankruptcy is aimed at ending the treadmill of ever-increasing debt. Once bankruptcy has occurred, the effects on prices (*consumer price index, GDP price measures, wholesale price indexes*), *interest rates,* profits (*corporate profits*), and taxes (*government economic transactions*) depend on actions taken by creditors who have lost income due to unpaid debts.[5] If creditors pass the costs along to consumers, they lead to higher prices and interest rates. If creditors absorb the costs, they lead to lower profits and in turn lower tax receipts.

Table 6.1

Bankruptcy Filings: Personal (Chapters 7, 11, 13)

Year ending December	Filings	Annual percentage change
1995	874,642	12.1
1996	1,125,006	28.6
1997	1,350,118	20.0
1998	1,441,701	6.8
1999	1,281,586	−11.1
2000	1,217,972	−5.0
2001	1,452,030	19.2
2002	1,539,555	6.0
2003	1,625,208	5.6
2004	1,563,145	−3.8
1995–2004 (annual average)		6.7

Recent Trends

From 1995 to 2004, personal bankruptcy filings rose in each year, except for declines in 1999, 2000, and 2004 (Table 6.1). The year-to-year percentage changes fluctuated considerably. The average annual change from 1995 to 2004 was an increase of 6.7 percent.

The 1,563,145 filings in 2004 included 1,117,766 under Chapter 7; 946 under Chapter 11; and 444,428 under Chapter 13 (the total filings figure included five cases under other chapters of the federal bankruptcy statute). There are no data distinguishing voluntary from involuntary filings, although the bulk are thought to be voluntary.

Reference from Primary Data Source

Administrative Office of the United States Courts, Statistics Division. *Statistical Tables for the Federal Judiciary.* Quarterly.

Notes

1. For a comprehensive coverage of personal bankruptcy, see Kim Kowalewski, *Personal Bankruptcy: A Literature Review,* CBO Paper, Congressional Budget Office, September 2000.

The Bankruptcy Reform Act of 1978 established minimum federal standards for the type of property and the dollar value of debt that are protected from payment to creditors. The Bankruptcy Reform Act of 1994 raised minimum-protection levels. The federal statute allows states to raise the dollar value and add to the types of property above the federal minimums, but all bankruptcy proceedings are conducted in federal courts. The Bankruptcy Abuse, Prevention, and Consumer Protection Act of 2005 made it more difficult for debtors to file for bankruptcy under Chapter 7 without paying some of their debt. In addition, the Act allowed state-based asset protection trusts (also called self-settled trusts) to be exempt from payments to creditors in bankruptcy proceedings, except for those trusts that are shown by the Trustee to have been established with the "actual intent to hinder, delay, or defraud" the payment of a particular claim.

2. Secured debt represents a loan backed by a borrower's collateral, such as a house, car, or financial securities. Credit card debt is unsecured debt.

3. Paul Paquin, and Melissa Squire Weiss, *An Analysis of the Determinants of Personal Bankruptcies,* Capital One Financial Corporation, Falls Church, VA (October 1997); and Visa U.S.A. Inc., *Consumer Bankruptcy: Causes and Implications,* July 1996.

4. Kowalewski, *Personal Bankruptcy,* p. xi, and Appendix B, p. 45.

5. WEFA Group, Resource Planning Service, *The Financial Costs of Personal Bankruptcy,* Burlington, MA, February 1998. The study was funded by Visa and MasterCard.

7
Capacity Utilization

Capacity utilization measures the proportion of equipment and structures used in production by the manufacturing, mining, electric, and gas utilities industries. It covers the same industries as the *industrial production index*. When production rises faster than capacity, the capacity utilization rate (CUR) increases, but when production rises more slowly (or declines), the CUR decreases.

Where and When Available

Capacity utilization is prepared monthly by the Federal Reserve Board (FRB). It is published in a statistical release (G.17) and in the monthly statistical supplement to the quarterly FRB journal, the *Federal Reserve Bulletin* (www.federalreserve.gov).

The data are available in the middle of the month after the month to which they refer, the same day as the *industrial production index*. Preliminary data are provided for the preceding month; these are revised in the subsequent three months. Annual revisions are made in the fall.

Content

The capacity utilization rate, expressed as a percentage, is the ratio of the *industrial production index* to equipment and structures capacity. The formula is:

$$\text{CUR} = \frac{\text{Industrial production index}}{\text{Equipment and structures capacity}} \times 100 \qquad (7.1)$$

Because the numerator is discussed in the chapter on the *industrial production index,* this section explains the denominator, or capacity.

The capacity number represents the economy's ability to produce goods and power assuming the existing equipment and structures facilities are used over the normal operating period for each industry—this ranges from a typical 35-to-40-hour workweek to continuous operations seven days a week. The capacity measure aims at achieving a level of sustainable maximum output within a realistic work schedule that allows for normal downtime and assumes a sufficient availability of labor, materials, and services used in production. Capacity gradually increases over time as each year more equipment and structures investment is added than physical facilities are scrapped. This long-term upward trend shows no cyclical fluctuation. Industries rarely operate at a CUR of 100 percent and thus typically have unused or spare capacity available to expand production when demand increases.

The industrial composition of the CUR is made up of manufacturing (84 percent), mining (7 percent), and utilities (9 percent).

The CUR data are seasonally adjusted.

Methodology

Because the *industrial production index* in the numerator of the CUR is already prepared, the primary task for developing the CUR is to provide a measure of capacity. For most industries, direct measures of capacity, such as the number of items that can be produced if the industry is operating at a CUR of 100 percent, are not available. Consequently, indirect measures of capacity are widely used. For most manufacturing industries, these are derived from year-end surveys of capacity utilization conducted in manufacturing industries by the Census Bureau (Survey of Plant Capacity). Capacity is inferred from these year-end CUR survey data by dividing them by the *industrial production index* for each industry.[1] The resultant capacity numbers are modified to reflect supplementary information on direct measures of capacity for selected manufacturing industries and on the value of stock of existing capital facilities derived from a perpetual inventory of investment data.

Capacity estimates in the mining and utilities industries are based on data from the U.S. Departments of Energy and the Interior and from industry sources. Also, for those industries where direct measures of capacity are not available, capacity is estimated based on long-term trends connecting peak levels of output.

The monthly trends between the year-end levels of capacity are obtained by connecting the year-end points by a straight trend line. Monthly movements of the current year are extrapolated based on the monthly trend of the previous year.

Accuracy

There are no estimates of revisions for the CUR data. However, the revision measures of the *industrial production index* (IPI) are a close approximation of revisions for the CUR data, because the volatile IPI is the numerator and the steady growth of capacity is the denominator of the CUR. The typical revision to the monthly IPI level between the preliminary estimate and the third monthly revision is plus or minus 0.28 percent. The typical revision to the monthly movement is plus or minus 0.22 percentage point. In about 85 percent of the cases, the direction of change in the preliminary estimate is the same as in the third revision.

Relevance

The CUR is used as an indicator of future equipment and structures investment. Generally, the higher the CUR, the greater the tendency for equipment and structures shortages to exist, which in turns leads to additional investment. However, it is important to analyze the CUR together with trends in the *gross domestic product* and business profits (see *corporate profits*) for clues to future investment. There is no specific CUR level that indicates a shortage of capacity or signals additional investment. The difference between 100 percent utilization and the CUR theoretically represents the unused capacity that is available to increase production to meet an increased demand. In practice, however, CURs typically do not top the 90th percentile, except for utilities, in continuous processing industries such as paper, chemicals, or petroleum refining, or during wartime when mobilization is high and less efficient facilities are put into production.

The CUR is also used to assess future inflation in a direct relationship. However, statistical linkages between the CUR and price movements are not strong.

Recent Trends

From 1995 to 2004, the CUR for manufacturing, mining, and utilities industries combined ranged from 82 to 85 percent from 1995 to 2000,

Table 7.1

Capacity Utilization (percent)

	All industries	Manufacturing	Mining	Utilities
1995	83.7	82.8	87.9	90.0
1996	82.7	81.4	90.1	90.5
1997	83.7	82.8	91.1	89.1
1998	82.9	81.8	88.9	91.2
1999	82.2	81.1	86.1	92.5
2000	82.0	80.6	90.1	92.4
2001	76.6	74.5	89.8	88.9
2002	75.3	73.5	85.5	87.6
2003	75.5	73.7	86.6	84.9
2004	78.1	76.7	86.5	85.1

declined to 75 to 76 percent during 2001–03, and rose to 78 percent in 2004 (Table 7.1). The movements and levels of this overall CUR were similar to those for manufacturing industries; the most noticeable difference was that the manufacturing level was typically 1.0 to 1.5 percentage points lower than the total CUR for all industries.

Both the mining and utilities CURs were several percentage points higher than those for manufacturing. The mining industries CUR typically ranged from 88 to 90 percent from 1995 to 2001, dropped to 85.5 percent in 2002, and rose to 86.5 percent in 2003–04. The utilities industries ranged from 90 to 92.5 percent from 1995 to 2000, and then declined to lows of 85 percent in 2003–04.

Reference from Primary Data Source

Board of Governors of the Federal Reserve System. *Statistical Supplement to the Federal Reserve Bulletin.* The *Statistical Supplement* is monthly and the *Federal Reserve Bulletin* is quarterly.

Note

1. This formula works as follows:

$$\frac{\text{Capacity utilization}}{\text{Production}} = \frac{\text{Production}}{\dfrac{\text{Capacity}}{\text{Production}}} = \frac{\text{Production}}{\text{Capacity}} \times \frac{1}{\text{Production}} = \text{Capacity}$$

8
Consumer Attitude Indexes

Two organizations provide indicators of consumer attitudes. They focus on households' perceptions of general business and employment conditions, and of their personal financial well-being, plus their attitudes toward purchasing big-ticket items that last a relatively long time—homes, cars, furniture, and major household appliances. The indicators of both organizations are covered here: the "consumer confidence index" (CCI) of The Conference Board, and the "consumer sentiment index" (CSI) of the University of Michigan. Both indexes measure similar phenomena but, because the methodologies differ and the concepts are not identical, there are periods when their movements differ. Both are constructed as diffusion indexes, which suggest an indication of the direction of the movement from one period to the next, but not of the size of the movement. The characteristics of The Conference Board and Michigan measures are described separately. This is followed by a summary of the main methodological differences between them, and then by highlights of the relevance and recent trends of both.

Consumer Confidence Index

The consumer confidence index reflects consumers' attitudes toward the economy, local job markets, and their own financial condition.

Where and When Available

The consumer confidence index is prepared monthly by the Consumer Research Center of The Conference Board. It is published in two Conference Board monthly reports, *Consumer Confidence Survey* and *Business Cycle Indicators* (www.conference-board.org).

The CCI data are available the last Tuesday of the same month to which they refer. The data are revised for the previous month.

Content

The consumer confidence index represents the combined effects of household perceptions of local area business conditions, household perceptions of available jobs in local areas currently and six months ahead, and expected household income six months ahead. A rising index means consumers are more optimistic, and a declining one signifies greater pessimism. While there are no absolute values that define optimism and pessimism, comparisons of the index levels with previous periods indicate whether consumers are more optimistic or pessimistic than in past periods.

The CCI is based currently on 1985 = 100.

The CCI is seasonally adjusted.

Methodology

Data for the consumer confidence index are obtained from a monthly household survey conducted by TNS-NFO for The Conference Board. The survey is mailed to approximately 5,000 households in the forty-eight mainland states and the District of Columbia, and the response rate is about 70 percent (3,500 households). A completely new group of households is surveyed each month.

The CCI is constructed by giving equal weight to each of five questions. There is one question each on the survey respondents' local area business conditions currently and six months ahead, one question each on jobs in the local area currently and six months ahead, and one question on expected household income six months ahead. In constructing the index, the positive responses are expressed as a percentage of the sum of the positive and negative responses. Neutral answers are not counted. Depending on the question, positive answers are referred to as "good," "better," "plenty," "more," "higher"; negative responses are referred to as "bad," "worse," "hard to get," "fewer," "lower"; and neutral responses are referred to as "normal," "same," "not so many" in the month. Mathematically, the formula is:

$$\text{CCI} = \frac{\text{Positive}}{\text{Positive} + \text{Negative}} \times 100 \qquad (8.1)$$

This type of index, which provides an indication of the direction but not of the magnitude of the movement from one period to the next, is a diffusion index (diffusion indexes are discussed further in the "Content" section of the *PMI* chapter). In contrast, traditional indexes of economic activity provide the actual direction and magnitude of the movement.

Accuracy

The sampling error (for one standard error) for the consumer confidence index is 1.5 percentage points. For example, if the estimated CCI were 100.0, in two of three cases the "true" index would be somewhere between 98.5 and 101.5. For further information on the interpretation of sampling and nonsampling errors, see the Appendix.

Consumer Sentiment Index

The consumer sentiment index reflects consumers' attitudes toward the economy and their own financial condition, and perceptions about buying big-ticket durable goods.

Where and When Available

The consumer sentiment index is prepared monthly by the Survey Research Center of the University of Michigan. It is published in the monthly report, *Surveys of Consumers* (www.athena.sca. isr.umich.edu).

The CSI data are available within the first five to ten days of the month after the month to which they refer. The monthly data are not revised.

Content

The consumer sentiment index combines three main categories of household attitudes toward the economy in one number: (1) expected business conditions in the national economy for one and five years ahead, (2) personal financial well-being compared with one year earlier and expected one year later, and (3) whether the current period is a good or bad time to buy furniture and major household appliances. Upward movements of the index suggest that consumers are becoming more optimistic, and downward movements suggest a growing pessimism. While there are no absolute values that define optimism and pessimism, comparisons of the index levels with previous periods indicate whether consumers are more optimistic or pessimistic than in past periods.

Supplementary information for interpreting the reasons for changes in household attitudes is included in *Surveys of Consumers*. The full report includes data on attitudes toward such items as employment, prices, interest rates, shortages, and government policies.

The CSI is based currently on 1966: 1Q = 100.

The CSI is not seasonally adjusted.

Methodology

Data for the consumer sentiment index are obtained from a telephone survey of a sample of households conducted by the Survey Research Center. Approximately 670 households are contacted monthly in the forty-eight mainland states and the District of Columbia, with a response rate of about 75 percent (500 households). The sample is designed as a rotating panel in which one-half of the survey respondents are new each month and one-half are carryovers from the survey panel of six months earlier.

Five questions are used in constructing the index. There is one question each on expected national economic conditions one year and five years ahead; one question each on personal financial well-being contrasting the current period with one year earlier and with one year ahead; and one question on whether the current period is a good time to buy furniture and major household appliances. Equal weight is given to each question. In valuing the answers, positive, negative, and neutral answers are used. Depending on the question, positive answers are "up," "better," "good"; negatives are "down," "worse," "bad"; and neutrals are "same," "no change," "uncertain" in the month. The percentage of negative responses is subtracted from the percentage of positive responses (the percentages of the positive and negative responses are calculated relative to the sum of the positive, negative, and neutral responses), and 100 is added to the difference to avoid negative numbers. Mathematically, the formula is:

$$\text{CSI} = \left(\frac{\text{Positive}}{(\text{Positive} + \text{Negative} + \text{Neutral})} \times 100 \right) - \qquad (8.2)$$

$$\left(\frac{\text{Negative}}{(\text{Positive} + \text{Negative} + \text{Neutral})} \times 100 \right) + 100$$

This type of index, which provides an indication of the direction but not of the magnitude of the movement from one period to the next, is a diffusion index (diffusion indexes are discussed further in the "Content" section of the *PMI* chapter). In contrast, traditional indexes of economic activity provide the actual direction and magnitude of the movement.

Accuracy

The sampling error (for one standard error) for the consumer sentiment index is 1.3 percentage points. For example, if the estimated consumer sentiment index were 100.0, in two of three cases the "true" index would be somewhere between 98.7 and 101.3. For further information on the interpretation of sampling and nonsampling errors, see the Appendix.

Main Differences Between the Conference Board and Michigan Indexes

While the consumer confidence index and consumer sentiment index basically measure the same phenomena, there are clear differences in their methodologies associated with the index content, wording of questions, seasonal adjustment, household samples, data collection, and questionnaire response estimation. The main differences are summarized below.

Index content. The CCI excludes the purchase of big-ticket items, while the CSI includes them. The CCI includes questions on current and expected job opportunities, while the CSI excludes them.

Wording of questions. For general business conditions, the CCI focuses on the respondents' local economy currently and with a short-term six-month outlook, while the CSI focuses on the national economy with a long-term one-to-five-year outlook. For personal financial well-being, the CCI looks at household income six months ahead, while the CSI asks how well off the respondent is financially compared with one year earlier and what expectations are for one year ahead.

Seasonal adjustment. The CCI is seasonally adjusted, while the CSI is not seasonally adjusted.

Monthly household sample. The CCI sample of respondents is 3,500 households, while the CSI sample of respondents is 500 households.

Data collection. The CCI uses a mail questionnaire, while the CSI uses a telephone interview.

Survey response estimation. The CCI and CSI apply different weights for positive and negative answers to survey questions.

Revisions. The CCI data are revised for the previous month, while the CSI data are not revised.

Relevance

Perceptions by households of the strength of general business conditions and of their personal financial conditions are closely linked to households' feelings of optimism and pessimism about the economy. In theory, when households are optimistic, they are more willing to increase spending and incur debt to finance the higher spending. When households are pessimistic, they are likely to cut back on spending, pay off debts, and build nest-egg savings. A household's decision to buy a home or big-ticket durable goods is typically based on advance planning and is heavily influenced by the household's perception of changing economic conditions.

When there are sustained changes in one direction over a period of time, the consumer confidence index (CCI) and the consumer sentiment index (CSI) are fairly good predictors of shifts in future household spending and saving. However, the index levels are hard to distinguish one from the other.

The CCI and the CSI are classified as leading indicators of economic activity by The Conference Board. In addition, the University of Michigan's "index of consumer expectations," which is based only on the three questions in the CSI relating to the future (the CSI has five questions), is a component of the leading index of the *leading, coincident, and lagging indexes.* Because the monthly and even quarterly movements show erratic increases and decreases, both indexes should be viewed over longer periods to discern a change from past trends.

Recent Trends

From 1995 to 2004, the CCI and CSI had similar upward and downward movements, except for 2002 (Table 8.1). The CCI had consistently larger

Table 8.1

Consumer Attitude Indexes

	Consumer Confidence Index[a] (1985 = 100)	Consumer Sentiment Index[b] (1966: IQ = 100)
1995	100.0	92.2
1996	104.6	93.6
1997	125.4	103.2
1998	131.7	104.6
1999	135.3	105.8
2000	139.0	107.6
2001	106.6	89.2
2002	96.6	89.6
2003	79.8	87.6
2004	96.1	95.2

[a]The Conference Board. [b]University of Michigan.

year-to-year changes than the CSI. Both indexes were at their highest levels in 2000 and at their lowest levels in 2003.

References from Primary Data Sources

The Conference Board. *Consumer Confidence Survey* and *Business Cycle Indicators*. New York, NY. Monthly.
University of Michigan, Survey Research Center. *Surveys of Consumers*. Ann Arbor, MI. Monthly.

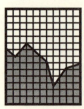

9
Consumer Credit

Consumer credit represents loans by banks, finance companies, and retail stores to households for financing consumer purchases of goods and services and for refinancing existing consumer debt.

Where and When Available

Measures of consumer credit are prepared monthly by the Federal Reserve Board (FRB). They are published in a statistical release (G-19) and in the monthly statistical supplement to the quarterly FRB journal, the *Federal Reserve Bulletin* (www.federalreserve.gov).

The data are available approximately five weeks after the month to which they refer. The data are revised as revisions in the database are received.

Content

The consumer credit data include credit cards and loans for items such as automobiles, mobile homes, education, boats, trailers, or vacations. They include loans with a fixed repayment schedule of one or more payments (nonrevolving credit) and loans where borrowers have the option to repay any amount above a given minimum (revolving credit). Securitized consumer loans—loans made by finance companies, banks, and retailers that are sold as securities—are included. The data exclude home mortgages, but probably include an unknown amount of consumer loans used for business purposes. Automobile leasing is also excluded from the consumer credit data.

The data reflect consumer credit outstanding at the end of the month.

The monthly change in consumer credit outstanding is the net effect of credit extensions and repayments during the month. Separate data on credit extended and repaid during the month are not available.

The consumer credit data are seasonally adjusted.

Methodology

Monthly data on consumer credit are based on the following: monthly surveys of a sample of commercial banks conducted by the Federal Reserve Board; monthly surveys of consumer finance companies, including auto finance companies, conducted by the Federal Reserve Board; quarterly reports filed by savings institutions with the Office of Thrift Supervision; monthly surveys of credit unions conducted by the Credit Union National Association; monthly U.S. Treasury reports on federal direct student loans; and monthly surveys of retail sales conducted by the Bureau of the Census. Benchmark data are available quarterly for commercial banks; annually for retailers (accounts receivable), and every five years for finance companies.

Accuracy

There are no estimates of sampling or revision error for the consumer credit data.

Relevance

Consumer credit supplements *personal income and saving* as a source of consumer purchasing power. In turn, consumer purchasing power impacts *retail sales*. While consumer credit outstanding typically increases, the rate of increase is faster during expansions than during recessions. The occasional monthly declines in consumer credit occur mostly during recessions. Thus, consumer credit accentuates the cyclical movements of consumer spending, particularly for durable goods. Households generally borrow more during periods of rapidly growing personal income, because prosperity leads to optimism regarding financial commitments (see *consumer attitude indexes*).

Consumer credit outstanding is also viewed as a burden on households because they must pay the principal and interest on the loans. The ratio of consumer credit outstanding to personal income and household

Table 9.1

Consumer Credit Outstanding (seasonally adjusted)

December	Credit outstanding (billions of dollars)	Annual percentage change (December to December)
1995	1,141.0	14.4
1996	1,242.9	8.9
1997	1,313.1	5.7
1998	1,416.8	7.9
1999	1,530.4	8.0
2000	1,705.1	11.4
2001	1,842.2	8.0
2002	1,924.2	4.5
2003	2,011.3	4.5
2004	2,109.6	4.9

debt-service payments for consumer and mortgage loans (scheduled periodic payments of principal and interest as a percentage of disposable personal income) are commonly used measures of this burden. As this percentage rises during expansions, the growing consumer credit can be expected to depress further consumer borrowing. The ratio of consumer credit outstanding to personal income is a component of the lagging index of the *leading, coincident, and lagging indexes.*

Recent Trends

From 1995 to 2004, the rate of increase in consumer credit outstanding fluctuated considerably (Table 9.1). The annual increase declined from 14 percent in 1995 to 6 percent in 1997, rose to 11 percent in 2000, declined to 4.5 percent in 2002 and 2003, and rose to 4.9 percent in 2004.

Reference from Primary Data Source

Board of Governors of the Federal Reserve System. *Statistical Supplement to the Federal Reserve Bulletin.* The *Statistical Supplement* is monthly, and the *Federal Reserve Bulletin* is quarterly.

10
Consumer Credit Delinquency

Consumer credit delinquency (CCD) rates are household loans with over-due payments of thirty days or more as a percentage of all consumer loans outstanding. The data represent loans by commercial banks and savings and loan associations for household expenditures associated with general personal use, vehicles, housing, and education. The loans are financed by installment, bank card, revolving, mortgage, and home equity credit.

Where and When Available

The consumer credit delinquency data are prepared quarterly by the American Bankers Association. They are published in the *Consumer Credit Delinquency Bulletin* (www.aba.com).

The CCD data are available approximately ten weeks after the reference calendar quarter. For example, the data for January, February, and March are published about the third week of June. The CCD data are not revised.

Content

The consumer credit delinquency data represent household loans extended by commercial banks and savings and loan associations that are delinquent as a percentage of the total number of loans outstanding at the end of each month. Delinquency rates are provided separately for the number and the dollar value by type of closed-end and open-end loan. Closed-end loans are for a specified item and must be paid back within a limited period (personal, automobile, mobile home, recreational vehicle, marine financing, property improvement, home equity and second mortgages, and education loans).

Open-end loans continue so long as the necessary payments are made to maintain them (bank card credit, revolving credit, home equity lines of credit).

The CCD data for the combined total of closed-end loans except education is also provided. In addition, repossession rates for defaulted loans (number of repossessions per month per 1,000 loans outstanding) are provided for automobile, mobile home, and marine financing loans. The data are shown for the national total and by state. The data exclude loans by thrift institutions, consumer finance companies, charge accounts by retail stores, and nonbank credit cards.

The CCD data are seasonally adjusted for the national total. The state data are not seasonally adjusted.

Methodology

The consumer credit delinquency data are obtained from a quarterly survey of a sample of commercial banks and savings and loan associations (S&Ls). Approximately 3,000 large commercial banks based on consumer loan portfolio size are surveyed; they account for 60 to 70 percent of the consumer loan portfolios managed by commercial banks. The surveyed S&Ls represent approximately 25 percent of all S&Ls. The CCD data are based solely on the reports from these banks and S&Ls.

The sample of surveyed banks and S&Ls is updated annually. The survey sample is not a probability sample.

Accuracy

There are no estimates of sampling or revision error for the consumer credit delinquency data.

Relevance

Analytic interest in the consumer credit delinquency data is related to *consumer credit, retail sales,* personal consumption expenditures in the *gross domestic product, bankruptcies: personal,* and *mortgage delinquency and foreclosure.* CCDs become more pronounced when household debt loads (consumer and mortgage scheduled debt-service payments in relation to disposable personal income) become vulnerable to reductions in personal income (*personal income and saving*) associated with *unemployment,* stock market losses (*stock market price aggre-*

Table 10.1

Consumer Credit Delinquency Rate (number of delinquent loans as a percentage of all loans outstanding)

December, seasonally adjusted	
1995	2.12
1996	2.34
1997	2.43
1998	2.35
1999	2.27
2000	2.40
2001	2.34
2002	2.16
2003	1.89
2004	1.68

gates and dividend yields), personal sickness, divorce, and so on. Other factors affecting CCDs are changes in bank lending standards (the willingness of banks to lend money as indicated in a monthly survey of senior loan officers conducted by the Federal Reserve Board), and changes in the promotion by banks and other credit card companies to households whose financial ability to pay off large debts is considered questionable. Reverse movements occur when CCD rates decline.

Rising CCD rates cause lenders to raise their credit standards for loans to risky borrowers, and/or to raise interest rates to risky borrowers that discourage them from additional borrowing, which tend to restrain spending growth. Analogously, declining CCD rates have the opposite effects and tend to stimulate spending growth. Rising and declining CCD rates are one precursor of movements in *bankruptcies: personal.*

Recent Trends

From 1995 to 2004, the consumer credit delinquency rate fluctuated within a narrow range during 1995–2001, and then declined in the latter part of the period (Table 10.1). The CCD trended downward from 2.40 in 2000 to 1.68 in 2004.

Reference from Primary Data Source

American Bankers Association. *Consumer Credit Delinquency Bulletin.* Washington, DC. Quarterly.

11
Consumer Price Index

The consumer price index (CPI) gauges the overall rate of price change for a fixed basket of goods and services bought by households. Because it prices the same items (with only limited exceptions) every month, this measure of inflation or deflation reflects the cost of maintaining the same purchases over time. The CPI does not conform to a theoretical cost-of-living index.

Where and When Available

The consumer price index is prepared monthly by the Bureau of Labor Statistics in the U.S. Department of Labor. The data are published in a news release, the *CPI Detailed Report,* and the monthly BLS journal, *Monthly Labor Review* (www.bls.gov).

The data are published in the middle of the month immediately following the month to which they refer. The monthly not-seasonally-adjusted data are rarely revised. The seasonally adjusted data are revised annually for several previous years based on new seasonal factors.

Content

The consumer price index records price changes in food and beverages, housing, apparel, transportation, medical care, recreation, education and communication, and other goods and services. Thousands of items within these broad groups are priced every month. It is published in two versions, the CPI-U and the CPI-W. The CPI-U represents all urban households including urban workers in all occupations, the unemployed, and retired persons; it accounts for about 87 percent of the noninstitutional population.[1] The CPI-W represents urban wage and clerical workers employed in blue collar occupations; it accounts for about 32 percent of the noninstitutional population. Both the CPI-U and the CPI-W exclude rural households, military personnel, and persons in institutionalized housing such as prisons, old-age homes, and long-term hospitals. A third CPI measure, the C-CPI-U (chain CPI-U) introduced in 2000, is discussed below under "Methodology."

CPIs are calculated for the nation as a whole, for broad geographic regions, and for large metropolitan areas. They therefore provide differential national and geographic measures of price movements over time. However, the CPI does not reflect the actual dollar *level* of living costs in the nation or in one area compared with another—it reveals only the inter-area differences in price movements.[2]

The weights of the CPI are based on the proportions of household budgets that consumers actually spend for particular goods and services. The spending patterns are updated every two years. For example, the CPI for 2004 and 2005 reflects spending patterns during 2001–02 and the CPI for 2006 and 2007 reflects spending patterns during 2003–04.

The CPI is based on actual transaction prices, which take into account such variations as premiums or discounts from the list price, sales and excise taxes, import duties, and trade in allowances when the used-car trade-in is part of the new-car price. The CPI reflects price movements for the same or similar item exclusive of enhancement or reduction in the quality or quantity of the item (see "Methodology" below).

The CPI is not a cost-of-living (COL) index. A COL index is a theoretical construct associated with the minimum expenditures necessary to maintain a constant standard of living over time. The CPI is not a cost-of-living (COL) index because the CPI measures price movements for purchasing only the same items between two periods, regardless of the availability of lower-priced substitutes, except for substitution among certain product categories, as noted below under "Methodology." The CPI also does not include other attributes of a COL index, such as accounting for household preferences between work and leisure, how changes in income tax rates affect the household's after-tax income and consequently the financial ability to buy the same goods and services over time, and social problems of crime and pollution that cause households to move to other areas or buy protective items. Also, the CPI is not a standard-of-living concept that prices spending patterns aimed at achieving certain standards of nutrition, housing, health, and so on that society considers appropriate.

The CPI is currently based on 1982 – 84 = 100.

The CPI data are seasonally adjusted.

Methodology

The monthly consumer price index (CPI) data are obtained primarily from surveys of retail and service establishments, utilities, and households. Surveyors visit or telephone the same retail and service establishments and price the same items if still available (or close substitutes) every month or bimonthly, depending on the city and item in the survey sample. For a small number of items such as used cars, airfares, and postal rates, the Bureau of Labor Statistics receives monthly reports on prices from trade sources and the Postal Service. Because housing rents are not volatile, and in order to reduce survey costs, rent information is obtained by less frequent visits (every six months) to one of six survey panels of apartments and single-family homes. The monthly rent change represents the change between rentals in the current month and six months earlier for the same panel of housing units. For example, the same panels are surveyed at six-month intervals for January and July, February and August, and so on, with each month's change represented by the sixth root of the six-month change. This procedure ensures that each panel is representative of the entire sample.

The current CPI weights for 2006 and 2007, which represent the proportion of household budgets spent on the various components, reflect consumer purchasing patterns during 2003–04. Weights for the main product categories are based on surveys of households to determine their actual purchasing patterns. As noted previously under "Content," the CPI spending patterns are revised every two years.

In order to more closely approximate the substitution effects of price shifts within generic product categories that represent closely related products, the Bureau of Labor Statistics uses geometric-mean estimating for these items. The geometric mean maintains the item share of *expenditures,* as distinct from *quantities,* constant from the base period. For example, in the category of laundry equipment, consumer preferences between washers and dryers are updated every year. This substitution within generic categories is done where it is considered most appropriate, which occurs in categories accounting for about 61 percent of the CPI. Food and beverages, apparel, and other goods and services are based on the geometric mean exclusively; in addition, selected shelter and government services charges are based on the geometric mean.

The remaining 39 percent of the CPI is based on arithmetic-mean indexing of fixed quantity weights between major spending pattern revisions. Use of the arithmetic means for selected categories reflects the fact that there is little ongoing substitution for these items. For example, rental housing is often based on a contract period; alternative electric, natural gas, and water utilities under deregulation typically are not available to households; and medical services are often determined by insurance plans.

It is important to keep in mind that this substitution is confined to generic product categories; it is not done between dissimilar categories such as between laundry equipment and kitchen appliances. Geometric averaging, in contrast to arithmetic averaging, treats price increases and decreases symmetrically, without the distortion of shifting bases.[3]

A new type of CPI, the C-CPI-U (chain CPI-U), was introduced in 2000. The C-CPI-U has a more comprehensive use of geometric averaging than the CPI-U and CPI-W. In addition to geometric averaging within generic product categories, the C-CPI-U includes geometric averaging at the overall index level from the base period to the current period. This is referred to as a superlative index.

If the quality or quantity of an item in the monthly survey has changed, an adjustment is made to reflect the improvement or decline. The goal is to price products having the same functional characteristics over time. For example, when an apartment building is renovated to include an elevator, if the rent increases by the cost of installing the elevator, the market-rent increase is represented as zero price change in the CPI. By contrast, if a loaf of bread becomes smaller but the price remains the same, the price of bread per unit has in fact increased and is represented as a price increase in the CPI. And when a new car with better safety features than those in the previous model increases in price less than the cost attributable to the improved safety features, the difference between the market price increase and the cost of making the safety improvements is represented as a price decrease in the CPI. The rent index assumes a small loss of quality as a housing unit ages. Thus, if the money rent of an apartment remains constant, the CPI would assume that the rent on an apartment of unchanging quality has increased.

Use of hedonic price measurement substantially lessens the problem of accounting for quality change. The word "hedonic" reflects its root meaning of pleasure, as the characteristics of a product in a hedonic index are assessed for the pleasure, or utility, they give the buyer. Hedonic price measurement, which requires considerable amounts of data, substantially lessens the problem of accounting for complex issues of quality change for which the production cost method is inadequate. A hedonic price index traces the effects of a group of attributes of a product that influences the price of an item, through both (a) the utility of the attributes to the buyer (demand), and (b) the cost of providing the attributes to the producer (supply). Currently hedonic indexes in the CPI are used for apparel, television sets, audio equipment, and college textbooks.

Because the data needed to make the necessary adjustments are not always available, the CPI contains an unknown amount of price change caused by quality and quantity changes. More generally, adjustments for quality change in the CPI are often complex and require special attention by the analyst preparing the estimates. Thus, the basis for some quality adjustments is ambiguous or relies on assumptions that are difficult to verify, which limits the accuracy of the adjustments. For example, scientific breakthroughs in various human diseases have resulted in longer life spans and an improved quality of life. But the task of putting a dollar value on the extended life spans and better quality of life, versus the increased costs of medical procedures and medicines in achieving these benefits, has not yet been solved for inclusion in the CPI. Another example is the greater variety of products available in stores from more countries resulting from the increased globalization of foreign trade.[4] But estimates of the impact of a greater variety of products that increase the quality of such goods, and consequently lower their CPI-measured price, are based on broad assumptions that need more refined statistical measurement for inclusion in the CPI.

Accuracy

The sampling error (for one standard error) of the monthly percentage change in the consumer price index (CPI) is plus or minus 0.06 of a percentage point. For example, if the estimated increase in the CPI from one month to the next were 0.30 percent, in two of three cases the "true" increase would be somewhere between 0.24 and 0.36 percent. For further information on the interpretation of sampling and nonsampling errors, see the Appendix.

Relevance

The consumer price index (CPI-U) is the most widely quoted number on price movements. In the formulation of macroeconomic fiscal and monetary policies (see "Relevance" under *gross domestic product*), trends in the CPI are a major guide in determining whether economic growth should be stimulated or restrained. The CPI is also contrasted with *unemployment* to analyze the tradeoff between inflation and unemployment, which is referred to as the Phillips Curve. Low inflation and low unemployment are primary goals of economic policies, as formulated in the Full Employment and Balanced Growth Act of 1978 (Humphrey-Hawkins Act).

The CPI is used in a variety of ways to adjust for cost escalation in commercial activities and in government programs: price change adjustments to wages, pensions, and income maintenance payments for cost-of-living allowances; price change adjustments in business contracts; and indexing of federal individual income tax brackets to limit inflation-induced bracket creep. Many labor–management union contracts are based on the CPI-W. In addition, the CPI is used to deflate various economic indicators to adjust for price change such as the consumer expenditure component of the *gross domestic product.*

Supplementary CPI measures are published that exclude price movements of food and energy products. Because these products sometimes have volatile price movements that are unrelated to cost pressures in the overall economy, their exclusion provides the "core inflation" rate, which is also referred to as the "underlying rate of inflation."

Recent Trends

From 1995 to 2004, the CPI-U and the CPI-W both increased within a range of approximately 1.5 to 3.5 percent annually (Table 11.1). The annual percentage changes in both indexes were the same in two years, differed by one percentage point in six years, and differed by 0.2 and 0.3 percentage point each in one year. The CPI-U increased more than the CPI-W in 1996, 1998, 2001, 2002, 2003, and 2004, and the CPI-W

Table 11.1

Consumer Price Index (annual percentage change)

	CPI-U	C-CPI-U	CPI-W
1995	2.8	NA	2.9
1996	3.0	NA	2.9
1997	2.3	NA	2.3
1998	1.6	NA	1.3
1999	2.2	NA	2.2
2000	3.4	NA	3.5
2001	2.8	2.3	2.7
2002	1.6	1.2	1.4
2003	2.3	2.1	2.2
2004	2.7	2.2	2.6
	1995–2004 (annual average)	2001–2004 (annual average)	1995–2004 (annual average)
	2.4	1.95	2.3

NA = not available

increased more than the CPI-U in 1995 and 2000. The C-CPI-U increased less than the CPI-U and the CPI-W in all years since the C-CPI-U was published. Over the entire nine-year period, the CPI-U increased at an average annual rate of 2.4 percent, and the CPI-W increased at an average annual rate of 2.3 percent. From 2001 to 2004, the C-CPI-U increased at an average annual rate of 1.9 percent (see Table 11.1).

Reference from Primary Data Source

Bureau of Labor Statistics, U.S. Department of Labor. *CPI Detailed Report* and *Monthly Labor Review.* Monthly.

Notes

1. The noninstitutional population represents people who are not in hospitals, nursing homes, jails, etc.

2. For possible future work on developing experimental inter-area price indexes to permit comparisons of price *levels* between local areas, see the Preface under "Data Sharing and Confidentiality of Federal Government Statistical Data." Also, for research on preparing inter-area price levels for the consumer price index, see Bettina H. Aten, "Report on Interarea Price Levels," Bureau of Economic Analysis, U.S. Department of Commerce, April 25, 2005. Available from the Bureau of Economic Analysis, www.bea.gov.

3. For example, a price increase from $4 to $5 in the ratio of 1.25 is 25 percent, while a price decrease from $5 to $4 in the ratio of .80 is –20 percent. The arithmetic mean shows the price increase as more important than the price decrease ([1.25 + .80]/2 = 1.025), while the geometric mean gives the same weight to both the price increase and the price decrease (1.25 x .80 = 1). Technically, geometric averaging is the nth root of the product of n numbers, and arithmetic averaging is the sum of n numbers divided by n.

4. Christian Broda, and David Weinstein, "Are We Underestimating the Gains from Globalization for the United States?" *Current Issues in Economics and Finance,* Federal Reserve Bank of New York, April 2005; idem, "Globalization and the Gains from Variety," NBER Working Paper 10314, National Bureau of Economic Research, February 2004.

12
Corporate Profits

Corporate profits are the returns to corporate enterprise from current operations. Profits occur when operating income (receipts) exceeds operating expenses (costs), and losses (negative profits) occur when expenses exceed income. Because profits are the difference between income and expenses, both elements affect profits. From one year to the next, for example, profits decline when income rises less than expenses or when income declines more than expenses, while profits increase when income rises more than expenses or when income declines less than expenses.

Where and When Available

Corporate profits measures are prepared quarterly for all industries by the Bureau of Economic Analysis in the U.S. Department of Commerce as part of the *gross domestic product*. The data are published in a news release and in the BEA monthly journal, *Survey of Current Business* (www.bea.gov). The profits data are available approximately fifty-five days after the quarter to which they refer; they are revised one month later and annually every summer.

Content

The corporate profits data are based on those used in calculating the *gross domestic product* (GDP). They are closer to the definitions of corporate profits in federal income tax returns than to those in company financial reports to stockholders. Profits are measured both before and after the payment of federal, state, and local income taxes. Undistributed corporate profits are the profits retained in the business after corporate income taxes are paid and dividends are distributed to stockholders. (Profits also accrue to unincorporated sole proprietorships and partnerships; corporations differ from unincorporated businesses in the method of designating ownership in the company, liability of owners, and income taxes.)

The following items highlight the main characteristics of corporate profits in the GDP that diverge from the definitions used in corporate federal income tax returns:

- Corporations encompass the following: (1) institutions required to file federal corporate income tax returns—for-profit corporations, savings and loan associations, mutual savings banks, and cooperatives, and (2) certain institutions not required to file federal corporate income tax returns—Federal Reserve Banks, federally sponsored credit unions, private noninsured pension funds, and nonprofit organizations that primarily serve business.
- The national measure of corporate (*gross national product*) profits shown in Table 12.1 includes profits from subsidiaries of U.S. companies abroad and excludes profits from subsidiaries of foreign companies in the United States. This measure is modified in the GDP through the rest-of-the-world sector, which conforms profits to the domestic measure by excluding profits from subsidiaries of U.S. companies abroad and including profits from subsidiaries of foreign companies in the United States.
- Inventory profits and losses are modified in the "inventory valuation adjustment" to eliminate profits or losses on inventory holdings due to changes in inventory prices.
- Depreciation allowances on equipment and structures are modified in the "capital consumption adjustment" to reflect the economic lifetime of capital facilities actually used in business practice in place of the service lives specified for these facilities in the income tax laws, and to reflect the current cost of replacing the existing equipment and structures in place of the original acquisition cost.
- Capital gains and losses from the sale of property are excluded from profits, except for the bid/ask price spreads on sales of securities by security dealers and brokers.

- Depletion allowances for using up nonreplaceable mineral reserves of mining corporations are added to profits.
- Charges for bad debts are treated as changes in asset valuation rather than as a deduction from profits.
- The corporate profits data are seasonally adjusted.

Methodology

Corporate profits are estimated every quarter from the *Quarterly Financial Report* (QFR) prepared for manufacturing, mining, and trade corporations by the U.S. Bureau of the Census. The QFR profits data are based on definitions used in company reports to stockholders. These are supplemented by company stockholder reports published in the press for certain industries not covered in the QFR, and indirect data on the economic activity for other industries such as construction. The above quarterly data are revised in subsequent years based on the annual *Statistics of Income* information for all industries, which is derived from federal corporate income tax returns and prepared by the U.S. Internal Revenue Service. These include the effects of IRS audits of corporate income tax returns. Special adjustments to the reported data for the GDP estimates of profits are made for institutional coverage, inventories, depreciation, capital gains and losses, depletion, and bad debts, as noted above under "Content."

Accuracy

The average revision error of corporate profits in the gross domestic product as a percentage of the quarterly change in profits is plus or minus 11.6 percentage points from the estimates eighty-five days after the quarter to the annual estimates three years later.

Relevance

Profits are the returns to investment and risk taking and are the prime motivating factor of the private-enterprise economy. Past profits and anticipated future profits directly affect business actions on *employment, inventory-sales ratios,* and equipment and structures investment. When business conditions are buoyant, entrepreneurs and executives are optimistic about the future and likely to expand their work force, inventories,

Table 12.1

Corporate Profits (billions of dollars)

	Profits before taxes, including IVA and CCAdj	Annual percentage change
1995	696.7	16.1
1996	786.2	12.8
1997	868.5	10.5
1998	801.6	−7.7
1999	851.3	6.2
2000	817.9	−3.9
2001	767.3	−6.2
2002	886.3	15.5
2003	1,031.8	16.4
2004	1,161.5	12.6
1995–2004 (annual average)		5.8

Note: Based on gross national product measure. See text under "Content" for difference with gross domestic product measure.

IVA = inventory valuation adjustment; CCAdj = capital consumption adjustment

and investment in capital facilities. By contrast, when business conditions are depressed, entrepreneurs and executives are pessimistic about the future and are likely to retrench employment, inventories, and investment.

Profits are one of the more volatile elements of the economy in that they tend to rise faster than the overall economy during business expansions and to decline more sharply than the rest of the economy during business recessions. While some corporations lose money, it is rare for all corporations in total to lose money. The last time total corporate profits of all companies were negative was in the depth of the Great Depression in 1931 and 1932.

Undistributed profits, also referred to as retained earnings, are profits after the payment of dividends to stockholders. Undistributed profits are internally generated funds available to business for use in operations, in investment, or in the balance sheet as an addition to surplus (external funds are obtained from *bank loans: commercial and industrial* and selling new equity stock). Undistributed profits fluctuate more than dividends since companies do not change dividend payments frequently. Company actions to change dividends are an indicator of business optimism, as a dividend increase indicates an optimistic outlook, while a dividend decrease indicates a pessimistic outlook.

Recent Trends

From 1995 to 2004, corporate profits fluctuated with annual percentage increases in double digits during 1995–97 and 2002–04, and annual decreases of 4 to 8 percent in 1998, 2000, and 2001 (Table 12.1). Over the entire nine-year period, corporate profits increased at an average annual rate of 6 percent.

Reference from Primary Data Source

Bureau of Economic Analysis, U.S. Department of Commerce. *Survey of Current Business*. Monthly.

13
Distribution of Income

The distribution of income data represent relative measures of income inequality. They show the proportions of total money income received by households in ascending steps on the income ladder. The data are often referred to with the qualitative designation of low-, middle-, and high-income groups. They are typically shown in statistical quintiles, which array the number of households from the lowest to the highest fifths based on income. For example, in 2003, the 20 percent of households with the lowest incomes received 3.4 percent of all money income, while the 20 percent of households with the highest incomes received 49.8 percent of all money income. Quintile income groups provide a relative measure of income distribution by comparing the position of one income group with that of others. In contrast, a single number, referred to as the Gini index of income inequality, signifies the overall extent of inequality in the income distribution.

Where and When Available

The Bureau of the Census in the U.S. Department of Commerce prepares annual measures of the distribution of income. The data are published annually in *Income, Poverty, and Health Insurance in the United States* (www.census.gov).

The income measures are available in August/September after the year to which they refer. Revisions for previous years are made in the annual publication.

Content

The official measures of the distribution of income represent money income of households both before and after the payment of such items as federal and state income taxes, Social Security taxes, federal employee retirement taxes, property taxes, Medicare deductions, and union dues. Money income is defined as regularly received cash income, such as wages and salaries, profits from self-employment, Social Security, retirement, unemployment insurance, other income maintenance benefits, interest, dividends, rents, royalties, estates and trusts, educational assistance, alimony, child support, and financial assistance from outside the household (excluding gifts and sporadic assistance). Noncash benefits, such as food stamps, Medicare, Medicaid, and rent supplements, as well as income from nonrecurring sources such as capital gains and life insurance settlements, are excluded from money income. In addition to this official money-income measure, the Census Bureau prepares seventeen alternative income-distribution measures based on varying definitions of items included and excluded as cash and noncash income and on the inclusion and exclusion of certain taxes; these also are the basis for alternative estimates of the poverty population (see *poverty*).

Statistical quintiles, which are featured in this description, are one of various measures of income distribution (e.g., deciles, percentiles). Quintiles array the number of households from the lowest to the highest fifths based on income and are a commonly used method for highlighting income shares in the distribution of income data. In contrast, the Gini index of income inequality is a single overall measure of the income distribution. The Gini index is a number that indicates the extent of inequality throughout the entire distribution. The Gini index ranges from zero to one, with zero indicating perfect equality (all recipients receive equal amounts of income), and 1.0 indicating perfect inequality (one recipient receives all of the income).

Household income data are also published in dollar amounts before the payment of taxes in selected increasing intervals up to $99,999 (under $5,000, $5,000–$9,999, $10,000–$14,999, $15,000–$24,999, $25,000–$34,999, $35,000–$49,999, $50,000–$74,999, $75,000–$99,999, $100,000 and over). Unpublished income intervals from $100,000 to $249,999, in one total for $250,000 and over, and in uniform intervals of $2,500 for the entire distribution up to

$249,999 are available on the Census Bureau's Web site. Income intervals above $250,000 are not available, in order to maintain the confidentiality of the data.

The household income data represent the income received by the unit defined as a household. A household consists of all persons who occupy a housing unit. A household may include one or more families and/or one or more unrelated individuals. A family refers to two or more persons related by birth, marriage, or adoption and living together in a house, apartment, a group of rooms, or a single room intended for separate living quarters. An unrelated individual is a person fifteen years old and older who does not live with any relatives. A housing unit has direct access from the outside or through a common hall. The occupants of a housing unit do not live or eat with any other people in the structure. The definition of households excludes people living in group quarters (e.g., hotels, dormitories), or institutions (e.g., hospitals, jails, shelters, halfway houses), or having no residence (people living on the street).

The members of a household may or may not share their incomes for personal consumption.[1] Consequently, the household is not a perfect unit for measuring income distribution. But the household is a practical device for measuring the incomes of people living in housing units.

Methodology

The before-tax household income data are based on the Current Population Survey (CPS) conducted by the Census Bureau. The information is collected every March in an income supplement for the previous calendar year. The survey sample is approximately 60,000 households. Typically, 55,500 are interviewed and 4,500 are not available for interviews. For additional detail on the CPS, see *employment.*

Estimates of household income after the payment of taxes are based on tax simulations incorporating the CPS income figures with several other data sources. Federal and state income taxes are simulated based on data from the Internal Revenue Service's *Statistics of Income* and the Commerce Clearinghouse's *State Tax Handbook;* Social Security and federal employee retirement taxes are estimated using the legal percentage rates for these taxes; and property taxes are estimated from information in the U.S. Department of Housing and Urban Development's *American Housing Survey.*

The quintiles and the Gini index for the household income data are calculated using two methodologies—actual sorted data and grouped data. The actual sorted data are used for the before-tax estimates. The grouped data are in income intervals of $2,500 and are used for the after-tax estimates (see "Content," above).

Accuracy

The sampling error (for one standard error) for the quintile shares of income before taxes in 2004 rose in each quintile from 0.02 of a percentage point for the lowest quintile to 0.34 percentage point for the highest quintile of households. In the lowest quintile of households, the share of income before taxes in 2004 was 3.4 percent. For example, in two of three cases the "true" share of income was somewhere between 3.398 and 3.402 percent. For further information on the interpretation of sampling and nonsampling errors, see the Appendix.

A comparison of the household income estimates of the Census Bureau with the personal income estimates of the U.S. Bureau of Economic Analysis (see *personal income and saving*) for the year 2001, after placing both income estimates on a comparable definitional basis, indicated that total household income was 11 percent below total personal income.[2] The difference is attributed to underreporting by survey respondents on the CPS, which is the source of household income data, as contrasted with administrative records of income tax, unemployment insurance, Social Security, and other income programs that are the source of the personal income data. This overall underreporting is not taken into account in developing the income distribution data because determining the variations in underreporting among income groups is difficult.

Relevance

The income distribution focuses on differences in economic well-being among groups in the population. The data show the inequality of income shares in the population and how it changes over time. The designation of low-, middle-, and high-income group is qualitative. It varies with the income thresholds used to arrive at these classifications, and with the perception individuals have of who is rich, poor, or in the middle.[3] The user of income distribution data should be aware of the income thresholds associated with references to low-, middle-, and high-income groups.

A large disparity in the income distribution suggests a society that is divided into "haves" and "have nots," which raises both economic and social concerns. Economic growth is hindered when purchasing power and profit-motivated incentives are not broadly based. Socially, a large disparity results in increasing discord and despair among the population. Economic growth and social harmony are regarded as essential to a democratic and stable society, even while political and economic philosophies for achieving these goals differ.

The distribution of income is related to *poverty* and the *distribution of wealth*, as well as to *productivity*, *average weekly earnings*, and price movements in the *consumer price index*, *producer price indexes*, and *GDP price measures*. Inequality of income stems from many sources, such as the match of workers having particular skills with the job market for those skills, discrimination, inheritance, innate abilities, entrepreneurial spirit, and luck.

Recent Trends

From 1980 to 2004 (based on five-year intervals to 2000 and then 2003 and 2004), the share of money income received by each of the first four-fifths of the households declined (Table 13.1). Conversely, the top fifth of households showed an increasing share of the income from 1980 to 2004. The only exception occurred in the fourth-fifth category, which increased slightly from 2000 to 2004.

The same general pattern occurred both before and after the payment of federal and state income taxes, Social Security and federal employee retirement taxes, and property taxes, although the inequality increased slightly less for income after taxes. Before taxes, the share of total income going to the top fifth of households rose from 43.7 percent in 1980 to 49.8 percent in 2003 (6.1 percentage points). After taxes, the top fifth's share rose from 40.6 percent in 1980 to 46.2 percent in 2003 (5.6 percentage points). Income share estimates after taxes for 2004 were not available at the time of this writing.

The Gini index for income before taxes rose from 0.401 in 1980 to 0.466 in 2004. Thus, on an overall basis, income inequality increased over the twenty-three-year period.

Table 13.1

Distribution of Income: Household Shares (in 2003 dollars)

Households (quintiles)	Income (percentage)						
	2004	2003	2000	1995	1990	1985	1980
Income before taxes							
Lowest fifth	3.4	3.4	3.6	3.7	3.9	4.0	4.3
Second fifth	8.7	8.7	8.9	9.1	9.6	9.7	10.3
Third fifth	14.7	14.8	14.8	15.2	15.9	16.3	16.9
Fourth fifth	23.2	23.4	23.0	23.3	24.0	24.6	24.9
Highest fifth	50.1	49.8	49.8	48.7	46.6	45.3	43.7
Total	100.0	100.0	100.0	100.0	100.0	100.0	100.0
Gini index of income inequality	0.466	0.464	0.462	0.450	0.428	0.419	0.403

Mean money income in quintiles in 2004: lowest fifth: $10,264; second fifth: $26,241; third fifth: $44,455; fourth fifth: $70,085; highest fifth: $151,593

	2004	2003	2000	1995	1990	1985	1980
Income after taxes							
Lowest fifth	NA	4.0	4.5	4.5	4.5	4.6	4.9
Second fifth	NA	10.0	10.5	10.5	10.8	11.0	11.6
Third fifth	NA	15.9	16.5	16.4	16.9	17.2	17.9
Fourth fifth	NA	24.0	24.1	23.9	24.3	24.7	25.1
Highest fifth	NA	46.2	44.4	44.6	43.5	42.6	40.6
Total	NA	100.0	100.0	100.0	100.0	100.0	100.0

Note: Components may not sum to totals, due to rounding. NA = Not available at time of writing.

Reference from Primary Data Source

Bureau of the Census, U.S. Department of Commerce. *Income, Poverty, and Health Insurance Coverage in the United States.* Annual.

Notes

1. Paul Ryscavage, *Income Inequality in America* (Armonk, NY: M.E. Sharpe, 1999), p. 29.

2. John Ruser, Adrienne Pilot, and Charles Nelson, "Alternative Measures of Household Income: BEA Personal Income, CPS Money Income, and Beyond," May 2004. Available from the Census Bureau, www.census.gov.

3. Ryscavage, *Income Inequality in America,* pp. 9 and 35.

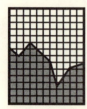

14
Distribution of Wealth

The distribution of wealth represents the material assets, liabilities, and net worth (assets minus liabilities) of households. The distribution focuses on the percentage shares of wealth accounted for by households. Assets cover financial and nonfinancial categories: cash, securities, and other financial holdings, and personal property, real property, and other nonfinancial holdings. Liabilities comprise debt associated with consumer credit, mortgage loans, and other borrowing.

Where and When Available

The Federal Reserve Board (FRB) prepares the distribution of wealth data for a single year every three years. A summary of the data is published in the quarterly FRB journal, *Federal Reserve Bulletin* (www.federalreserve.gov).

The wealth data are available approximately two years after the year to which they refer. The wealth measures are not scheduled to be revised; they are revised on an ad hoc basis when a specific issue arises.

Content

Distribution-of-wealth data are provided as a balance sheet of the assets, liabilities, and net worth for families. They are available on a statistically consistent basis for 1989, 1992, 1995, 1998, and 2001. Earlier wealth data for the 1960s, 1970s, and 1983 are not statistically consistent with the 1989 and later data. Wealth data are planned for every three years for 2004, 2007, and so on.

In the distribution of wealth data, a family is defined as a couple whether married or living together as partners, as well as individuals living in the household who are financially interdependent with the couple or with other individuals in the household. Thus, this definition of a family is closer to the definition of a household in the U.S. Census Bureau's data on income distribution, in which an individual is not classified as a family, than it is to the definition of family in the Census Bureau's data (see *distribution of income*).

Assets

Financial and nonfinancial asset data represent the cumulation of previous incomes that have been saved or invested.

Financial Assets

- Transaction accounts: checking, savings, and money market accounts, other
- Certificates of deposit
- Savings bonds
- Other government and commercial bonds
- Publicly traded corporate stocks
- Mutual funds
- Retirement accounts
- Cash value life insurance
- Other financial assets

Nonfinancial Assets

- Vehicles: automobiles, sport utility vehicles, trucks, motorcycles, motor homes, recreational vehicles, airplanes, boats
- Primary residence
- Other residential property
- Equity in nonresidential property
- Business equity: sole proprietorships, partnerships, corporations, other
- Other nonfinancial assets: artwork, jewelry, precious metals, antiques, other tangible assets

The values of these assets incorporates the effects of capital gains and losses. Capital gains and losses are the difference between the current and sales price of an asset. Capital gains or losses that result from changes in the value of such assets as stocks, real estate, and businesses are realized as income only when the asset is sold. Unrealized capital gains and losses are those in which the asset has not yet been sold and are included in the wealth measures. Thus, as the prices of stocks, businesses, or real estate assets rise or fall, the wealth estimates rise or fall accordingly.

Liabilities

Liabilities data refer to debts incurred from borrowings. Some of the liabilities are financial obligations associated with the financial and non-financial assets mentioned above.

- Home secured debt: home mortgages and home equity borrowing
- Other residential debt
- Installment borrowing
- Other lines of credit
- Credit card balances
- Other debt: loans on insurance policies, loans against pension accounts, borrowings on margin accounts, other loans

Methodology

The distribution-of-wealth data are obtained from the Survey of Consumer Finances sponsored by the Federal Reserve Board. The NORC at the University of Chicago (formerly the National Opinion Research Center at the University of Chicago) has conducted the survey for the FRB since 1992.

The 2001 survey is based on information obtained from a probability sample of 4,499 households. The sample includes an oversampling of wealthy households that hold a disproportionately large share of such assets as noncorporate businesses and tax-exempt bonds to ensure that sufficient survey returns are available for developing these estimates. The data were gathered during May–December 2001, primarily from interviews conducted in person, plus telephone interviews when more convenient for the respondent.

Accuracy

Standard errors (for one standard error) due to sampling and imputations for the distribution-of-wealth data based on the net worth held by various

Table 14.1

Net Worth and Standard Errors of Percentile Groups of Families: 2001
(percentiles of families)

	0–49.9	50–89.9	90–94.9	95–98.9	99–100	Total
Share of dollar net worth (percentage)	2.8	27.4	12.1	25.0	32.7	100.0
Standard errors	0.1	0.7	0.7	1.1	1.4	

Source: Arthur B. Kennickell, *A Rolling Tide: Changes in the Distribution of Wealth in the U.S., 1989-2001,* Federal Reserve Board, Washington, DC. September 2003, Table 5, p. 9.

percentile groupings of families for 2001 are shown in Table 14.1. In the 0–49.0 percentile of families, the standard error was 0.1 of a percentage point and the share of dollar net worth was 2.8 percent. For example, in two of three cases the "true" share of the dollar net worth was somewhere between 2.7 and 2.9 percent. For further information on the interpretation of sampling and nonsampling errors, see the Appendix.

Relevance

The distribution of wealth shows the disparity of economic well-being among households. In highlighting differences in the material well-being of the population, the wealth measures summarize the relative economic well-being and economic power derived from income and saving flows over time and the intergenerational transfer of wealth. The wealth data are the resultant inventory of "haves" and "have nots" emanating from income and saving flows and intergenerational transfers.

The distribution of wealth is related to the *distribution of income* and *poverty.* Inequality of income stems from many sources, such as the match of workers having particular skills with the job market for those skills, discrimination, inheritance, innate abilities, entrepreneurial spirit, and luck.

Recent Trends

From 1989 to 2001 (based on three-year points), movements in the distribution of net worth (assets minus liabilities) among families grouped

Table 14.2

Distribution of Dollar Net Worth (percentage)

| | Percentiles of families | | | | | |
	0–49.9	50–89.9	90–94.9	95–98.9	99–100	Total
1989	2.7	29.9	13.0	24.1	30.3	100.0
1992	3.3	29.7	12.6	24.4	30.2	100.0
1995	3.6	28.6	11.9	21.3	34.6	100.0
1998	3.0	28.4	11.4	23.3	33.9	100.0
2001	2.8	27.4	12.1	25.0	32.7	100.0

Note: Components may not sum to totals, due to rounding.
Source: See Table 14.1.

by percentile showed a general increasing inequality of wealth, though the inequality patterns fluctuated among the five survey years (Table 14.2). In 2001, the lowest 50 percent of families in terms of net worth accounted for 2.8 percent of the net worth held by all families, while the highest one percent of families in terms of net worth held 32.7 percent of the net worth held by all families.

References from Primary Data Source

Ana M. Aizcorbe, Arthur B. Kennickell, and Kevin B. Moore, "Recent Changes in U.S. Family Finances: Evidence from the 1998 and 2001 Survey of Consumer Finances," *Federal Reserve Bulletin,* January 2003.
Arthur B. Kennickell, *A Rolling Tide: Changes in the Distribution of Wealth in the U.S., 1989–2001,* Federal Reserve Board, September 2003.

15
Employment

Employment represents workers engaged in gainful work. There are two official measures of employment prepared by the U.S. Bureau of Labor Statistics. One is a count of jobs and is based on a survey of employer establishments, and the other is a count of employed persons and is based on a survey of households. Both measures reflect similar phenomena, but because the definitions and methodologies differ, there are periods when their movements differ substantially.

The two surveys are described separately, first the establishment survey and then the household survey. This is followed by a summary of the main technical differences between them, and then by highlights of the relevance and recent trends of both.

Establishment Survey

Where and When Available

Employment data are provided monthly by the Bureau of Labor Statistics (BLS) in the U.S. Department of Labor. The data are published in a news release and in two BLS monthly journals, *Monthly Labor Review* and *Employment and Earnings* (www.bls.gov).

The data are available on the third Friday after the week containing the twelfth of the month. Thus, the information is released on the first or second Friday of the month following the month in question. The exception to the third Friday rule is that if January 1, 2, or 3 or a federal holiday falls on the third Friday, the release date is moved one day earlier. On the day the data are released, the commissioner of labor statistics reports on recent employment and unemployment trends to the Joint Economic Committee of Congress. Preliminary data are provided for the immediately preceding month; these are revised in the subsequent two months. Annual revisions are made in February of the following year.

Content

Employment data cover the number of paid nonfarm civilian jobs on employer payrolls in U.S. enterprises and governments. To be counted, a job must be on the payroll of a business, a nonprofit organization, or the federal or a state or local government. All paid jobs are counted equally, from the lowest pay scales to company executives and officers, as are full-time and part-time jobs. Since some individuals hold two or more jobs, the number of jobs exceeds the number of working persons. Included in the employment data are residents of Canada and Mexico who commute to jobs on employer payrolls in the United States, and institutionalized persons (e.g., those confined to penal or mental facilities) and residents of old-age homes on payroll jobs. The employment data exclude farm workers, self-employment, jobs in private households, railroad employment, religious organization employment, elected officials, unpaid family work, military personnel on active duty in the armed forces (but uniformed military personnel who hold civilian jobs are included in the job count), and employees of the Central Intelligence Agency, Defense Intelligence Agency, National Geospatial-Intelligence Agency, and National Security Agency.

Persons on paid leave for illness or vacation are counted as employed because the job continues as a payroll cost. Those temporarily not working because of illness, vacation, strike, or lockout and who are not paid are not counted as employed.

The establishment employment data are seasonally adjusted.

Methodology

The employment data are based on employer payroll records that represent employees on payrolls during pay periods that include the twelfth day of the month. The data are obtained from a survey of a sample of approximately 160,000 businesses and government agencies including 400,000 individual worksite establishments in 2004. The sample includes employers with only one work location as well as those with several establishments (an establishment is defined as the physical location of an employer's operations, with companies and other organizations operating in more than one location having several establishments). The survey sample covered approximately one-third of all nonfarm employment in 2004.

The survey sample became a full probability sample in 2003. The monthly estimates are based on changes in employment by the same establishments reporting in the preceding month. In order to reduce the reporting burden, all but the largest establishments are rotated out of the sample after participating in the survey for an extended period of time. Employers having single or multiple establishments in their unemployment insurance (UI) tax accounts that have more than 1,000 employees are in the establishment sample continuously, that is, they are not rotated out of the sample. Employers pay their UI taxes to the Bureau of Public Debt in the U.S. Department of the Treasury.

The surveys of industry, nonprofits, and state and local governments are conducted for BLS by the state governments' employment agencies. The monthly data are collected primarily by electronic data interchange, touch data entry, and computer-assisted telephone interviewing, and secondarily by Fax and mail. Data covering all federal civilian workers, including the Department of Defense, are provided by the U.S. National Finance Center. Armed forces military personnel and employees of the Central Intelligence Agency, Defense Intelligence Agency, National Geospatial-Intelligence Agency, and National Security Agency are excluded from the job count.

The monthly employment data are benchmarked and revised every year. The benchmark is based primarily on the universe of the UI employment data, which account for approximately 97 percent of the total employment of the establishment survey. The remaining 3 percent of total employment is obtained mainly from records of the Railroad Retirement Board and from the U.S. Census Bureau's *County Business Patterns* (CBP); the CBP data reflect employment statistics from administrative records of the U.S. Internal Revenue Service's Employer's Quarterly Federal Tax Return (Form 941) for small employers, and from the Census Bureau's annual Company Organization Survey for large employers. The benchmark data are prepared for March of the previous year, and the relative revisions for March are carried back through the previous eleven months and extrapolated forward to the current period.

The benchmark data become available in February of the current period with the release of the January data. For example, the employment data beginning with January 2006 that are released in February 2006 are based on the March 2005 benchmark data.

Because of the difficulty of obtaining timely information on the startup of new firms, the establishment survey collection is late in capturing the employment in these firms. To compensate for this understatement of jobs in new establishments, the survey data are augmented by an estimate derived from a statistical model. The model also implicitly adjusts for the late identification of establishments going out of operations.

Accuracy

The sampling error (for one standard error) for the establishment employment data is 0.2 percent for the monthly level and 67,700 jobs for the monthly change. For example, if the estimated monthly level of establishment employment were 130 million workers, in two of three cases the "true" level would be somewhere between 129,740,000 and 130,260,000 workers. And if the estimated increase in establishment employment from one month to the next were 200,000 workers, in two of three cases the "true" increase would be somewhere between 132,300 and 267,700 workers. For further information on the interpretation of sampling and nonsampling errors, see the Appendix.

Household Survey

Where and When Available

Employment data are provided monthly by the Bureau of Labor Statistics in the U.S. Department of Labor. The data are published in a news release and in two BLS monthly journals, *Monthly Labor Review* and *Employment and Earnings* (www.bls.gov).

The data are available on the third Friday after the week containing the twelfth of the month, which falls on the first or second Friday of the month following the month to which they refer. Thus, the information is released on the first or second Friday of the month following the month in question. The exception to the third Friday rule is that if January 1, 2, or 3 or a federal holiday falls on the third Friday, the release date is moved one day earlier. On the day the data are released, the commissioner of labor statistics reports on recent employment and unemployment trends to the Joint Economic Committee of Congress. The monthly data are revised every January for the previous five years based on updated seasonal factors.

Content

Employed persons represent noninstitutionalized individuals sixteen years old and older living in the United States who worked at least one hour as wage- and salary-paid employees, self-employed persons working in their own businesses, unpaid workers in a family business who worked at least fifteen hours a week, and civilian government workers in nonfarm and farm activities.[1] They include U.S. residents who commute to jobs in Canada and Mexico. Thus, the employed civilian population consists of wage and salary employees and those who work for profit, the latter being the self-employed and unpaid workers in family businesses who are assumed to share in the profits. All persons are counted equally if they are paid for an hour or more per week. If a person has two or more jobs, the job with the most hours worked in the week is the only one counted, and the hours worked for all jobs are assigned to that job. Supplemental data on the number of multiple jobholders are provided. Also, detail is provided by age, gender, race, Hispanic origin, educational attainment, marital status, and broad occupational and industry groupings.

Persons are defined as employed who are temporarily absent because of vacation, illness, bad weather, child-care problems, maternity or paternity leave, strike or lockout, job training, or other family or personal reasons, regardless of whether they are paid for the time off or are seeking other jobs. Included as employed are citizens of foreign countries who are temporarily in the United States but not living on embassy premises. Excluded from the employment data are all military personnel on active duty in the armed forces (including uniformed military personnel holding civilian jobs); residents of Canada and Mexico who commute to jobs in the United States; persons who work solely around their house (painting, repairing, other home housework); those who do volunteer work for religious, charitable, or other organizations; and institutionalized persons (e.g., those confined to penal or mental facilities) and residents of homes for the aged on payroll jobs.

The household employment data are seasonally adjusted.

Methodology

The household survey employment data are obtained from a monthly survey of households called the Current Population Survey (CPS). The CPS is a sample of about 60,000 households, which the U.S. Bureau of the Census conducts for the Bureau of Labor Statistics.[2] Responses are actually obtained from about 55,500 households; no responses are obtained from the remaining 4,500 households due to absence, impassable roads, refusals, or other reasons. The sample is representative of the distribution of households in small and large metropolitan areas and in rural areas. It undergoes a major revision every ten years to be consistent with the most recent decennial population census. The sample currently is based on the decennial 2000 census of population. The sample is also updated during intercensal years on a limited basis to reflect current changes in residential locations due to new construction based on *housing starts* data prepared by the Census Bureau and on estimates of international migration.

In order to reduce the reporting burden on any group of households, the sample is divided into eight subsamples (panels) that are rotated over a sixteen-month period. Each subsample is surveyed for four consecutive months, then dropped from the survey for eight months, and subsequently resurveyed for the following four months. At the end of the sixteen months, the subsample is eliminated from the sample and is replaced with a new panel of households. The result of this procedure is that every month 25 percent of the households in the sample are either new to the survey or are returning after an eight-month hiatus. Correspondingly, 25 percent of the sample households drop out of the survey every month.

The survey refers to the individual's employment status during the calendar week (Sunday through Saturday) that includes the twelfth of the month. The survey is conducted mainly by telephone interviews, supplemented by personal interviews as necessary.

The CPS survey data are also used to estimate *unemployment*.

Accuracy

The sampling error (for one standard error) for the household employment data is 326,000 workers for the monthly level and 212,000 workers for the monthly change. For example, if the estimated monthly level of household employment were 150 million workers, in two of three cases the "true" level would be somewhere between 149,574,000 and 150,326,000 workers. And if the estimated increase in household employment from one month to the next were 200,000 workers, in two of three cases the "true" change would be somewhere between –12,000 and 412,000 workers. For further information on the interpretation of sampling and nonsampling errors, see the Appendix.

Comparison of the Establishment and Household Employment Measures

This section summarizes the main differences between the employment data obtained from the establishment and household surveys.

Coverage

Employment data based on the establishment survey are limited to employees in nonagricultural industries (including government civilian workers) who are paid for their work or for their absence from the job. By contrast, employment data based on the household survey cover a broader range of employment, including farm workers, the self-employed, private household workers, unpaid workers in family businesses, plus those temporarily absent from work due to illness, vacation, strike, or lockout, even if they are not paid during their absence. The establishment data partially compensate for their smaller coverage by including workers of all ages, multiple jobs of workers, residents of Canada and Mexico who commute to the United States for work, and institutionalized persons and residents of homes for the aged on payroll jobs. By contrast, the household survey is limited to workers sixteen years and older, counts each worker only once regardless of how many jobs he or she may hold (supplementary data on multiple jobs of workers are available), excludes Canadian and Mexican residents commuting to jobs in the United States, but includes U.S. residents commuting to Canada and Mexico, and excludes institutionalized persons and residents of homes for the aged on payroll jobs.

Also, there are differences in the treatment of persons in the armed forces on active duty. The establishment survey distinguishes between uniformed personnel holding military or civilian jobs. Those holding military jobs are excluded and those holding civilian jobs are included in the employment count. By contrast, the household survey excludes both categories from the employment count.

In addition, the survey reference period differs between the two surveys. The reference period for the establishment survey is the *pay period* that includes the twelfth of the month, while the reference period for the household survey is the *calendar week* (Sunday through Saturday) that includes the twelfth of the month. Because pay periods vary in length, typically from one to two weeks but in some cases also longer, such as with monthly pay, the establishment survey counts workers over a longer period than the household survey, which can cause differences in the two measures if the employment movement is upward or downward during the pay period.

The net effect of these differences is that the household survey shows more employment than the establishment survey. Reconciliation of both measures, when they are put on as similar a basis as the available data will allow, reduces the difference substantially.[3] For example, in 2003, household survey employment exceeded establishment survey employment by 7.74 million before the reconciliation and only 258,000 after the reconciliation; and in 2004, household survey employment exceeded establishment survey employment by 7.77 million before the reconciliation and only 345,000 after the reconciliation.

Component Detail

The establishment survey details the industry composition and geographic location of jobs, which is useful in analyses of the industrial structure and location of employment. The household survey details the age, gender, race, Hispanic origin, educational attainment, marital status, and broad occupational and industry groupings of workers, which is useful for analyzing the worker characteristics of employment trends. Therefore, each measure has its particular uses because of the different detail provided.

Accuracy

Statistically, both surveys have strengths and weaknesses. The establishment survey has a better information source because the data are obtained from employer payroll records, which are used for tax and accounting records. But its use of a statistical model to compensate for the late introduction of new employer establishments into the survey sample may cause the monthly movements to be smoother than actually occurs in the workplace.

In contrast, the household survey obtains undocumented answers to survey questions from household members that suffer from such problems as the inability to obtain information on all persons in the sample household,[4] differences in the interpretation of the questions by different respondents in the same household from month to month, inability or unwillingness of respondents to provide correct information, and inability to recall information. The change in respondents from month to month by the rotation of the survey samples may cause more volatility in the changing monthly direction of employment than actually occurs in the workplace.

Overall, while each survey has shortcomings, I agree with the consensus view of the economics community that the establishment survey provides more reliable measures of monthly and annual employment movements than those of the household survey. In addition to the greater reliability of the employer payroll records of employment used in the establishment survey compared with the personal interviews in the household survey, I believe the much larger sample and the much smaller sampling error in the establishment survey make its employment estimates superior to those of the household survey.

Relevance

Employment is the main source of household incomes, which in turn, are spent on consumer goods and services. Because household spending (*retail sales* represent the goods component) accounted in the first half of the 2000s for 70 percent of the *gross domestic product,* employment is a key factor affecting economic growth. In addition, employment data based on the establishment survey are used as inputs to other indicators such as the *gross domestic product, industrial production index,* and *leading, coincident, and lagging indexes.*

The distribution of employment between high- and low-paying jobs also affects *personal income and saving.* The types of jobs held influence economic growth as well as living conditions (*distribution of income* and *distribution of wealth*), because the bulk of the population depends on employment as its main source of income.

The distinction in detail provided by both surveys—industry and ge-

Table 15.1

Employment: Alternative Definitions

	Establishment survey (nonfarm civilian jobs)	Household survey (All civilian workers)
Level (millions)		
1995	117.3	124.9
1996	119.7	126.7
1997	122.8	129.6
1998	125.9	131.5
1999	129.0	133.5
2000	131.8	136.9
2001	131.8	136.9
2002	130.3	136.5
2003	130.0	137.7
2004	131.5	139.3
Change (millions)		
1995–2000	14.5	12.0
2000–2004	−0.3	2.4
1995–2004	14.2	14.4
2000–01	0.0	0.0
2001–02	−1.5	−0.4
2002–03	−0.3	1.2
2003–04	0.5	1.6
Annual percentage change		
1995–2000	2.36	1.85
2000–2004	−0.06	0.44
1995–2004	1.28	1.22

ography for establishment survey and demographic for the household survey—means that at the disaggregated level, each survey has its unique uses, as noted above.

Recent Trends

From 1995 to 2004, establishment employment increased 14.2 million, and household employment increased 14.4 million (Table 15.1). Both surveys showed similar directional movements in employment in all years except 2003, when employment in the establishment survey declined while that in the household survey rose.

But there were sharp differences in the movements of both surveys between the intermediate periods of 1995–2000 and 2000–04 (both surveys showed zero change between 2000 and 2001). Over the 1995–2000 period, establishment employment increased 14.5 million and household employment increased 12.0 million, while over 2000–04, establishment employment decreased 0.3 million and household employment increased 2.4 million. Also, the 2002–04 establishment employment levels were below those in 2000 and 2001, while the 2003–04 employment levels in the household survey were above those in 2000 and 2001.

These differences also appeared in the relative measures of annual percentage change between 1995–2000 and 2000–04. These showed negative growth in establishment employment and marked lesser growth in household employment in 2000–04 compared with 1995–2000.

Reference from Primary Data Source

Bureau of Labor Statistics, U.S. Department of Labor. *Monthly Labor Review* and *Employment and Earnings*. Monthly.

Notes

1. Self-employed persons whose businesses are unincorporated are classified as self-employed, but those whose businesses are incorporated are classified as wage and salary employees because, technically, they are paid employees of a corporation.

2. A household consists of all persons—related family members and unrelated individuals—who occupy a housing unit and have no other usual address. A housing unit is intended as separate living quarters, and encompasses single-family houses, townhouses, condominiums, apartments, mobile homes, single rooms, and group quarters where residents share common facilities or receive formal or authorized care or custody. There were 112.0 million households in the United States in 2003.

3. There are a variety of "irreconcilable" statistical differences between the establishment and household employment data, including sampling errors, benchmarks, estimation methodologies, pay period versus calendar week data collections, and some independent contractors classified as wage and salary workers rather than as self-employed in the household survey.

4. Particularly minority men and undocumented aliens.

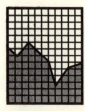

16
Employment Cost Index

The employment cost index (ECI) measures changes in labor costs to employers for money wages and salaries and noncash fringe benefits in nonfarm private industry and state and local governments for workers at all levels of responsibility. The ECI is not affected by shifts in the composition of employment between high-wage and low-wage industries or between high- and low-wage occupations within industries. Thus, the ECI represents labor costs for the same jobs over time. This contrasts with the shifting types of jobs in *average weekly earnings,*

Where and When Available

The employment cost index is prepared quarterly by the Bureau of Labor Statistics (BLS) in the U.S. Department of Labor. The data are published in a news release and in the BLS monthly journal, *Monthly Labor Review* (www.bls.gov).

The data are available during the last week of the month immediately following the quarter to which they refer (April for the first quarter, July for the second quarter, October for the third quarter, and January for the fourth quarter). No revisions are made to the ECI data, except for the re-estimation of seasonal factors for the most recent five years.

Content

The employment cost index data cover labor costs to employers. The costs include money wages and salaries; commissions; bonuses; fringe benefits such as paid leave for vacations, illness, holidays, and so on, and noncash health, retirement, and other fringe benefits. The data are provided for private nonfarm industries, including union and nonunion workers separately, and for state and local governments. Costs are included for all workers—production, nonsupervisory, supervisory, and executive. The wage and salary component of labor costs reflects straight-time pay only before payroll deductions, excluding premium rates for overtime, holidays, night work, and hazardous conditions. Production bonuses, incentive earnings, commission payments, and cost-of-living adjustments are included in straight-time wage and salary rates.

The benefit cost component reflects the cost of benefits. Benefit costs include paid vacation, sick, and holiday leave; life, health, and disability insurance; higher pay for overtime, weekends, holidays, shift differentials, and nonproduction bonuses such as referral bonuses and lump-sum payments in lieu of wage increases; legally required benefits for Social Security, Medicare, federal and state unemployment insurance, and workers' compensation, and other benefits for severance pay and supplemental unemployment plans.

Wages and salaries plus benefit costs are called compensation. Data are provided separately for compensation, wages and salaries, and benefit costs.

The ECI represents a fixed composition of industries and of occupations within industries. Therefore, movements in the index over time are not affected by shifts between higher- and lower-paying industries and occupations. By contrast, *average weekly earnings* are affected by such changes. In addition to industry and occupational detail, the ECI distinguishes compensation costs between union and nonunion workers.

The ECI is currently based on an index base of June 1989 = 100.

The ECI data are seasonally adjusted.

Methodology

The employment cost index data are based on an ECI survey of employer payrolls in the third month of the quarter (March, June, September, and December) for the pay period including the twelfth day of the month. The survey is a probability sample of approximately 9,700 private industry employers and 800 state and local governments, public schools, and public hospitals obtained for 10 occupational categories.

The index weights represent the wage and salary and fringe benefit costs of each occupation within an industry. This is average compensation per worker multiplied by the number of workers in each occupation/industry group. The employment data are obtained from the census of population and the compensation data are from the ECI survey. The composition of industry and occupational employment currently primarily reflects the distribution of the triennial occupational employment survey of the Bureau of Labor Statistics. The occupational/industry weights derived from that survey will be updated to 2002 in 2006. In contrast to the overall ECI, the component indexes for union and nonunion workers are based on current period distributions rather than fixed weights because of the changing union status of workers within a company; these are updated every quarter based on the current ECI survey of employer payrolls.

Accuracy

The sampling error (for one standard error) of the twelve-month percentage change in the employment cost index for compensation both for private industry workers and for state and local government workers is 0.2 of a percentage point. For example, if the estimated increase in the ECI over a twelve-month period were 4 percent, in two of three cases the "true" increase would be somewhere between 3.8 and 4.2 percent. For further information on the interpretation of sampling and non-sampling errors, see the Appendix.

Relevance

The employment cost index is the most comprehensive measure of underlying trends in employee compensation as a cost of production. It is used for analyzing changes in wages and salaries and fringe benefits in labor markets for various categories of occupations and industries, collective bargaining negotiations, and cost escalators in union and other business contracts, and for adjusting pay of federal government employees including members of Congress (if Congress elects to use it), federal judges, and senior government executives. In distinguishing between union and nonunion workers, it also provides data for contrasting compensation trends between union and nonunion companies.

The ECI is not strongly related to overall price movements in the *consumer price index, producer price indexes,* and *GDP price measures.* This probably reflects the fact that it does not adjust for productivity

Table 16.1

Employment Cost Index: Private Industry (annual percentage change)

12 months ending December	Compensation	Wages and salaries	Benefit costs
1995	2.6	2.8	2.2
1996	3.1	3.4	2.0
1997	3.4	3.9	2.3
1998	3.5	3.9	2.4
1999	3.4	3.5	3.4
2000	4.4	3.9	5.6
2001	4.2	3.8	5.1
2002	3.2	2.7	4.7
2003	4.0	3.0	6.4
2004	3.8	2.4	6.9

changes.[1] By contrast, *unit labor costs* data adjust for productivity changes and tend to parallel price movements.

Recent Trends

From 1995 to 2004, the employment cost index showed greater increases in annual compensation costs during 2000–04 compared with those during 1995–99 (Table 16.1). From 1995 to 1999, annual increases in compensation were in the 3.5-percent-and-under range, and from 2000 to 2004, the annual compensation increases were typically in the 4-percent range, though they declined from the peak 4.4 percent in 2000 to 3.8 percent in 2004. The greater compensation costs during 2000–04 reflected the much larger increases in benefit costs compared with those in wage and salary costs during the period. This reversed the earlier pattern of 1995–99, when wages and salaries showed greater increases than benefit costs.

Reference from Primary Data Source

Bureau of Labor Statistics, U.S. Department of Labor. *Monthly Labor Review.* Monthly.

Note

1. C. Alan Garner, "A Closer Look at the Employment Cost Index," *Economic Review,* Federal Reserve Bank of Kansas City, third quarter 1998.

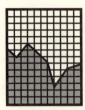

17
Farm Parity Ratio

The farm parity ratio provides a general indication of farmers' economic well-being. The ratio shows the relationship between (a) the prices farmers receive for sales of crop and livestock products, and (b) the prices farmers pay for production and living expenses. This relationship is a limited measure of the change in income because it does not include the effects of improvements in production technology or of the changing quantities and quality of farm products sold. The 1910–14 period is used as the base for comparison because prices of farm and nonfarm items were considered to have been generally in balance in that period by the legislators who passed the Agricultural Adjustment Act of 1939, establishing the parity ratio.

Where and When Available

The farm parity ratio is prepared monthly by the National Agricultural Statistics Service of the U.S. Department of Agriculture. It is published in the report *Agricultural Prices* (www.usda.gov/nass).

The data are available at the end of the month to which they refer. Revisions are made to each month in the following monthly estimates, and annually in January of the following year.

Content

The farm parity ratio is composed of the index of prices received for sales of crop and livestock products in the numerator, and the index of prices paid for farm production and living expenses in the denominator. The percentage change in both indexes reflects the movement from 1910–

14 to the current period. Currently, the ratio using 1990–92 = 100 is also provided to facilitate comparisons with other price indexes. Basing the ratio on 1990–92 does not affect percentage changes from one period to another, but the levels are different. Thus, when using the 1990–92 base, a comparison with 1910–14 is not readily observable unless back data are shown for the earlier period. When either ratio is above 100, farmers' purchasing power is higher than in the base period, and when either ratio is below 100, their purchasing power is less than in the base period.

The current weights in both the prices received and the prices paid indexes reflect the relative dollar importance of sales and expenses of the components of each index during 1990–92. In the prices-received index, crops account for 48 percent of the weight and livestock products for 52 percent. Crop products include food and feed grains, cotton, tobacco, oil-bearing crops (e.g., soybeans and peanuts), and fruits and vegetables. Livestock products include meat animals, dairy products, poultry, and eggs. The index represents about 90 percent of the cash receipts from all farm products. Of the excluded commodities, livestock products such as wool, horses, goats, and ducks account for 2 percent and crop products such as forest, nursery, greenhouse, and specialty crops account for 8 percent.

In the prices-paid index, farm production expenses are weighted 82 percent and living expenses are weighted 18 percent. Farm production costs include such items as feed, feeder livestock, seed, fertilizer, fuels, chemicals, equipment, cash rent, wages, interest, and real estate taxes. The living expense component is based on the *consumer price index* (CPI-U).

The farm parity ratio is currently based both on 1910–14 = 100 and 1990–92 = 100.

The farm parity ratio is not seasonally adjusted.

Methodology

Weights for the prices-received and prices-paid indexes are based on five-year moving averages. The moving-average weights capture changes over time in the composition of crop and livestock items that farmers produce and sell, and of the goods and services items used in their production, thus maintaining the weights on a generally up-to-date basis. Prices-received weights are based on farm cash receipts prepared by the Department of Agriculture's Economic Research Service, and prices-paid weights are based on the department's annual farm finance survey on costs and returns.

Current-period prices-received data are derived from department surveys of marketings and prices for various crop and livestock products. The data incorporate changes in the relative proportions of the various grades or qualities of the products sold. The data are not adjusted for changes in the quality of farm products.

Current-period prices-paid data are based on surveys of firms that sell to farmers and firms that purchase the item directly from farmers, such as feeder pigs, on the *producer price indexes* and the *consumer price index,* and on a quarterly department survey of farm labor wage rates (interim months are based on U.S. Bureau of Labor Statistics wage data). The prices-paid data for farm expenditures are not adjusted for changes in the quality of goods and services bought. The living-expense component of prices paid is adjusted for changes in quality in the consumer price index.

Accuracy

There are no estimates of sampling or revision error for the farm parity ratio.

Relevance

The farm parity ratio is a limited indicator of the economic well-being of farmers. While the ratio contrasts prices of farm products sold with production and living costs, it does not reflect improvements in farm production technology or changes in the quantity and quality of farm products sold. Thus, it is not an indicator of farm income. However, it portrays whether price movements are more or less favorable to farmers. Used with projections of the production of crop and livestock products, the parity ratio foreshadows the likely direction of changes in income. In addition, by focusing attention on the price component of farm income, the farm parity ratio is used as one guide for initiating or terminating farm marketing quotas for restricting shipments of particular products to market in order to bolster farm prices.

Recent Trends

From 1995 to 2004, the farm parity ratio generally declined, though it increased in 2003 and 2004 (Table 17.1). From peaks of 93 and 98 in

Table 17.1

Farm Parity Ratio (1990–92 = 100)

	Farm parity ratio	Prices-received index	Prices-paid index
1995	93	102	109
1996	98	112	115
1997	90	107	118
1998	89	102	115
1999	83	96	115
2000	80	96	120
2001	83	102	123
2002	79	98	124
2003	84	107	128
2004	90	119	133

Note: The parity ratio does not always equal the division of prices received by prices paid, due to rounding.

1995–96, the parity ratio declined to 79 in 2002, and then rose to 90 in 2004. The prices-received index fluctuated from year to year, while the prices-paid index increased continuously, except for 1998 and 1999.

Reference from Primary Data Source

National Agricultural Statistics Service, U.S. Department of Agriculture. *Agricultural Prices.* Monthly.

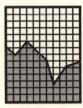

18
GDP Price Measures

There are two measures of price change associated with the *gross domestic product* (GDP): the chain-type price index and the implicit price deflator. The GDP price measures are the most comprehensive indicators of price change in the U.S. economy. They include the goods and services elements of consumer, investment, government, and international economic transactions in the GDP. Because of different methodologies used in their calculation, the two measures sometimes result in slightly different price movements.

Where and When Available

The GDP price measures are prepared quarterly by the Bureau of Economic Analysis (BEA) in the U.S. Department of Commerce. The data are published in "BEA News," a monthly news release and in the BEA monthly journal, *Survey of Current Business* (www.bea.gov).

The data are available during the fourth week of every month. Preliminary data for the immediately preceding quarter are provided in the month following the quarter (April for the first quarter, July for the second quarter, and so on). These are initially revised in the subsequent two months. More detailed revisions are made annually every August, and comprehensive benchmark revisions based largely on the quinquennial economic censuses are published about every five years.

Content

Two *gross domestic product* price measures—the chain-type index and the implicit price deflator—are developed for the entire GDP and for the consumer, investment, government, and international components. The two measures are based on the same composition of the goods and services and are virtually identical. The Bureau of Economic Analysis considers the chain-type index as the featured measure; the implicit price deflator is also provided because of its widespread use in the past.

The GDP price measures are currently based on 2000 = 100.

The GDP price measures are seasonally adjusted.

Methodology

The GDP chain-type price index weights change annually according to the composition of expenditures for goods and services items in each year. Two expenditure weights in adjacent years are used in calculating price movements. Price movements from one period to the next are based on the Fisher ideal index number formula.

The chain-type price measure is developed by applying price movements of the various goods and services items contained mainly in the *consumer price index, producer price indexes,* and the *import and export price indexes* to the expenditure weights noted above. These are supplemented with other price and cost indexes, including those for construction and defense prices and costs.

The chain-type price index movements are calculated using the geometric mean of two price movements based on alternative goods and services quantity weights (Fisher ideal index). The quantity weights for the most recent years and quarters are based on the annual GDP revisions each August. For years and for historical quarters, quantity weights for two different years are used. Price changes are calculated separately using the two weighting patterns, and the actual movement is the geometric mean of the two movements. Geometric averaging, in contrast to arithmetic averaging, treats price increases and decreases symmetrically, without the distortion of shifting bases.[1]

The implicit price deflator is calculated by dividing the index of current-dollar GDP by the chain-type quantity index of GDP, and multiplying by 100. Since it is a by-product of the estimation of real GDP, it does not involve the conventional index number construction of multiplying price movements by the weights and summing the products, as in the chain-type price index. Nevertheless, if it were not for certain technicalities, the chain-type index and the implicit price deflator would be identical. An example of these technicalities is that the quarterly price and quantity chain-type indexes are adjusted so that they average to their corresponding annual values. As a result, the formulas for quarterly chain-type prices and quantities are not exactly symmetrical.

Accuracy

There are no estimates of revision error for the GDP price measures.

Relevance

A unique feature of the GDP price measures is their inclusion of all components of the economy. This enables comprehensive analyses of the sources of price movements in the consumer, investment, government, and international components integrated in a statistically consistent framework.

In analyzing consumer price movements, it is useful to compare the movements of the chain GDP price for consumer expenditures with the *consumer price index* (CPI) and with the chain CPI that was introduced in 2000. Differences between the chain GDP price index and the CPI reflect variations in the coverage of certain goods and services items. The chain GDP price index represents spending of all consumers while the CPI refers only to spending by urban civilian households, the expenditure weights of the chain GDP price index are updated annually while the CPI weights are updated every two years, and the geometric averaging of the chain GDP price index contrasts with the arithmetic averaging of the CPI. While the chain CPI is based on similar geometric averaging as the chain GDP price index, differences between the chain GDP price index and the chain CPI still reflect variations in their coverage of certain goods and services items, spending of all consumers as distinct from spending by urban civilian households, and annual versus biennial updating of the expenditure weights.

Recent Trends

From 1995 to 2004, the GDP price measures ranged from annual increases of 1.1 percent in 1998 to 2.6 percent in 2004 (Table 18.1). The rate of price increase fluctuated throughout the period. The chain-type

Table 18.1

GDP Price Measures (annual percentage change)

	Chain-type price index	Implicit price deflator
1995	2.0	2.0
1996	1.9	1.9
1997	1.7	1.7
1998	1.1	1.1
1999	1.4	1.4
2000	2.2	2.2
2001	2.4	2.4
2002	1.7	1.7
2003	2.0	2.0
2004	2.6	2.6
1995–2004 (annual average)	1.9	1.9

index and the implicit price deflator had identical movements in all years. Over the entire nine-year period, both the chain-type index and the implicit price deflator increased at an average annual rate of 1.9 percent.

Reference from Primary Data Source

Bureau of Economic Analysis, U.S. Department of Commerce. *Survey of Current Business.* Monthly.

Note

1. For example, a price increase from $4 to $5 in the ratio of 1.25 is 25 percent, while a price decrease from $5 to $4 in the ratio of .80 is –20 percent. The arithmetic mean shows the price increase as more important than the price decrease ([25% – 20%]/2 = 2.5%), while the geometric mean gives the same weight to both the price increase and the price decrease (1.25 × .80 = 1). Technically, geometric averaging is the nth root of the product of n numbers, and arithmetic averaging is the sum of n numbers divided by n.

19
Government Economic Transactions: Expenditures, Receipts, Surplus/Deficit

Government economic transactions represent expenditures, receipts, and the resultant surplus/deficit for all levels of government—federal, state, and local. Government expenditures and receipts are underwritten by legislation appropriating funds to be spent and by tax laws specifying what items are to be taxed and the taxation rates. Actual expenditures and receipts are also influenced by the state of the economy. Expenditures and receipts are in balance when expenditures equal receipts, in surplus when receipts exceed expenditures, and in deficit when expenditures exceed receipts.

This discussion centers on the government expenditure and receipts data that are part of the national income and product accounts (see *gross domestic product*). This integrates government economic transactions with the macroeconomic measures of the overall economy. The government transactions data differ in content and timing from government budgets data of the federal, state, and local governments, though the differences are relatively small.

Where and When Available

The Bureau of Economic Analysis (BEA) in the U.S. Department of Commerce prepares quarterly measures of government expenditures, receipts, and the surplus/deficit of the federal government and of the total of all state and local governments in the BEA monthly journal, *Survey of Current Business* (www.bea.gov).

The BEA data on government economic transactions are available in the month after the quarter to which the data refer (April for the first quarter, July for the second quarter, and so on). The exception is data on corporate income taxes and thus the budget surplus/deficit position, which are prepared and revised in the subsequent months. These are revised annually every summer, and in the subsequent benchmark revisions of the national income and product accounts (see *gross domestic product*).

Content

Government expenditures consist of consumption expenditures, social benefits payments, interest payments on the public debt, and subsidies. Consumption expenditures are composed of compensation of government employees, purchases of goods and services from business, depreciation of government structures and equipment, and other smaller items. Social benefits payments include Social Security, Medicare, Medicaid, unemployment insurance, veterans benefits, and other income-maintenance payments to individuals. Grants-in-aid from the federal government to state and local governments are a federal expenditure, and grants-in-aid from state governments to local governments are a state and local expenditure. Government expenditures exclude transactions in financial assets and land.

Government receipts encompass government revenue from income, sales, and property taxes; contributions for social insurance; customs duties; grants-in-aid received by state and local governments, and fees, licenses, and other miscellaneous sources of revenue.

The main components of expenditures and receipts differ in content and magnitude between the federal government and state and local governments. For example, only the federal government spends for Social Security and for farm subsidies, and collects customs duties, while the federal government expenditures for defense far outweigh the state government outlays for the National Guard. By contrast, only the state and local governments spend for local schools and collect sales and property taxes, while state and local government expenditures for police far outweigh federal outlays for the Park Police, Federal Protective Service, Capital Police, and the Secret Service.

The surplus/deficit measure is referred to in the government economic transactions data as net government saving. The surplus/deficit designation is used here because of the common understanding of these terms.

Government debt, which is not included in government economic transactions, results from borrowing. The debt primarily represents the cumulative excess of annual deficits over annual surpluses in previous years, with an addition for any deficits in the current year. Also, some borrowing occurs in anticipation of spending in future years, particularly for capital construction projects of state and local governments.

Federal government economic transactions are generally on a cash basis, but with several exceptions. The primary exceptions are: For spending, payment of interest on the public debt is on an accrual basis, payment for large defense items such as airplanes and missiles are recorded on a delivery basis, and expenditures for ships and construction are recorded on a work-put-in-place basis, which is similar to an accrual basis. For receipts, business taxes are recorded on an accrual basis.

State and local government economic transactions are also generally on a cash basis. The exceptions are for interest payments and business taxes, which are on an accrual basis.

The government economic transactions data are seasonally adjusted.

Methodology

Federal government economic transactions for expenditures are based on reports of government agencies to the Office of Management and Budget. The Treasury Department provides monthly data on federal tax revenues, which are revised on an annual basis. The Bureau of Economic Analysis modifies these for the accrual, delivery-based, and work-put-in-place elements.

State and local government economic transactions for quarterly data are based on survey data of the U.S. Bureau of Labor Statistics and the U.S. Bureau of the Census for payrolls, construction, and taxes, and are supplemented by the trend of less recent actual data for the other components. The Bureau of Labor Statistics conducts a monthly survey of state and local government worker payrolls. The Census Bureau conducts a monthly survey of state and local government–owned new construction and a quarterly survey of state and local tax revenues. Annual state and local government economic transactions data are based on Census Bureau surveys of all state governments and a sample of local governments that provide spending and revenue information on a yearly basis. The Bureau of Economic Analysis estimates the accrual elements for the government economic transactions data.

Accuracy

There are no estimates of revisions of government economic transactions. Estimates of government current expenditures and gross investment that are part of the *gross domestic product* show a revision in the quarterly real (constant dollars) growth rate from the third month after the quarter to which they refer to succeeding annual revisions each August of an average of plus or minus 1.3 percentage points.

Relevance

Government economic transactions are integrated with the *gross domestic product,* which facilitates their use in analyzing overall economic trends. A surplus or deficit in government economic transactions data affects spending in the entire economy both directly and indirectly. High economic growth tends to raise tax receipts and lower outlays for unemployment insurance. This results in the direct effect of an increase in the surplus or a reduction in the deficit, with the effect of removing money from the income stream, and thus restraining spending, though not necessarily proportionately. In fact, the relationship is not always linear. For example, during the high economic growth for most of the 1980s, the deficit also rose for a few years, as the tax reductions of that decade significantly lessened the tax receipts that were generated by economic growth. To the extent that low economic growth leads to an increasing deficit or a reduction in the surplus, the direct effect is to add money to the income stream and thus stimulate spending, though not necessarily proportionately.

Government economic transactions also affect spending indirectly through *interest rates.* These effects are in opposition to the more direct effects. Because a surplus (or reduction in the deficit) reduces the debt (or slows the increase in the debt), it tends to lower interest rates and consequently stimulate private spending. Analogously, a deficit (or reduction in the surplus) increases debt (or slows the reduction in debt), resulting in higher interest rates, which tend to restrain spending. Again, the interaction of the surplus/deficit with interest rates is not always linear. For example, during periods of uncertainty when investors park their funds in safe U.S. government securities, the resultant smaller pool of funds for business and household borrowers leads to higher interest rates for the borrowers because of lower supplies of loanable funds. Thus, borrowers have to pay an interest premium in order to get lenders to provide loans. The net result of these contrasting direct and indirect effects determines the overall impact of government budgets on the economy.

In addition to government economic transactions impacting the economy, the economy impacts government transactions through feedback effects. Because economic growth (measured by the *gross domestic product*) affects tax revenues and spending for unemployment insurance, periods of high economic growth generally tend toward a budget surplus (or reduction in the deficit) and low growth periods tend toward a deficit (or reduction in the surplus).

The size and components of expenditures and receipts also influence the economy. The amount of total expenditures, as well its composition of civilian and defense programs, impacts *employment, average weekly earnings,* and industrial production (*industrial production index*). The amount of total receipts, as well as the component shares of income, sales, and property taxes, affects business and employment incentives and the *distribution of income.*

Recent Trends

From 1995 to 2004, government economic transactions fluctuated noticeably in relationship to the *gross domestic product* (Table 19.1). The federal government had both greater levels and greater fluctuations in expenditures and receipts than those of state and local governments. Consequently, the pattern of total government, the sum of the federal and the state and local governments, reflected the movements of the federal government more than those of the state and local governments.

As a percentage of the GDP, federal government expenditures declined from 21.7 percent in 1995 to 19.0 percent in 2000, rose to 20.4 percent in 2003, and declined to 20.0 percent in 2004. As a percentage of the GDP, state and local government expenditures declined from 13.2 percent in 1995 to 12.7 percent in 1997–98, rose to 13.7 percent in 2002, and declined to 13.4 percent in 2004.

As a percentage of the GDP, federal government receipts rose from 19.0 percent in 1995 to 20.9 percent in 2000, and then declined to 16.8 percent in 2004. As a percentage of the GDP, state and local government receipts rose from an average of 13.3 percent during 1995–2000 to 13.5–13.6 percent during 2001–04.

Table 19.1

Government Economic Transactions (percentage of the gross domestic product)

Calendar year	Expenditures			Receipts			Surplus/Deficit(−)		
	Federal	State and local	Total government	Federal	State and local	Total government	Federal	State and local	Total government
1995	21.7	13.2	32.4	19.0	13.4	29.9	−2.7	0.2	−2.5
1996	21.3	13.0	31.9	19.5	13.3	30.4	−1.8	0.3	−1.5
1997	20.6	12.7	30.9	19.9	13.2	30.7	−0.7	0.5	−0.2
1998	19.8	12.7	30.1	20.3	13.3	31.1	0.4	0.6	1.0
1999	19.3	12.8	29.6	20.4	13.3	31.2	1.1	0.5	1.7
2000	19.0	12.9	29.4	20.9	13.4	31.8	1.9	0.5	2.4
2001	19.4	13.5	30.2	19.9	13.6	30.7	0.5	0.0	0.5
2002	20.0	13.7	30.8	17.6	13.5	28.2	−2.4	−0.2	−2.7
2003	20.4	13.6	30.9	17.1	13.6	27.6	−3.3	0.0	−3.3
2004	20.0	13.4	30.3	16.8	13.5	27.3	−3.2	0.1	−3.1

For the surplus/deficit measures, as a percentage of the GDP, the federal government deficit declined from 2.7 percent in 1995 to 0.7 percent in 1997, shifted to a surplus that peaked at 1.9 percent in 2000 that dropped to 0.5 percent in 2001, and reverted to deficits during 2002–04 that were 3.3 and 3.2 percent in 2003–04. As a percentage of the GDP, the state and local government surplus was typically 0.5 percent during 1995–2000, dropped to zero surplus/deficit in 2001 and 2003, with a deficit of 0.2 percent in 2002, and was a surplus of 0.1 percent in 2004.

Reference from Primary Data Sources

Bureau of Economic Analysis, U.S. Department of Commerce. *Survey of Current Business*. Monthly.

20
Gross Domestic Product

The gross domestic product (GDP) is the broadest indicator of economic output and growth. It covers the goods and services produced and consumed in the private, public, domestic, and international sectors of the economy. Two measures of the GDP are provided, one from the viewpoint of demand that shows the market for goods and services, and the other from the viewpoint of supply, showing the resource costs in producing the goods and services. The GDP is a summary measure of the national income and product accounts, which are also referred to as the "national accounts."

In addition, the GDP is presented in two ways with respect to price levels. One is in current dollars that represent actual prices in every period, and the other is in chained dollars that abstract from changing prices over time. The current-dollar GDP is the market value of goods and services produced, which is the product of quantities and prices. The chained-dollar GDP, which is referred to as real GDP, represents the quantity of economic output and is the measure used to define the rate of economic growth. There are several alternative measures of real GDP growth based on variations in the component items. Indicators of price movements are provided for the total GDP and its major components (see *GDP price measures*).

Where and When Available

The gross domestic product is prepared quarterly by the Bureau of Economic Analysis (BEA) in the U.S. Department of Commerce. The data are published in a monthly news release and in the BEA monthly journal, *Survey of Current Business* (www.bea.gov).

The data are available during the fourth week of every month. Initial (referred to as "advance") data are provided in the month after the quarter to which they refer (April for the first quarter, July for the second quarter, and so on). These are revised in the subsequent two months (referred to as "preliminary" and "final," respectively), with more detailed revisions made annually every summer, and still more comprehensive benchmark revisions made about every five years.

Content

The composition of the two gross domestic product measures is shown in Table 20.1. The "product side" reflects demand or markets for goods and services, and the "income side" reflects the supply or costs of producing the goods and services. The two measures are conceptually equal, but they differ statistically because they are estimated independently and because of inadequacies in the data; this difference is called the "statistical discrepancy." As noted below under "Accuracy," each measure is equally valid for calculating economic growth rates.

The GDP is measured on a value-added basis. Only the value that is added in each stage of production, from raw materials to semifinished goods to final products, is counted. This prevents endless double-counting that would occur if goods and services purchased from other business for use in production were included.

The GDP data are seasonally adjusted.

Product Side: Demand Components

The component markets for the nation's output represent the demand aspects of the economy and are referred to as the product-side of GDP. The product-side total is the official GDP measure. It has the following main components:

Personal consumption expenditures represent spending by households for durable goods, nondurable goods, services, and the operating expenses of nonprofit organizations.

Gross private domestic investment represents business spending for equipment, nonresidential structures, and software by for-profit and nonprofit organizations; residential construction; and the change in business inventories, excluding profit or loss due to cost changes between the time of purchase and sale of inventoried goods (inventory valuation adjustment).

Table 20.1

Gross Domestic Product and Main Components: 2004

	Product side			Income side	
	$ Billions	Percentage		$ Billions	Percentage
Gross domestic product	11,735.0	100.0	Gross domestic product	11,735.0	100.0
Personal consumption expenditures	8,229.9	70.1	Compensation of employees	6,632.0	56.5
•Durable goods	993.9	8.5	•Wages and salaries	5,355.7	45.6
•Nondurable goods	2,377.0	20.3	•Supplements to wages		
•Services	4,859.0	41.4	and salaries	1,276.3	10.9
Gross private domestic investment	1,927.3	16.4	Proprietors' income[d]	902.8	7.7
•Nonresidential[a]	1,220.5	10.4	Corporate		
•Residential[b]	663.4	5.7	profits[e]	1,181.6	10.1
•Inventory change[c]	43.4	0.4	Rental income of persons[f]	165.1	1.4
Net exports of goods and services	−606.2	−5.2	Net interest	549.5	4.7
•Exports	1,175.5	10.0	Taxes on production		
•Imports	1,781.6	15.2	and imports[g]	841.1	7.2
Government consumption expenditures and gross investment	2,183.9	18.6	Consumption of fixed capital[h]	1,407.3	12.0
•Federal	809.9	6.9	Business transfer payments	82.1	0.7
•State and local	1,373.9	11.7			

(continued)

Table 20.1 *(continued)*

Product side			Income side	
$ Billions	Percentage		$ Billions	Percentage
		Less: Government subsidies less surplus of government enterprises	−33.5	−0.3
		Rest of the world[i]	−43.9	−0.4
		Statistical discrepancy[j]	50.9	0.4

Source: Bureau of Economic Analysis, U.S. Department of Commerce, *Survey of Current Business,* March 2005.

Notes: Components do not sum to totals, due to rounding. a. Business purchases of structures, equipment, and software. b. New housing construction and improvements. c. With inventory valuation adjustment. d. Profits of unincorporated businesses with inventory valuation and capital consumption adjustments. e. With inventory valuation and capital consumption adjustments. f. With capital consumption adjustment. g. Mainly sales and property taxes. h. Mainly depreciation allowances with capital consumption adjustment (CCA sign reversed with those of d, e, f above). i. Adjustment to place sum of income–side components on a domestic income basis, rather than a national income basis. j. Product–side total less sum of income–side components shown above. Balancing item between product–side and income–side totals.total less sum of income–side components shown above. Balancing item between product–side and income–side totals.

Government consumption expenditures and gross investment represent the federal, state, and local wages of government workers; purchases of civilian and defense goods, services, and structures, and the value of current services derived from government-owned equipment and structures (depreciation). Transfer payments for Social Security and other income-maintenance payments, federal grants to state governments and state grants to local governments, interest on the public debt, and subsidy payments to business are excluded. These latter items are part of total government spending (see *government economic transactions*).

Net exports of goods and services represent the international balance of exports minus imports in goods and services.

Income Side: Supply Components

The labor, capital, and tax costs in producing the nation's output are reflected in the supply aspects of the economy and are referred to as the income side of GDP. This side has the following main components:

Compensation of employees represents the money wages and salaries and noncash fringe benefits of workers that accrue at the time they are earned (supplements to wages and salaries).

Proprietors' income and *corporate profits* represent business profits of unincorporated businesses and corporations, excluding the profit or loss due to cost changes between the time of acquisition and time of sales of inventories (inventory valuation adjustment) or to cost changes in replacing existing capital facilities since their acquisition (capital consumption adjustment).

Rental income of persons represents the net income (income less expenses) to owners of residential and nonresidential real property who are not primarily engaged in the real estate business. Rental income includes nonmarket imputations of income for owner-occupied housing as if such housing were rented at the market price, plus royalties paid by businesses to individuals.

Interest is interest paid by the business sector to households and governments, minus interest received by businesses from these nonbusiness sectors. Interest paid and received between businesses cancels out. Interest includes nonmarket imputations for banking services provided to household and government customers without charge.

Consumption of fixed capital represents the charge for the using up (depreciation) of privately owned and government-owned equipment and structures, including owner-occupied housing. It includes adjustments for the changing costs of replacing existing capital facilities from their original purchase cost (capital consumption adjustment).

Taxes on production and imports represent sales and property taxes, customs duties, user fees, fines, rents and royalties paid to governments, and other miscellaneous payments to governments.

Real GDP

The GDP in chained dollars, referred to as "real GDP," represents the *quantity* of goods and services. Real GDP is the preeminent measure of the nation's economic growth. Real GDP eliminates the effect of price increases or decreases from one period to the next. By contrast, the GDP in current dollars, referred to as "nominal GDP," represents the *value* of goods and services produced in the prices of each period, and thus includes price and quantity.

The quantity index for real GDP growth is based on a chain-type index. The chain-type index utilizes price"weights," which change annually according to the prices of goods and services items in each year. Quantity movements from one period to the next are based on the Fisher ideal index number formula described below under "Methodology." This is the obverse of the chain-type price index, which employs quantity weights for its calculation (see *GDP price indexes*).

Other Summary GDP Measures

In addition to GDP, several variants of total GDP are provided to assist in economic analysis. These are based on adjustments related to inventories, international transactions, and statistical problems. The most widely cited one is final sales, which excludes the effect of inventory increases or decreases. This results in highlighting underlying demand as represented by purchases of goods and services by households, business, government, and foreigners, independent of whether the highly volatile business inventories in stores, warehouses, and factories are accumulating or depleting.

These summary measures of the nation's output that are closely related to the GDP are gross domestic income, final sales, final sales to domestic purchasers, gross domestic purchases, gross national product (GNP), and command-basis GNP. Typically, the largest difference in the quarterly and annual movements between GDP and the other summary measures occurs with final sales.

Methodology

The gross domestic product is calculated using secondary data that are initially compiled for other purposes, which limits control of the quality of the data for GDP requirements. Because of this dependence on secondary data, the BEA focuses sharply on unusual movements in this database and raises questions with the organizations providing the data to determine whether errors or special circumstances affect the figures. This close attention to the data base is done when the GDP components are first estimated and is repeated a second time when the total product and income sides are compared, particularly if there is a large difference (statistical discrepancy) between the two GDP aggregates.

This process sometimes uncovers data problems that in turn lead to modifying the initial estimates. In addition, special formulas are used to adjust inventories and depreciation to exclude profit or loss due to changing costs of inventories or of capital facilities between the time of purchase and their sale or replacement. These are referred to as the "inventory valuation adjustment" and "capital consumption adjustment," which are included in the product side under private investment and government investment, and in the income side under proprietors' income, corporate profits, rental income of persons, and consumption of fixed capital.

The data used in constructing the GDP come from many government agencies and private organizations that provide statistics obtained from surveys, income tax returns, and regulatory reports. The items in this database vary considerably in definition, collection technique, and timeliness, and thus are of uneven quality. Because the two measures of GDP on the product and income sides are developed independently from different data sources, the "statistical discrepancy" between the two GDP totals indicates the extent of the inconsistency in the two databases. Formally, the statistical discrepancy is the product side minus the income side.

Real GDP is prepared by dividing the current-dollar data for the various goods and services items primarily by the price levels of the *consumer price index, producer price indexes,* and the *import and export price indexes.* These are supplemented with other indicators of price change such as those for construction and defense prices and costs.

The movements in the chain-type quantity index for real GDP (which is an example of a Fisher ideal index) are calculated using the geometric mean of two more basic measures of these movements. For annual estimates and for recent quarters, these more basic measures are a Laspeyres index, which measures quantity movements in terms of the weights of previous-period prices, and a Paasche index, which measures quantity movements in terms of the weights of current-period prices. In each of these instances, quantities in the current and preceding periods are multiplied by prices for a single period (the current or preceding one).

Quarterly quantity indexes for historical periods use a slightly different formula, in that the two sets of price weights are for years instead of quarters. The first two quarters of the year use prices for the current and preceding year, while the last two quarters use prices for the current and following year. In the most recent quarters, prices in the following year are not yet known, so price weights are for the current and preceding quarter.

Accuracy

There are no estimates of sampling error for the gross domestic product data. The statistical discrepancy indicates the extent to which unknown errors in the databases, in which some are above and others below the "correct" values, do not cancel each other. However, because some of these errors are offsetting, the statistical discrepancy is a net figure of the consistency of the databases rather than a gross measure of all errors regardless of whether the high and low figures are offsetting. As noted earlier, the product side GDP is regarded as the official measure, although the availability of the product and income sides allows the calculation of alternative growth rates that provide a lower and upper range for use in analysis (by comparing movements of the product side against the product side minus the statistical discrepancy). Thus, one way of viewing the accuracy of the GDP data is to treat it as being within the growth rate range indicated by the product and income sides movements.

Another perspective of GDP accuracy is provided by considering the size of the revisions to the provisional GDP data.[1] These are shown in terms of the confidence that the percentage growth rates in GDP are likely to be revised upward or downward within a specified range based on past experience. For example, the growth rate of the estimate of real GDP that is published in the third month after the quarter to which it refers is revised in the succeeding annual revisions each August as follows: in two of three cases in a range of –1.2 to 2.0 percentage points and in nine of ten cases in a range of –2.6 to 3.1 percentage points. Thus, if the growth rate reported in the third month after the quarter is 3.0 percent, there is a two-thirds probability that after the annual revisions, the figure will be in the range of 1.8 to 5.0 percent, and a 90 percent chance that it will be in the range of 0.4 to 6.1 percent.

Relevance

The gross domestic product provides the overall framework for analyzing and forecasting economic trends. It has the unique attribute of integrating the markets for goods and services (demand or spending) with the production of the goods and services (supply or costs) in one format. Because the costs of production also generate wage and profit incomes, the GDP measures are the basis for analyzing the feedback effects between spending and incomes from one period to the next.

The analyses used to assist the president and Congress in formulating

Table 20.2

Gross Domestic Product (billions of dollars)

	Current dollars	Real GDP (billions of chained 2000 dollars)	Annual percentage change in real GDP
1995	7,397.7	8,031.7	2.5
1996	7,816.9	8,328.9	3.7
1997	8,304.3	8,703.5	4.5
1998	8,747.0	9,066.9	4.2
1999	9,268.4	9,470.3	4.5
2000	9,817.0	9,817.0	3.7
2001	10,128.0	9,890.7	0.8
2002	10,469.6	10,048.8	1.6
2003	11,971.2	10,320.6	2.7
2004	11,734.3	10,755.7	4.2
		1995–2000 (annual average)	4.1
		2000–2004 (annual average)	2.3
		1995–2004 (annual average)	3.3

fiscal policies and the Federal Reserve in formulating monetary policies focus on real GDP growth. These economic policies are aimed at maximizing *employment* growth and minimizing *unemployment* and inflation (*consumer price index, producer price indexes,* and *GDP price measures*). Fiscal policies refer to federal spending and taxes (*government economic transactions*), and monetary policies refer to *interest rates*. Analyses of the cyclical expansion and recession movements and of the longer-term periods that span several business cycles are the backdrop for deriving implications of adopting particular fiscal and monetary policies for moderating cyclical fluctuations and stimulating noninflationary long-term economic growth. The GDP is the overall framework of such analyses, although it is supplemented importantly with assessments from other indicators.

Recent Trends

From 1995 to 2004, the real gross domestic product's annual growth rate accelerated from 2.5 percent in 1995 to a range of 3.7 to 4.5 percent during 1996–2000 (Table 20.2). Growth rates during the recession of 2001 and the recovery years of 2002 and 2003 were 1 to 3 percentage points below those of the 1995–2000 period, although the growth rate accelerated from the 2001 recession low of 0.8 percent, rising to 4.2 percent in 2004. Over the entire nine-year period, real GDP increased at an average annual rate of 3.3 percent. Within this period, real GDP increased at an average annual rate of 4.1 percent during 1995–2000, and 2.3 percent during 2000–04.

Reference from Primary Data Source

Bureau of Economic Analysis, U.S. Department of Commerce. *Survey of Current Business.* Monthly.

Note

1. For a discussion of the magnitude of the revisions, see Dennis J. Fixler and Bruce T. Grimm, "Reliability of the NIPA Estimates of U.S. Economic Activity," *Survey of Current Business,* February 2005.

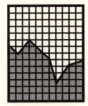

21
Help-Wanted Advertising Index

The help-wanted advertising index tracks employers' advertisements for job openings in the classified section of newspapers in fifty-one labor market areas. The index represents job vacancies resulting from turnover in existing positions due to such reasons as workers changing jobs or retiring, and from the creation of new jobs. It excludes unadvertised job vacancies and jobs advertised in nonclassified sections of newspapers such as display ads in business or news sections.

Where and When Available

Measures of the help-wanted advertising index are provided monthly by The Conference Board. The data are published in a news release and in The Conference Board's monthly report, *Business Cycle Indicators* (www.conference-board.org).

The data are available twenty-five to thirty days after the month to which they refer. The data are revised in the following month.

Content

The help-wanted advertising index covers jobs in many fields—professional, technical, crafts, office, sales, farm, custodial, and so on. They include a higher proportion of all junior and middle-level vacancies than of managerial, executive, or unskilled levels. In addition to the national help-wanted index, local indexes for fifty-one labor markers are provided. The help-wanted index does not distinguish job vacancies by occupational skills.

The help-wanted advertising index is currently based on 1987 = 100. The help-wanted data are seasonally adjusted.

Methodology

The help-wanted advertising data are obtained from classified advertisements in one daily (including Sunday) newspaper in each of the fifty-one labor markets (fifty-one cities including their suburbs). Newspapers are selected according to how well their ads represent total jobs in the local labor market area. The fifty-one labor markets accounted for approximately 45 percent of nonagricultural employment in 2002.

The index reflects the number of job advertisements. Each advertisement is weighted equally regardless of whether it is an ad for one job or for multiple positions or whether for full-time or part-time work. Advertisements of both employers and employment agencies and advertisements for the same job on successive days are included in the count.

Index weights for the fifty-one labor markets are based on the proportion of nonagricultural employment accounted for by each of the labor markets. The index is based on 1987 weights. Within each market area, help-wanted advertisements in the Sunday newspaper are weighted according to the ratio of the average Sunday advertising volume to average daily advertising volume.

The help-wanted advertising index does not include employer online advertising for jobs, although future research may be done on the feasibility of incorporating online advertising into the index. Beginning in 2005, The Conference Board instituted a monthly data series on new online job advertisements, *The Conference Board Help-Wanted Online Data Series.* This new online series is considered developmental.

Accuracy

There are no estimates of sampling or revision error for the help-wanted advertising index.

Relevance

The help-wanted advertising index indicates the direction of employers' hiring plans. In theory, it provides an advance signal of future changes in *employment* and cyclical turning points. In practice, the help-wanted index leads the downturn from the expansion peak to a recession, but it lags the turning point in moving from recession to expansion, based on analyses conducted as part of the *leading, coincident, and lagging indexes.* The lag in the recovery from a recession results from the tendency of employers to increase average weekly hours of existing workers when business improves or to call back workers on layoff before advertising for new workers. In the past two recoveries of 1991–92 and 2002, the lag also reflects the much smaller increase in employment than in previous recoveries.[1] Also, during the past two recoveries of 1991–92 and 2002–03, job losses were far more structural than cyclical as compared to previous recoveries, resulting in proportionately more permanent job losses that make it more difficult to find new employment than cyclical job losses, in which at least some rehiring occurs along with a cyclical upturn.[2]

The help-wanted index tends to be inversely related to *unemployment.* When help-wanted advertisements increase, unemployment usually declines, while when help-wanted advertisements decrease, unemployment usually rises. But the help-wanted movements typically do not parallel unemployment movements because of changing advertising practices. For example, during periods of low unemployment, employers may rely more heavily on help-wanted advertisements than on alternative means of finding workers. During periods of high unemployment, employers may find workers more easily through alternative means such as through workers initiating the contact on their own or on the advice of a friend.

Some advertised jobs may not be filled because employers are not satisfied with the applicants, there is an overall shortage of applicants, or employers decide not to fill the jobs.

The help-wanted index does not measure overall job vacancies, nor does it provide data on occupational skills. Therefore, the index cannot be compared with unemployment data to assess job shortages and surpluses in labor markets.

The *Job Openings and Labor Turnover* survey provides a more comprehensive measure of employer recruitment for specific job openings in the overall economy than that of the help-wanted advertising index.

Recent Trends

From 1995 to 2004, the help-wanted advertising index fluctuated in a narrow range of 83 to 89 during 1995–2000, and then dropped sharply to 38 in 2003 and 2004 (Table 21.1).

Table 21.1

Help-Wanted Advertising Index (1987 = 100)

Year	Index count
1995	85
1996	83
1997	87
1998	89
1999	87
2000	83
2001	58
2002	44
2003	38
2004	38

Reference from Primary Data Source

The Conference Board. *Business Cycle Indicators.* New York, NY. Monthly.

Notes

1. Stacey L. Schreft and Aarti Singh, "A Closer Look at Jobless Recoveries," *Economic Review,* Federal Reserve Bank of Kansas City, second quarter 2003.

2. Erica L. Groshen and Simon Potter, "Has Structural Change Contributed to a Jobless Recovery?" *Current Issues in Economics and Finance,* Federal Reserve Bank of New York, August 2003.

22
Home Sales: New and Existing Houses

Sales of new and existing privately owned homes represent the number of single-family unattached houses and townhouses for new home sales; and the number of single-family unattached houses and townhouses, plus the number of condominium and cooperative apartments in multi-family buildings for existing home sales. Each house or apartment is counted as one unit regardless of the sale price. New homes are newly constructed houses that are sold by the developer to the first owner. Existing homes are houses that are at least one year old.

(Data on the inventories of new and existing homes for sale are provided by the same organizations that prepare the sales data. I note these data on unsold homes to alert the reader to their availability, though they are not covered here.)

New Homes

Where and When Available

Measures of new home sales are prepared monthly by the Bureau of the Census in the U.S. Department of Commerce and the U.S. Department of Housing and Urban Development. They are published in a news release, *New Residential Sales* (www.census.gov).

The data are available approximately one month after the month to which they refer. They are revised in the three succeeding months.

Content

A new home sale is recorded when a sales contract is signed or a buyer's deposit is accepted. Although some contracts or deposits are conditional and subsequently canceled, the data are not revised to show this change
  The new-home-sales data are seasonally adjusted.

Methodology

Data on new home sales are obtained from a monthly survey of a sample of builder or owner developers conducted by the Bureau of the Census. Imputations are made to the new-home-sales data to allocate late reports of home sales data to the month when the sale occurred, and to account for those sales taking place prior to the issuance of a building permit, where one is required.

Accuracy

The sampling error (for one standard error) for new home sales data is 6 percent. For example, if the monthly new-home-sales were estimated at one million units, in two of three cases the "true" sales would be somewhere between 940,000 and 1,060,000 units. For further information on the interpretation of sampling and nonsampling errors, see the Appendix.

Existing Homes

Where and When Available

Existing home sales are prepared monthly by the National Association of Realtors (NAR). They are published in a news release and in the monthly NAR newsletter, *Real Estate Outlook: Market Trends and Insights* (www.realtor.org).
  The data are available twenty-five days after the month to which they refer. They are revised one month later and annually every February.

Content

Existing homes are houses that are at least one year old. An exception is a newly constructed house that is first sold more than one year after being put on the market, in which case it is defined as a new house. Sales of existing homes include transactions conducted through a real estate broker and those made directly by the owner.

The existing home sales data are seasonally adjusted.

Methodology

Data on existing home sales are obtained from monthly surveys of local areas based on a sample of over 600 boards/associations of realtors and multiple-listing systems conducted by the National Association of Realtors (NAR). The NAR sample and its multiple-listing systems account for approximately 35 percent of all existing home sales. Through the methodology, the data capture estimates of sales made directly by the owner.

The local area data are primarily for metropolitan areas, but they are considered to be representative of nonmetropolitan counties surrounding the metropolitan areas, based on biennial information in the *American Housing Survey* of the U.S. Department of Housing and Urban Development. The local area data are summed to the four broad Census Bureau regions of the United States, the Northeast, South, Midwest, and West. The regional data are in turn augmented by an inflation factor to account for total sales of each region, including those not captured in the sample of realtor and multiple-listing reporting systems. The inflation factor, which is revised approximately every five years, is based on sales data in the American Housing Survey and the decennial Census of Housing. The sales data for the four regions are then summed to the national total.

Accuracy

There are no estimates of sampling or revision error for the existing home sales data.

New and Existing Homes

Relevance

Close to 70 percent of all households own single-family homes. A home is typically the largest single item bought by householders (outlays of comparable magnitude are associated with financing college educations and major medical bills). Economic output increases far more by the

Table 22.1

Home Sales: New and Existing Houses (thousands of units)

	New homes[a]	Existing homes[b]	Ratio, existing homes to new homes
1995	667	3,852	5.8
1996	757	4,167	5.5
1997	804	4,371	5.4
1998	886	4,966	5.6
1999	880	5,190	5.9
2000	877	5,171	5.9
2001	908	5,332	5.9
2002	973	5,631	5.8
2003	1,086	6,183	5.7
2004	1,200	6,784	5.7

[a]Single-family unattached houses and townhouses; [b]Single-family unattached houses and townhouses, and condominium and cooperative apartments in multifamily buildings.

purchase of a new house than of an existing house because of the materials and construction work required in building a new house, although renovation work is sometimes done when an existing house is purchased. While existing home sales have a much smaller direct impact on the economy than new home sales, existing and new home sales are in fact closely linked because existing home owners often can afford to buy a new home only by selling their existing home. Also, both new and existing home sales generate purchases of furniture, appliances, and other house furnishings, which is a secondary stimulus to the economy.

Home sales are sensitive to changes in economic conditions related to employment, personal income and saving, interest rates, housing starts, housing affordability index, and mortgage delinquency and foreclosure. Although housing is a necessity of living, home sales are highly cyclical because households are most likely to purchase a home during prosperous times when they can best afford it, but they tend to defer a home purchase during depressed times when they can least afford it.

Recent Trends

From 1995 to 2004, there were far more sales of existing homes than of new homes (Table 22.1). Sales of existing homes were five to six times as high as sales of new homes.

New home sales rose from 667,000 in 1995 to 1.2 million in 2004.

These sales increased continuously over the nine-year period, except for small declines in 1999 and 2000.

Sales of existing homes rose from 3.9 million in 1995 to 6.8 million in 2004. These sales increased continuously over the nine-year period, except for a small decline in 2000.

References from Primary Data Sources

Bureau of the Census, U.S. Department of Commerce, and U.S. Department of Housing and Urban Development. *New Residential Sales.* Monthly.
National Association of Realtors. *Real Estate Outlook: Market Trends and Insights.* Washington, DC. Monthly.

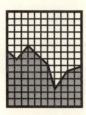

23
House Prices: New and Existing Houses

There are two measures of house prices for privately owned single-family houses. One represents sales prices for newly constructed houses and adjusts for the price effect of changes in the size and various characteristics of new houses. However, this measure does not adjust for the price effect of building new houses in less developed locations that lowers the price of the purchased lot. The other price measure represents the resale price and the house revaluations required to obtain mortgage refinancing of existing houses. This measure adjusts for the price effect of resales and mortgage refinancing related to changes in the characteristics of the same neighborhoods. However, the measure does not adjust for the price effect of structural and landscaping improvements made to the same houses.

The price measures for new and existing houses are described separately. This is followed by a comparison of the relevance and recent trends of both price measures.

New Houses

Where and When Available

The new house price index is prepared quarterly by the Bureau of the Census in the U.S. Department of Commerce. It is published in the news release, *Price Index of New One-Family Houses Sold* (www.census.gov).

The data are available four weeks after the quarter to which they refer. They are revised in the succeeding quarter.

Content

The new house price index is based on the actual sales price of single-family houses (the price index excludes houses built for the exclusive use of the land owner). The sales price covers the value of the house structure, the developed lot, selling expenses, and the seller's profit. The index covers detached single-family houses and attached townhouses, including condominiums and cooperatives, whether financed with conventional, Federal Housing Administration, or Veterans Administration mortgages.

The sale is recorded when a sales contract is signed or a deposit is accepted, regardless of the stage of construction. If that sale falls through and the house is sold to a different buyer, the index still records the sales data of the initial transaction and thus does not reflect the price or timing of the sale to a different buyer. Analogously, subsequent price changes due to changes in amenities after the initial sale is recorded are not included in the index.

The new house price index represents a constant set of structural characteristics and amenities within different regions of the United States. Examples of the characteristics are floor space, number of bedrooms, garage or carport, kitchen appliances, heating system, exterior wall material, and number of fireplaces. This maintenance of a constant quality house means that index changes over time reflect price changes only. The physical characteristics that are used to develop the constant quality price index are updated approximately every ten to fifteen years.

However, no direct adjustment is made in the index for the price effect of new houses being constructed in less developed geographic areas. Less developed areas have lower land costs than do more developed areas (the Henry George effect), which lowers the price of the purchased lot. An indirect adjustment for the lower cost of lots in the new house price index may be reflected in the inclusion of four separate regional indexes (Northeast, Midwest, South, West) and in a metropolitan area variable in the statistical regression used to calculate the index (see "Methodology" below). These indirect measures distinguish *between* regions, such as the much greater construction of new housing in the South than in the Northeast, highlighting the greater availability of undeveloped land and lower land costs in the South. The indirect measure also distinguishes *between* metropolitan areas and the entire region, with the region having lower land costs because it includes the rural component. But these indirect measures do not adjust for differences in land costs *within* regions and *within* the metropolitan area of a region.

The new house price index is prepared for the United States and four broad regions of the country.

The new house price index is currently based on 1996 = 100.

The new house price index is not seasonally adjusted.

Methodology

The new house price index data on the physical characteristics of the house (floor space, number of bedrooms, etc.) are obtained from monthly interviews with homebuilders or owners of a sample of houses that were sold. Approximately 13,000 interviews are conducted each year. The new house price index is referred to as a hedonic price index (for a brief description of hedonic price indexes, see the "Methodology" section of the *consumer price index*).

A statistical regression model is used to relate the characteristics of each house with its sale price. The model is developed for detached houses in separate strata for four regions of the country (Northeast, Midwest, South, West) and in a fifth stratum for all attached townhouses in the country. The U.S. index is derived by combining the four regional indexes and the attached townhouse index based on the following percentage weights that reflect the relative importance of new house construction among the five categories:

Northeast	6.2
Midwest	15.9
South	40.3
West	27.1
Attached townhouses	10.5
Total	100.0

The data on house sales in the new house price index are obtained from the Census Bureau's Survey of Construction. The sales data are based on a monthly survey of a sample of homebuilders. The quarterly sales data used in the index are the three-month total in each calendar quarter (e.g., first-quarter sales are the sum of January, February, and March sales).

Accuracy

The statistical regression model error in the new house price index in two of three cases is plus or minus 0.5 percent.

Existing Houses

Where and When Available

The price index for existing houses is prepared quarterly by the Office of Federal Housing Enterprise Oversight, an independent agency under the U.S. Department of Housing and Urban Development. The data on the existing house price index are published in a news release, *House Price Index* (www.ofheo.gov).

The data are available two months after the quarter to which they refer. All data are revised each quarter as revised or more complete information is received.

Content

The existing house price index is based on repeat sales or house revaluations required to obtain mortgage refinancing of existing mortgages. The index covers the same houses that have been purchased or securitized through secondary mortgage transactions by the Federal National Mortgage Corporation (Fannie Mae) or the Federal Home Loan Mortgage Corporation (Freddie Mac). The index is confined to house sales of single-family detached houses and to financing by conventional mortgages. Thus, the index excludes townhouses and houses financed with Federal Housing Administration or Veterans Administration mortgages.

The existing house price index adjusts for the price effect of changing demographic, socioeconomic, or land use characteristics in the same neighborhoods over time. However, the index does not adjust for improvements to the house or landscaping over time, for depreciation of the house, or for maintenance of the house.

The existing house price index is prepared for the United States, regions, states, and metropolitan areas.

The existing house price index is currently based on 1980 (first quarter) = 100.

The existing house price index is seasonally adjusted.

Methodology

The existing house price index incorporates repeat mortgage refinancings of repeat sales or refinancing of the same house that may occur years apart, in the quarter that the transaction occurs. The data are based on a sample of secondary mortgage transactions that are purchased or securitized by Fannie Mae or Freddie Mac. The repeat transactions data for the same house are identified by matching street addresses consistent with U.S. Postal Service standards.

Greater weight is given in the index to sales price changes of repeat sales or refinancing of houses that occur in short rather than long time periods between transactions because (a) differential depreciation rates for similar properties are more likely over longer periods of time, and (b) local area real estate values are affected by changing demographic and socioeconomic characteristics in individual neighborhoods over time. The existing house price index is developed using a statistical regression model.

The existing house price index is limited to mortgage loans that do not exceed a "conforming loan limit." Purchases of mortgages by Fannie Mae or Freddie Mac may not exceed the conforming loan limit. The conforming loan limit is based on the amount of the mortgage loan, not on the value of the house. In 2004, the conforming loan limit was $333,700, which thus included houses of higher value.

Accuracy

The statistical regression model error in the existing house price index in two of three cases is less than plus or minus one percent.

New and Existing Houses

Relevance

House prices are one factor affecting the demand for housing. Other factors include mortgage interest rates (*interest rates*), *unemployment,* disposable personal income (*personal income and saving*), household debt (*consumer credit*), and housing affordability (*housing affordability index*).

Recent Trends

From 1995 to 2004, the new house price index increased at a lesser rate than that of the existing house price index, except for 1996, 1997, and

Table 23.1

House Prices: New and Existing Houses (year-to-year percentage change)

	New houses (annual average)	Existing houses (fourth quarter to fourth quarter
1995	2.7	4.5
1996	4.9	2.6
1997	5.9	4.6
1998	3.2	5.0
1999	7.5	5.2
2000	5.8	7.6
2001	3.0	7.6
2002	7.3	7.6
2003	7.7	8.2
2004	10.6	11.2

1999, when the new house price index increased at a greater rate than the existing house price index (Table 23.1). The directional year-to-year movements of the two indexes also occasionally varied. In 1998 and 2000, the rate of increase in the new house price index declined, while that of the existing house price index rose, and in 1996, the rate of increase in the new house price index rose, while that in the existing house price index declined. Another variation occurred in 2001 and 2002, when the rate of increase in the new house price index first declined and then rose, while the increase in the existing house price index was stable in both years.

References from Primary Data Sources

Bureau of the Census, U.S. Department of Commerce. *Price Index of New One-Family Houses Sold.* Quarterly.
Office of Federal Housing Enterprise Oversight, U.S. Department of Housing and Urban Development. *House Price Index.* Quarterly.

24
Housing Affordability Index

The housing affordability index (HAI) measures the extent to which families with the median income can afford an existing single-family, median-price house. The index gauges whether (a) the required monthly mortgage payments are below the threshold income/price relationship (house is affordable), or (b) the required mortgage payments are above the income/price relationship (house is not affordable). The index includes the effects of family incomes, house prices, thirty-year fixed-rate mortgages, adjustable-rate mortgages, a down payment of 20 percent, and a qualifying income standard for prospective buyers to obtain a mortgage.

Where and When Available

The housing affordability index is prepared monthly by the National Association of Realtors. The data are published in the *Real Estate Outlook: Market Trends and Insights* (www.realtor.org).

The index is published the last week of the month following the month to which the data refer, and it is revised every month. Annual revisions are made every March.

Content

The housing affordability index indicates a threshold for determining the extent to which monthly mortgage payments for an existing single-family median-price house can be met by the median-income family. The threshold number is 100. When the index is above 100, the median-price house is affordable for a median-income family; and when the index is below

100, the house is not affordable. For example, an index of 100 means the family has the exact amount of income required to finance the house; an index of 115 means the family income is 15 percent higher than necessary to finance the house; and an index of 90 means the income is 10 percent lower than necessary to finance the house. In addition to the composite index, supplementary indexes are provided separately for fixed-rate mortgages, adjustable-rate mortgages, and first-time buyers.

The HAI is derived from the interrelationships of the median-price house, a down payment of 20 percent, fixed and adjustable mortgage interest rates, median family income, and a qualifying income standard for prospective buyers to obtain a mortgage.

The median-price house means that the prices of 50 percent of existing single-family houses sold are above the median threshold price and 50 percent of the homes sold are below the threshold price. The median-price house is determined by the sales prices of houses of all sizes (e.g., houses with varying amounts of square footage) and of all amenities (e.g., houses with and without central air conditioning).

Family income is defined as gross income before the payment of income taxes. The median family income means that 50 percent of the families have incomes above the threshold and 50 percent have incomes below the threshold. The median-income family is based on families of all sizes. A family refers to two or more individuals related by birth, marriage, or adoption and living together in a house, apartment, or rooms intended for separate living quarters.

Mortgage interest rates cover conventional loans for thirty-year fixed-rate mortgages and conventional loans for adjustable-rate mortgages.

The qualifying income standard for a prospective house buyer to obtain a mortgage is based on the percentage of gross monthly family income that monthly mortgage principal and interest expenses (assuming a down payment of 20 percent) would be. Under the standard, in order for a family to obtain a mortgage, the monthly housing expense may not exceed 25 percent of the monthly gross income. Housing expense excludes real estate taxes, homeowner insurance, and housing maintenance.

The HAI is not seasonally adjusted.

Methodology

The housing affordability index is calculated as the percentage that median gross monthly income is of the qualifying income standard for obtaining a mortgage. Mathematically, the formula is:

$$\begin{matrix} \text{Housing} \\ \text{affordability} \\ \text{index} \end{matrix} = \frac{\text{Median family monthly gross income}}{\text{Qualifying monthly income standard}} \times 100 \quad (24.1)$$

The median family income data are based on annual income information obtained in the Current Population Survey (CPS) of the U.S. Bureau of the Census (see *distribution of income* for the CPS methodology). The annual income data from the previous one to two years are updated to the current month by using statistical regressions to project historical trends.

The median house price data are based on a monthly survey of realtors and multiple listing systems of housing sales by the National Association of Realtors. See *home sales: new and existing houses* for the methodology of the NAR survey.

The mortgage interest data are based on the effective interest rate for loans closed from a monthly survey of mortgage lenders by the Federal Housing Finance Board. The effective interest rate includes the contract rate plus fees and charges.

The housing expense data are derived from other existing data. The mortgage principal is the house price noted above less 20 percent for the down payment. The interest rate is the effective interest rate noted above.

The composite HAI (fixed-rate plus adjustable-rate mortgages) is a weighted average of the fixed-rate and adjustable-rate HAIs. The weights are based on the proportion of mortgages closed on fixed-rate and adjustable-rate loans obtained from the Federal Housing Finance Board.

Accuracy

There are no estimates of sampling or revision error for the housing affordability index.

Relevance

The housing affordability index suggests prospects for owners and buyers to match a house sale price with the income required to finance the purchase. The higher the index is above 100, the greater the pool of prospective buyers who can afford to buy a house, and so the greater the number of likely home sales. By contrast, the lower the index is below

Table 24.1

Housing Affordability Index (actual income as a percentage of required income)

	Composite	Fixed-rate mortgages	Adjustable-rate mortgages
1995	132.4	126.6	143.3
1996	133.3	129.6	142.9
1997	134.0	130.8	145.3
1998	141.1	139.7	151.0
1999	139.1	136.3	150.4
2000	129.2	127.6	141.3
2001	135.7	135.7	145.5
2002	133.9	131.6	147.1
2003	138.4	125.7	140.5
2004	132.6	121.1	135.4

100, the smaller the pool of prospective buyers and the smaller the number of likely house sales. Because sales of existing houses provide owners with the income to buy new or other existing houses, sales of existing houses generate income and employment through the construction of new houses plus the purchase of furniture, appliances, and other house furnishings typically associated with moving into a newly purchased house (see *home sales: new and existing houses*).

Recent Trends

From 1995 to 2004, the annual averages of the housing affordability indexes for the composite, fixed-rate mortgages, and adjustable-rate mortgages were well above 100 (Table 24.1). The composite HAI fluctuated within a range of 129.2 (2000) and 141.1 (1998), with peak levels in 1998, 1999, and 2003, and low levels in 1995, 2000, and 2004. The fixed-rate HAI ranged between 121.1 (2004) and 139.7 (1998). The adjustable-rate HAI ranged between 135.4 (2004) and 151.0 (1998).

Reference from Primary Data Source

National Association of Realtors. *Real Estate Outlook: Market Trends and Insights.* Washington, DC. Monthly.

25
Housing Starts

The housing starts data represent the beginning of construction of new privately owned single-family homes, townhouses, and multifamily apartment buildings. Each single-family house and each separate apartment within apartment buildings (including cooperative and condominium buildings) is counted as one housing start. Housing starts exclude publicly owned housing, mobile homes, group quarters such as hotels and dormitories, additions and alterations to existing housing, and conversions from nonresidential structures to residential use.

Where and When Available

Housing starts data are prepared monthly by the Bureau of the Census in the U.S. Department of Commerce. The data are published in a news release and in the report *Housing Starts* (www.census.gov).

The data are available during the third week of the month after the month to which they refer. Each monthly report contains revised data for the two previous months. The seasonally adjusted data are revised every year for the preceding two years based on revised seasonal factors.

Content

A housing start is the beginning of construction of a privately owned residential structure containing one or more housing units. A housing unit is a dwelling of one or more rooms intended for occupancy as separate living quarters by a family or group of unrelated individuals living together. Each housing start represents a housing unit. A housing start is counted as occurring in the month that excavation work begins for the foundation, or of a residential structure rebuilt on an existing foundation. While each single-family house and apartment unit is counted as one housing start, the effect of differences in size and amenities of each start with respect to the volume of construction work is captured only in data on the dollar value of new housing construction put in place.

In addition to national totals, housing starts data are published for the Northeast, Midwest, South, and West regions of the country.

The housing starts data are seasonally adjusted.

Methodology

Housing starts data are estimated separately for housing in local areas that require building permits for construction and for housing in non-permit-issuing localities. For the permit-issuing areas, two monthly sample surveys are used: (1) a mail survey of 8,700 of 20,000 permit-issuing localities to determine the total number of permits issued, and (2) a survey of 900 areas by on-site interviewers to determine in which month construction started on housing units that were authorized in previous months and the current month. The information obtained on-site about the rates of construction started for permits issued for each month to date is applied to the current permit figures to develop the total number of housing starts every month. The data are adjusted upward to reflect housing starts for which late reports are received and for housing starts begun before a building permit was issued. These upward adjustments are based on factors derived from annual reviews plus more up-to-date monthly modifications of the extent to which these events occur.

Private housing starts in nonpermit areas are estimated from monthly on-site surveys of ongoing construction work in a sample of eighty localities.

Accuracy

The sampling error (for one standard error) of the housing starts data is 3 percent. For example, if the monthly housing starts were estimated at two million units, in two of three cases the "true" housing starts would be somewhere between 1,940,000 and 2,060,000 units. For further information on the interpretation of sampling and nonsampling errors, see the Appendix.

Table 25.1

Housing Starts (thousands)

	Total	Single-family percentage of total	Multifamily percentage of total
1995	1,354	79	21
1996	1,477	79	21
1997	1,474	77	23
1998	1,617	79	21
1999	1,641	79	21
2000	1,569	78	22
2001	1,603	79	21
2002	1,705	80	20
2003	1,848	81	19
2004	1,957	82	18

Relevance

New housing construction is important to the overall economy. Construction results in the hiring of workers, the production of construction materials and equipment, and the sale of large household appliances such as ranges and refrigerators. In addition, when owners or tenants occupy the housing, they often buy new furniture, carpeting, and other furnishings.

The rate of new housing construction is heavily influenced by growth in the number of households in the long run, and by the growth of inflation-adjusted household incomes and by the level and movement of mortgage interest rates over shorter periods. Because housing lasts for many years and there is little need to replace it frequently, the purchase of new housing usually is deferred until incomes and interest rates make it affordable (see *housing affordability index*). Housing starts are stimulated when incomes of workers at all earnings levels rise steadily or interest rates are low or declining, and they are restrained when incomes of workers at all earnings levels do not rise steadily or interest rates are high or rising (see *distribution of income* and *interest rates*).

Housing starts are related to *home sales: new and existing houses*. Building permits for the construction of new housing (see "Methodology"), which are a precursor of housing starts, are a component of the leading index of the *leading, coincident, and lagging indexes*.

Recent Trends

From 1995 to 2004, housing starts rose from 1.35 million units in 1995 to 1.96 million units in 2004 (Table 25.1). Increases occurred in all years except 1997 and 2000. The single-family share of all housing units, typically 79 percent during 1995–2001, rose to 82 percent in 2004.

Reference from Primary Data Source

Bureau of the Census, U.S. Department of Commerce. *Housing Starts.* Monthly.

26
Housing Vacancy Rate

The housing vacancy rate represents housing units that are not occupied and that are physically suitable for occupancy. The housing vacancy data cover year-round and seasonal housing in multifamily rental apartments, single-family houses, townhouses, condominiums, cooperatives, and mobile homes.

Where and When Available

The housing vacancy rate is prepared quarterly by the Bureau of the Census in the U.S. Department of Commerce. The data are published in a news release and in the report, *Housing Vacancy Survey* (www.census.gov).

The data on housing vacancies are available about the fourth week of the month following the quarter to which they refer. They are revised approximately at ten-year intervals with the incorporation of new benchmark data from the decennial censuses.

Content

Housing vacancies comprise year-round and seasonal housing units that are not occupied and are physically suitable for occupancy. Housing vacancy data are provided for the United States, four Census geographic regions, metropolitan areas, and outside metropolitan areas, and for selected characteristics of the house, such as the number of rooms and contract rent.

A housing unit is a single-family house, an apartment in a multifamily building (including townhouses, condominiums, and cooperatives), or a mobile home that is owned or rented and is occupied or intended for occupancy as separate living quarters by a family or a group of individuals living together. A housing unit excludes people living in group quarters (e.g., dormitories, barracks, transient hotels or motels, except in cases where people consider the hotel their usual residence,) and in institutions (e.g., hospitals, jails, shelters, halfway houses).

A housing unit is defined as vacant if no one is living in it when the housing enumerator conducts the survey, except when the household occupants are only temporarily absent when the housing survey is taken. A vacant unit may be one that is entirely occupied by persons who have a usual residence elsewhere. A household consists of all persons—related family members and unrelated individuals—who occupy a housing unit and have no other usual address.

When a seasonal housing unit, which is intended for use only during certain seasons of the year, is occupied by a household that has a usual residence elsewhere, it is counted as vacant, while the housing unit that is the usual residence of the household is counted as occupied. An unoccupied housing unit is not considered vacant if it is exposed to the elements so that the roof, walls, windows, or doors do not protect the interior from the elements, or if there is positive evidence (such as a sign on the house or block) that the unit is condemned or is to be demolished.

The housing vacancy data are not seasonally adjusted.

Methodology

The housing vacancy data are obtained from a monthly sample survey of households, called the Current Population Survey (CPS), which is conducted by the U.S. Bureau of the Census. The CPS is the same survey that is used to obtain the monthly household employment and unemployment data (see *employment* and *unemployment*). The housing occupancy and vacancy data are obtained by the enumerators at the same time that they obtain the employment and unemployment data. The CPS is a probability sample of households that is currently drawn from the 2000 census of population and is updated in subsequent years using changes in residential locations associated with new housing construction data prepared by the Census Bureau.

Survey responses for the employment data in the CPS are obtained from approximately 55,000 households each month. About 6,400 additional vacant units are surveyed for the housing vacancy data. The count of occupied housing units is the same as the count of households.

Information on vacancies is obtained from neighbors, real estate agents, property managers of rental property, or the owner of the property.

The housing vacancy rate is calculated as a percentage separately for rental housing and for homeowner housing:

$$\text{Rental vacancy rate} = \frac{\text{Vacant for-rent housing units}}{\text{Renter occupied housing units} + \text{vacant for-rent housing units} + \text{rented units awaiting occupancy}} \times 100 \quad (26.1)$$

$$\text{Homeowner vacancy rate} = \frac{\text{Vacant for-sale housing units}}{\text{Owner occupied housing units} + \text{vacant for-sale housing units} + \text{sold units awaiting occupancy}} \times 100$$

Accuracy

The sampling error (for one standard error) for the rental housing vacancy rate is 0.2 of a percentage point. The sampling error (for one standard error) for the home owner housing vacancy is less than 0.05 of a percentage point. For example, if the estimated rental housing vacancy rate were 10 percent, in two of three cases the "true" vacancy rate would be somewhere between 9.8 and 10.2 percent. For further information on the interpretation of sampling and nonsampling errors, see the Appendix. These error ranges may vary as the vacancy rate varies.

Relevance

The housing vacancy rate is a broad indicator of the relative shortage or surplus of existing housing. The lower the vacancy rate, the greater the potential for additional housing, while the higher the vacancy rate, the smaller the potential for additional housing. This generalization may be weakened if there is a shift in preference between rental and homeowner housing. For example, a rise in the rental vacancy rate may reflect an increasing preference for homeowner housing, in which case new single-family construction could increase despite the rise in rental vacancies.

In assessing the need for additional housing, vacancy rates should be

Table 26.1

Housing Vacancy Rates (percent)

	Rental housing	Homeowner housing
1995	7.6	1.5
1996	7.8	1.6
1997	7.7	1.6
1998	7.9	1.7
1999	8.1	1.7
2000	8.0	1.6
2001	8.4	1.8
2002	8.9	1.7
2003	9.8	1.8
2004	10.2	1.7

supplemented with information on household growth, incomes, and rentals and sales by locality. Vacancy rates may also suggest a strengthening or lessening of rental levels and *housing prices.*

Recent Trends

From 1995 to 2004, the rental housing vacancy rate generally rose from 7.6 percent in 1995 to 10.2 percent in 2004 (Table 26.1). The increase was particularly pronounced from 2001 to 2004. The homeowner housing vacancy rate fluctuated around 1.6–1.8 percent over the 1995–2004 period. In general, the rental housing vacancy rate was about five times the level of the homeowner vacancy rate.

Reference from Primary Data Source

Bureau of the Census, U.S. Department of Commerce. *Housing Vacancy Survey.* Quarterly.

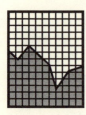

27
Import and Export Price Indexes

The import and export price indexes measure price changes in agricultural, raw material, and manufactured products for goods bought from and sold to foreigners, plus a limited number of transportation services. They represent increases and decreases in prices of internationally traded goods due to changes in the *value of the dollar* and changes in the markets for the items.

Where and When Available

Import and export price indexes are provided monthly by the Bureau of Labor Statistics (BLS) in the U.S. Department of Labor. The data are published in a news release and in the BLS monthly journal, *Monthly Labor Review* (www.bls.gov).

The data are published two to three weeks after the month to which they refer. They are revised in the following three months. Major benchmark revisions, which include updating the weighting structure, are made every year.

Content

The import and export price indexes cover most internationally traded goods. The broad product categories of the indexes are food, feeds, and beverages; industrial supplies and materials; capital goods; automotive vehicles, parts, and engines; and consumer goods, excluding automotive. Goods exclusively for military use (based on U.S. Customs Bureau definitions), works of art, commercial aircraft, and ships are excluded.

Supplementary international price indexes for transportation services are provided for air freight rates, air passenger fares, crude oil tanker freight rates (imports only), and ocean liner freight rates (imports only). These services are not included in the above indexes for goods.

The indexes reflect movements for the same items exclusive of enhancement or reduction in the quality or quantity of the item. Prices represent the actual transaction value including premiums and discounts from list prices and changes in credit terms and packaging. Prices usually are based on the time the item is delivered, not the time the order is placed.

The price definition for imports is the value at the foreign port of export loaded on the carrier (free on board, f.o.b.) or the value at the U.S. border including overseas transportation and insurance costs (cost, insurance, freight, c.i.f.). Import duties are excluded from the price.

The price definition for exports is the value at the U.S. port of export before loading on the carrier (free alongside ship, f.a.s.) or loaded on the carrier (free on board, f.o.b). Regardless of variations in the pricing basis, it is more important that the same products maintain consistent definitions over time. Thus, the same definition of prices is maintained for individual products to ensure consistency in the monthly price movements.

The import and export price indexes are currently based on 2000 = 100.

The import and export price indexes are not seasonally adjusted.

Methodology

The price data are obtained by a Bureau of Labor Statistics mail survey of a sample of importers and exporters, including a limited number of foreign trade brokers. In addition, prices of crude petroleum imports are based on U.S. Department of Energy data, and those for grain exports (excluding rice) are based on U.S. Department of Agriculture data. The overall response rate to the BLS survey rises from 75–80 percent for the initial estimate for the month to 85–90 percent as late responses to the survey are incorporated in the third revised estimate of the month.

Price quotations are sought for the first transaction of the month, which typically occurs within the first week of the month. The weights of the indexes are obtained from the Census Bureau's foreign trade data and are reweighted annually with a two-year lag.

If the reported import or export price includes a change in the quality (performance) or quantity (size) of the item, the Bureau of Labor Statistics attempts to adjust the price to compensate for the improvement or decline in quality or quantity. The adjustment is made to ensure that price movements reflect items having the same functional characteristics over time. The quality and quantity adjustments are based on performance and size data in relation to production costs supplied by the importers and exporters. Because the data to make the necessary adjustments are not always available, the import and export price indexes contain an unknown amount of price change caused by quality or quantity changes.

Accuracy

There are no estimates of sampling or revision error for the import and export price indexes.

Relevance

The import and export price indexes are used in analyzing the effect of changes in the competitive position of U.S. imports and exports. This includes their linkage to the volume of imports and exports and the *balance of trade,* and their relationship to domestic price change in the *consumer price index, producer price indexes,* and *GDP price measures.* The international price indexes are also used in evaluating the effect of changes in the *value of the dollar* on import and export prices. The extent of "pass-throughs" of price changes that partly or fully offset changes in the value of the dollar can be calculated through the preparation of supplementary trade-weighted exchange rates.

In addition, the international price indexes are used to adjust other economic indicators for price change such as the merchandise trade data in the *balance of trade,* the *balance of payments,* and the exports and imports components of the *gross domestic product.*

Recent Trends

From 1995 to 2004, "all imports" prices fluctuated within an annual range of –6.1 to 6.5 percent, compared with nonpetroleum imports prices that fluctuated within a range of –3.6 to 3.9 percent (Table 27.1). The narrower range of nonpetroleum imports reflects the volatility of petroleum prices. "All imports" prices changed more than nonpetroleum imports prices in all years except 1999. In most years, "all exports" prices and nonagricultural exports prices changed less than all imports and

Table 27.1

Import and Export Price Indexes (annual percentage change)

	Import prices		Export prices	
	All imports	Nonpetroleum imports	All exports	Nonagricultural exports
1995	4.6	3.9	5.1	4.6
1996	1.0	−0.7	0.6	−0.9
1997	−2.5	−2.2	−1.3	−0.3
1998	−6.1	−3.6	−3.3	−2.5
1999	0.9	−1.4	−1.3	−0.6
2000	6.5	1.0	1.6	1.8
2001	−3.5	−1.5	−0.8	−1.0
2002	−2.5	−2.3	−1.0	−1.3
2003	3.0	1.1	1.5	1.1
2004	5.6	2.6	3.9	3.3
1995–2004 (annual average)	0.2	−0.8	−0.03	−0.04

nonpetroleum imports prices. Over the entire nine-year period, the annual increases and decreases in "all imports" prices averaged 0.2 percent and for nonpetroleum imports prices averaged –0.8 percent, which indicated a relatively small change in the price levels from 1995 to 2004. The nine-year change for "all exports" averaged –0.03 percent and for nonagricultural exports averaged –0.04 percent, which indicated virtually zero change in the price levels from 1995 to 2004.

Reference from Primary Data Source

Bureau of Labor Statistics, U.S. Department of Labor. *Monthly Labor Review.* Monthly.

28
Industrial Production Index

The industrial production index (IPI) measures the change in output in U.S. manufacturing, mining, and electric and gas utilities industries. Output refers to the physical quantity of items produced, as distinct from sales value, which combines quantity and price. The index covers the production of goods and power for domestic sales in the United States and exports. It excludes production in the agriculture, construction, transportation, communication, trade, finance, and service industries; government output; and imports. While the excluded industries and imports are not directly in the index, they are indirectly incorporated to the extent that the manufacturing, mining, and utilities industries use them as intermediate items, in which case they are a component of the product or power produced.

Where and When Available

The industrial production index is prepared monthly by the Federal Reserve Board (FRB). It is published in a statistical release (G. 17) and in the monthly statistical supplement to the quarterly FRB journal, the *Federal Reserve Bulletin* (www.federalreserve.gov).

The data are available in the middle of the month after the month to which they refer, the same day as the *capacity utilization* measure. Preliminary data are provided for the preceding month; these are revised in the subsequent three months. Annual revisions are made in the fall.

Content

The industrial production index is provided from two perspectives: (a) output originating in the producing industries (supply), and (b) selected consumer and business markets of the items produced (demand). The component groups of the supply perspective are the producing industries: manufacturing, mining, and electric and gas utilities. For the market perspective, these components are categorized as products according to their typical usage. These are: consumer goods, business equipment, defense and space equipment, intermediate products including construction and business supplies, and materials including energy and nonenergy materials, parts, and containers.

The IPI is currently based on 1997 = 100.

The IPI data are seasonally adjusted.

Methodology

The industrial production index weights are updated annually based on an index number formulation in which the geometric mean of the value-added weights in the previous year and the current-year is used (Fisher ideal index). This is similar to the weighting used in the *GDP price indexes* and in the chain index of the *consumer price index* (C-CPI-U). Because the value-added data from the Census Bureau annual surveys are available with a lag of approximately two years, weights in the current year are extrapolated by the movements of *producer price indexes* in each industry for the most recent period. This procedure utilizes price movements in order to account for significant shifts in the value-added weights on an up-to-date basis, such as sharp declines in computer and semiconductor prices. "Value added" generally refers to the wages, profits, and depreciation of capital facilities in the producing industry, that is, the value an industry adds to goods and services it buys from other industries, although there are technical differences in the definition of value added as it is used in the Census Bureau surveys from that in the *gross domestic product.*

The monthly movements of the index are based on the following source information in the third monthly revision: production of actual items (48 percent); production worker hours in producing industries (30 percent); electric kilowatt-hour consumption by producing industries (18 percent), and various estimating techniques (4 percent). In the annual revisions, monthly movements of the IPI components that were estimated from in-

Table 28.1

Industrial Production Index (1997 = 100)

	All industries	Manufacturing	Mining	Utilities
1995	89.4	88.1	96.7	97.2
1996	93.2	92.2	98.3	100.0
1997	100.0	100.0	100.0	100.0
1998	105.8	106.6	98.5	102.6
1999	110.6	112.2	93.6	105.5
2000	115.4	117.3	95.8	108.6
2001	111.3	112.3	96.7	108.1
2002	111.0	111.9	92.6	111.4
2003	110.9	111.9	92.2	111.9
2004	115.5	117.2	91.4	114.8
1995–2004 (annual average percentage change)	2.9	3.2	–0.6	1.9

direct sources (kilowatt hours and worker hours) are corrected to reflect more extensive direct data on production, which are obtained mainly from the Census Bureau's *Annual Survey of Manufactures.*

Accuracy

The typical revision to the monthly industrial production index level between the preliminary estimate and the third monthly revision is plus or minus 0.28 percent. The typical revision to the monthly movement is plus or minus 0.22 of a percentage point. In about 85 percent of the cases, the direction of change in the preliminary estimate is the same as in the third revision.

Relevance

The coverage of the industrial production index makes it a sensitive gauge of the most cyclical aspects of the economy. Although the industries covered amounted to only 16 percent of the *gross domestic product* in 2003, they account for the bulk of the more volatile movements in expansions and recessions. Consequently, the IPI tends to rise more in expansions and fall more in recessions than the overall economy. The IPI is a component of the coincident index of the *leading, coincident, and lagging indexes.*

Recent Trends

From 1995 to 2004, the industrial production index for all industries combined increased from 89.4 in 1995 to 115.4 in 2000, declined to 110.9 in 2003, and rose to 115.5 in 2004 (Table 28.1). Manufacturing had similar movements as the all-industries total. Mining peaked at 100 in 1997, and then declined to 91.4 in 2004. Utilities rose in all years, from 97.2 in 1995 to 114.8 in 2004, except for zero change in 1997 and a decline in 2001. The average annual percentage change in the IPI over the nine-year period was: all industries (2.9 percent), manufacturing (3.2 percent), mining (–0.6 percent), and utilities (1.9 percent).

Reference from Primary Data Source

Board of Governors of the Federal Reserve System. *Statistical Supplement to the Federal Reserve Bulletin.* The *Statistical Supplement* is monthly, and the *Federal Reserve Bulletin* is quarterly.

29
Interest Rates

Interest is the cost of borrowing money, and interest rates are the price of money. An interest rate, also referred to as a yield, is the annualized percentage that interest is of the principal of the loan. Loans are extended and paid back through the use of debt instruments. The value (i.e., the price) of the debt instrument, such as a bond, fluctuates due to actual and anticipated inflation movements until its maturity date, when the principal is repaid; during this period, the price of the debt instrument moves inversely to the interest rate, with a price rise accompanied by an interest rate decline, and vice versa. Interest rates differ for various loans due to the length and risk of the loan. Generally, short-term loans have lower interest rates than long-term loans, and loans subject to little risk of not being repaid have lower interest rates than those with higher risk.[1]

Where and When Available

Measures of interest rates for different types of debt instruments are reported on a daily, weekly, or monthly basis by the Federal Reserve Board, U.S. Department of the Treasury, Federal Reserve Bank of New York, Federal Housing Finance Board, Moody's Investors Service, and Standard & Poor's Corporation. Interest rates are published in news releases of the source organizations. Several interest rates are published in the Federal Reserve's weekly statistical release H.15 (www. federalreserve.gov). Other general Web sites for interest rates include: Bloomberg Financial (www.bloomberg.com), Wall Street Journal Interactive Edition (www.wsj.com), Barrons (www.barrons.com),

MarketWatch (www.marketwatch.com), Bankrate (www.bankrate.com), and Interest (www.interest.com).

The data are available within a day to a week after the period to which they refer.

Content

The nine annualized interest rate measures covered here show the different costs of borrowing for short-term, medium-term, and long-term loans of high quality that are authorized by debt instruments such as notes and bonds. Loans of high quality have the least risk of nonpayment. While all nine types are high-quality loans, some are more secure than others—for example, U.S. Treasury securities are default-free, and thus are the highest quality. Loan periods may be broadly defined as up to one year (short-term), one to three years (medium-term), and more than three years (long-term). Some interest rates are for new loans, while others are for outstanding loans that are traded in securities markets. The loans are made in transactions involving households, nonbank industries, commercial banks, and federal, state, and local governments.

Depending on the type of debt instrument, interest rates are measured according to one of three methods: (a) paying a certain amount at regularly specified intervals with a bond coupon or through negotiated terms of the loan, (b) the extent to which the par value (redemption price when the security expires) of a noncoupon security is above the discounted market price of the security, or (c) a hybrid of regular interest and a premium or discounted market price from the par value of the security.

Interest rates are not seasonally adjusted.

Selected Debt Instruments and Interest Rates

The nine interest rates are summarized below (U.S. Treasury notes and bonds for three- and ten-year maturities make up two of the nine interest rates). Sources of the interest rate data are in parentheses.

U.S. Treasury Three-Month Bills (U.S. Department of the Treasury): Short-term default-free borrowing of new issues sold at a discount from the par value.

U.S. Treasury Notes and Bonds with Average Constant Maturities of Three and Ten Years (Federal Reserve): Yields on actively traded medium-term and long-term default-free outstanding issues sold with a coupon interest rate and at a premium or discount from the par value. These are averages of securities that encompass a range of remaining maturities from under one year to twenty years and do not represent a particular issue.

Federal Funds (Federal Reserve Bank of New York): Loans between commercial banks to enable the borrowing bank to meet its reserve requirements with the Federal Reserve. They are primarily overnight loans but also include term loans ranging from a few days to over one year. The daily effective rate is a composite of the varying interest rates on the different loan maturities.

Discount Rate, primary credit (Federal Reserve): Short-term borrowing by commercial banks from regional Federal Reserve. This rate is available to banks only with adequate capitalization and supervisory ratings for soundness. The borrowing, which ranges from overnight to a few weeks, is used variously to maintain certain reserve levels over a two-week period, to meet huge outflows at the end of a day, to keep bank reserves from falling close to or below legal minimum requirements, or for any other purpose including financing the sale of *federal funds*. The primary credit discount rate is set above the federal funds rate (immediately above), so it is a backup to the lower federal funds rate in the event of particular short-term needs. Federal Reserve secondary credit is available at interest rates above the primary credit discount rate to banks lacking satisfactory capitalization or supervisory ratings.[2]

High-Grade Municipal Bonds (Standard & Poor's): Long-term outstanding general obligation and revenue issues of municipalities sold with a coupon interest rate and at a premium or discount from the par value. The interest from the coupon rate is exempt from federal taxes.[3]

Corporate AAA Bonds (Moody's Investors Service): Long-term public utilities and other nonfinancial outstanding issues judged to be the best quality with the smallest degree of investment risk. They are sold with a coupon interest rate and at a premium or discount from the par value.

Prime Rate Charged by Commercial Banks (Federal Reserve): Reference rate for small business loans, home equity loans, and credit card loans. Bank loans to large businesses are more often priced with reference to the London Interbank Offered Rate (LIBOR) denominated in dollars and other currencies as well as with reference to other rates.

New-Home Mortgage Yields (Federal Housing Finance Board): The effective rate at closings of conventional first mortgage loans for fixed- and variable-rate mortgages for newly built, single-family, nonfarm houses amortized, on average, over ten years. This rate includes the contract interest rate and all fees, commissions, discounts, and points paid by the borrower and/or seller to the lender in order to obtain the loan. The ten-year amortization period is an approximation of the average life of a conventional mortgage.

(The Federal Home Loan Mortgage Corporation provides a real-time home mortgage rate based on mortgage commitments [prospective interest rates] for new and existing single-family homes. This differs from the above FHFB rate, which represents closings [actual interest rates] for new homes on a monthly basis. The FHLMC rate is noted here to acquaint the reader with an indicator of future mortgage interest rates.)

Methodology

Procedures used in calculating interest rates for the nine debt instruments are summarized below.

U.S. Treasury Three-Month Bills: The discounted price of the auction conducted every Monday as a percentage of the par value of the securities is the weekly yield. These weekly yields are averaged to obtain the monthly figure.

U.S. Treasury Notes and Bonds with Average Constant Maturities of Three and Ten Years: Yield curves are constructed by plotting interest rates on the vertical axis of a graph and years to maturity on the horizontal axis. A line is drawn through the middle of the plotted points and the interest rate is read from the line that corresponds to three and ten years. The daily closing market bid yields are averaged to obtain the weekly number, and the weekly numbers are averaged for the monthly yield.

Federal Funds: Daily rates for federal funds of varying maturities are obtained from federal funds brokers in New York City. The daily effective rate is the average of these rates weighted by the volume of loans transacted through brokers at each rate.

Federal Reserve Primary Credit Discount Rate: These administered rates of the twelve regional Federal Reserve Banks must be approved by the Federal Reserve Board. The rates of all twelve regional banks are the same, except for periods of a day or two when changes are not made simultaneously. Officially, the rate for the Federal Reserve Bank of New York is used, but in practice the New York rate is the same as those of the other regional banks.

High-Grade Municipal Bonds: The yields of general obligation and revenue issues for fifteen municipalities with remaining maturities of approximately twenty years are averaged using equal weights for each issue. The Wednesday closing is used as the weekly yield.

Corporate AAA Bonds: These are yields for public utilities and other nonfinancial issues with remaining maturities of at least twenty years. The number of bonds included in the indicator changes as the universe of bonds meeting the AAA standard changes. They are averaged using equal weights for each issue and calculated daily.

Prime Rate Charged by Commercial Banks: The daily rate charged by the majority of the twenty-five largest domestically chartered commercial banks based on assets. The rate is identical in at least thirteen of the banks, and is referred to as the predominant rate.

New Home Mortgage Yields: A sample of savings and loan associations, commercial banks, mutual savings banks, and mortgage bankers is surveyed for yields on mortgage loans for newly built, single-family nonfarm houses. The survey covers mortgage closings during the last five working days of the month. Interest rates of the various lenders are weighted by the share of the mortgages originated by each type of lender. The weights are updated quarterly.

Accuracy

There are no estimates of sampling or revision error for the interest rate data.

Relevance

Interest rates have a significant impact on borrowing and spending. Designations of "low" or "high" interest rates are based on borrowers' assessments of past levels and prospective movements. If interest rates are expected to rise, there is an incentive to borrow immediately, but if interest rates are expected to fall, there is an incentive to delay borrowing. Interest rates react to and influence movements of the *gross domestic product* and the *value of the dollar.* The Federal Reserve focuses on interest rates as the ultimate tool in conducting monetary policy to foster economic growth and moderate inflation.

Yield curves represent differential interest rates for short-term, medium-term, and long-term debt instruments. The yield curve reflects expectations of future interest rates, inflation, and business cycle move-

Table 29.1

Interest Rates (percent)

	U.S. Treasury 3-month bills: new issues	U.S. Treasury 3-year constant maturities	U.S. Treasury 10-year constant maturities	Federal funds	Primary credit discount rate: Federal Reserve Bank of New York	High-grade municipal bonds	Corporate AAA bonds	Prime rate charged by commercial banks	New home mortgage yields
1995	5.51	6.25	6.57	5.83	5.21*	5.95	7.59	8.83	7.87
1996	5.02	5.99	6.44	5.30	5.02*	5.75	7.37	8.27	7.80
1997	5.07	6.10	6.35	5.46	5.00*	5.55	7.26	8.44	7.71
1998	4.81	5.14	5.26	5.35	4.92*	5.12	6.53	8.35	7.07
1999	4.66	5.49	5.65	4.97	4.62*	5.43	7.04	8.00	7.04
2000	5.85	6.22	6.03	6.24	5.73*	5.77	7.62	9.23	7.52
2001	3.45	4.09	5.02	3.88	3.40*	5.19	7.08	6.91	7.00
2002	1.62	3.10	4.61	1.67	1.17*	5.05	6.49	4.67	6.43
2003	1.02	2.10	4.01	1.13	2.12	4.73	5.67	4.12	5.80
2004	1.38	2.78	4.27	1.35	2.34	4.63	5.63	4.34	5.77

*The primary credit discount rate was instituted in 2003. This rate differs from the discount rate that was used before 2003, which included secondary credit.

ments. The interest rate spread of the ten-year Treasury bond less the federal funds rate is a component of the leading index of the *leading, coincident, and lagging indexes*. The prime interest rate is a component of the lagging index of the *leading, coincident, and lagging indexes*.

The federal funds rate and the primary credit discount rate are the only indicators in this book that are acted on by a government authority solely to affect their performance and consequently that of the economy. The federal budget is acted on directly, but the federal budget is not associated solely with influencing the economy (see *government economic transactions*).

Recent Trends

From 1995 to 2004, interest rates drifted lower, except for increases in some issues in 1999, 2000, and 2004. The declines were greater in short-term and medium-term issues than in long-term issues (Table 29.1). Interest rates in 2004 ranged from 1.35 percent for federal funds to 5.77 percent for new home mortgage yields.

General Reference for Several Interest Rates

Board of Governors of the Federal Reserve System. *Selected Interest Rates,* Statistical Release H.15. Weekly.

Notes

1. In the early 1960s, an attempt was made to lessen the differential between short-term and long-term interest rates, which was referred to as "Operation Twist." See Franco Modigliani and Richard Sutch, "Innovations in Interest Rate Policy," *American Economic Review,* March 1966.

2. The primary credit discount rate was instituted in 2003. Before 2003, the discount rate included banks in today's definition with both primary and secondary credit ratings.

3. The yield includes both the coupon rate and the purchase price. When the purchase price is the same as the principal of the bond (par value), the yield is the coupon rate. When the purchase price is above par (premium) or below par (discount), the yield differs from the coupon rate. When the purchase price is at a premium, the yield is below the coupon rate; when the purchase price is at a discount, the yield is above the coupon rate. Capital gains and losses, which are associated with the difference between the par value and the purchase price of the bond, are subject to the liability for federal taxes.

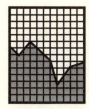

30
International Investment
Position of the United States

The international investment position of the U.S. represents the difference between the value of foreign assets held by U.S. parties abroad and the value of U.S. assets held by foreign parties in the United States. It is commonly referred to as the overall creditor or debtor status of the nation, although technically it only partially represents debt because it also includes equity ownership of foreign companies. Nevertheless, in this discussion, the creditor and debtor designations will be used because they reflect the general perception of the meaning of the data. If American assets abroad exceed foreign assets in the United States, the United States is a creditor nation, and if foreign assets in the United States exceed American assets abroad, the United States is a debtor nation.

Where and When Available

The Bureau of Economic Analysis (BEA) in the U.S. Department of Commerce provides annual measures of the U.S. international investment position. They are published in a news release and in the BEA monthly journal, *Survey of Current Business* (www.bea.gov).

The data are available each July for the preceding year. Annual revisions to the historical data for several of the preceding years are also provided each July.

Content

International investments include capital equipment and structures in manufacturing and other industries, stocks, bonds, loans, the official U.S.

gold stock, and the U.S. reserve position and special drawing rights in the International Monetary Fund. The net investment position of the U.S. is defined as foreign assets held by U.S. parties abroad (assets) minus U.S. assets held by foreigners (liabilities). The net investment position reflects the total U.S. and foreign assets outstanding at the end of each year.

The investment position data include the actual capital flows at current costs in the *balance of payments* plus valuation changes to the existing holdings of assets from previous acquisitions. Investment position data consist of transactions throughout the year and valuation adjustments to positions outstanding at the beginning of the year.

The annual change in the investment position is attributable to four factors: (1) capital flows of private and government assets, (2) valuation adjustments due to price changes, (3) valuation adjustments due to exchange rate movements, and (4) methodological changes of coverage, statistical discrepancies, and valuation of assets. Methodological changes result in a break in the comparability of the data series.

Methodology

The main data sources used in developing the investment position indicator are: U.S. Treasury Department surveys conducted by the Federal Reserve Bank of New York on international assets and liabilities; BEA surveys of foreign direct investment abroad and in the United States; bilateral financial data provided by other countries; and the value of the dollar based on Federal Reserve Board and Treasury Department measures. Breakdowns of the factors contributing to the changes in position from year to year are also derived from these data.

Direct investment and portfolio investment are two major components of international investment. Direct investment is associated with a long-term interest in and control of corporate and noncorporate business enterprises. It is defined as when a foreign investor owns 10 percent or more of the voting securities or equivalent equity of an enterprise. Portfolio investment is associated with short-term activity in financial markets that emphasizes the ability to move funds between countries and investments. It is defined as when a foreign investor owns less than 10 percent of the voting securities or equivalent equity of a business enterprise. Portfolio investment also includes the total amount of an investor's holdings of foreign private and government bonds and other debt instruments.

The valuation of the investment position is made in current-cost and

market-value prices. Current cost is the dollar outlay necessary to replace the tangible equipment, structures, and land assets of direct investments. Market value is the dollar worth of the direct investment
tangible assets as measured by stock market prices, which also implicitly includes the value of intangible assets such as patents, trademarks,
management, and name recognition.

Portfolio investments are measured only in market-value prices. Thus,
the alternative current-cost and market-value price measures of the investment position reflect these distinctions only for direct investment.
Separate measures of historical cost of direct investment represent the
original purchase price of tangible assets; however, historical-cost estimates are not included in the investment position measures.

Accuracy

There are no estimates of sampling or revision error in the international
investment position data. Increases and decreases in the position from
year to year attributable to methodological changes in the data sources
indicate the net effect of inconsistencies in the various data sources. This
is an overall minimum assessment of the inconsistencies because offsetting errors among the data elements reduce the net effect. In addition, the
statistical discrepancy in the *balance of payments* shifts between a net
inflow of unrecorded funds into the United States and a net outflow of
unrecorded funds from the United States. If the unrecorded flows are capital
funds, foreign assets in the United States would be understated (inflows)
or overstated (outflows). For all of these reasons, the international investment position is an order of magnitude rather than a precise number.

Relevance

The international investment position reflects the international industrial and financial base of the United States. A creditor status signifies
that Americans own more capital abroad than foreigners own in the United
States, while a debtor status indicates that Americans own less capital
abroad than foreigners own in the United States. Because a creditor nation is less dependent on outside sources of financing than a debtor nation, its capital funding requirements are less vulnerable to changes in
international financial markets. Therefore, a creditor nation is more independent than a debtor nation in conducting monetary policies that

Table 30.1

International Investment Position of the United States (billions of dollar)

	Net investment position (current cost)	Net investment position (market value)	U.S. assets abroad (current cost)	Foreign assets in the U.S. (current cost)
1995	−458.5	−305.8	3,486.3	3,944.7
1996	−495.1	−360.0	4,032.3	4,527.4
1997	−820.7	−822.7	4,567.9	5,388.6
1998	−895.4	−1,070.8	5,095.5	5,990.9
1999	−766.2	−1,037.4	5,974.4	6,740.6
2000	−1,381.2	−1,581.0	6,238.8	7,620.0
2001	−1,919.4	−2,339.4	6,308.7	8,228.1
2002	−2,107.3	−2,445.1	6,645.7	8,752.9
2003	−2,156.7	−2,372.4	7,641.0	9,797.7
2004	−2,484.2	−2,542.2	9,052.8	11,537.0

influence its economy with respect to *interest rates* and the *value of the dollar.*

A creditor nation has a net inflow and a debtor nation has a net outflow of interest and dividend incomes paid on international loans and investments. If a nation is a creditor, the income flows increase exports, which results in a surplus (or reduction in the deficit) in its balance of payments. If the nation is a debtor, the income flows increase imports, which results in a deficit (or reduction in the surplus) in its balance of payments. The income flows also tend to raise the wealth and standard of living in creditor nations relative to debtor nations. However, creditor nations risk adverse actions by debtor nations—default on foreign debt and expropriation of foreign-owned properties.

Recent Trends

From 1995 to 2004, the United States became an increasingly net debtor nation (Table 30.1). The net debt in 2004 was $2.48 trillion (current cost) and $2.54 trillion (market value). The growing net debt reflected a continuous trend of slower growth of U.S. assets abroad than of foreign assets in the United States.

Reference from Primary Data Source

Bureau of Economic Analysis, U.S. Department of Commerce. *Survey of Current Business.* Monthly.

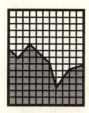

31
Inventory–Sales Ratios

The inventory–sales ratio represents the monthly turnover rate of inventories at current sales rates. For example, a ratio of 1.6 means that existing inventories will be used up in 1.6 months if sales continue at the current rate (assuming that inventories are not replenished during the period). The ratio is calculated with inventories in the numerator and sales in the denominator.

Where and When Available

The Bureau of the Census in the U.S. Department of Commerce prepares monthly inventory–sales ratios. They are published in the report, *Manufacturing and Trade Inventories and Sales* (www. census.gov).

The data are available forty-five days after the month to which they refer; they are revised in the next month. Annual revisions are made in the spring of the following year.

Content

The Census Bureau's inventory–sales ratios reflect inventories and sales of manufacturers, merchant wholesalers, and retailers. They include materials and supplies, work in process, and finished goods of manufacturers, including service installation costs; they also include merchandise of wholesalers and retailers who resell them without further processing, including service installation costs of retailers.

The inventory–sales ratios are provided in current dollars.

The inventory–sales ratios are seasonally adjusted.

(An alternative measure of inventory–sales ratios, referred to as private inventories to final sales ratios, is provided as part of the *gross domestic product* measures. These measures are not included in this book, but are briefly noted here to alert the reader to their existence. Final sales exclude sales of crude materials, supplies, and semifinished goods that become intermediate products in the production process. They also exclude sales of finished goods from manufacturers to wholesalers and retailers and from wholesalers to retailers who resell them in the same state, and thus provide unduplicated sales values of products from manufacturers to wholesalers to retailers. This contrasts with the inventory–sales ratios in this book that include the duplication of such sales. The inventory–final sales ratios are provided quarterly in current and in price-adjusted dollars. The inventory–final sales ratios are relevant for analysts who prefer the use of unduplicated sales of products as described above.)

Methodology

The inventory and sales data are obtained from the Census Bureau's monthly surveys of manufacturers, merchant wholesalers, and retailers. The inventory data are defined at current cost valuation, which is the book-value acquisition cost before the companies convert inventories to a LIFO (last-in, first-out) valuation. The sales data for manufacturers represent shipments and the sales data for wholesalers and retailers represent sales.

Accuracy

There are no estimates of sampling or revision error for the inventory–sales ratios for the combined total of manufacturing and trade industries. Estimates of sampling error are available for the wholesale and retail trade components separately.

Relevance

Inventory–sales ratios impact future production levels. Inventories are a business cost, which businesses finance by borrowing funds or tying up their own money. Thus, high inventory–sales ratios suggest that busi-

Table 31.1

Inventory-Sales Ratio (manufacturing and trade industries)

1995	1.48
1996	1.46
1997	1.42
1998	1.43
1999	1.40
2000	1.41
2001	1.44
2002	1.40
2003	1.38
2004	1.31

nesses will tend to cut back on orders to suppliers because it is expensive to hold goods that are not selling rapidly. The resulting lower manufacturers' orders lead to declines in the *industrial production index* and *employment.* Analogously, low inventory–sales ratios suggest increased orders to replenish inventories, because the ability to furnish items readily off the shelf and maintain a wider selection of goods for customers will promote sales. In this case, the growth in orders results in higher production and employment.

These general tendencies hold true, more or less, depending on the extent to which inventory movements result from deliberate action by businesses to build up or deplete inventories through sales incentives, cost cutting, changes in production and orders (planned inventory change), or from unanticipated inventory accumulation or depletion due to unexpected surges or weaknesses in customer demand (unplanned inventory change). Unplanned inventory changes may affect future production more because of the surprise effect they have on business expectations. Unanticipated changes are not quantifiable because the inventory data do not distinguish the planned and unplanned components. The Census Bureau's inventory–sales ratio for manufacturing and trade combined is converted to price-adjusted dollars for inclusion as a component of the lagging index of the *leading, coincident, and lagging indexes.*

Recent Trends

From 1995 to 2004, the inventory–sales ratio for manufacturing and trade inventories combined generally declined from 1.48 in 1995 to 1.31

in 2004 (Table 31.1). The nine-year decline was interrupted by increases in 1998 and 2001.

Reference from Primary Data Source

Bureau of the Census, U.S. Department of Commerce. *Manufacturing and Trade Inventories and Sales.* Monthly.

32
Job Gains and Losses

Job gains and losses represent gross job increases and decreases, not just the employment net change of the gains minus the losses. Employment gains cover job increases in existing business establishments and job increases in establishments newly starting in business. Employment losses cover job decreases in existing businesses and job decreases in businesses going out of business. The formal title of this program is Business Employment Dynamics. Job gains and losses is a new economic indicator that was first published in 2004.

Where and When Available

The job gains and losses data are prepared quarterly by the Bureau of Labor Statistics in the U.S. Department of Labor. The data are published in *Business Employment Dynamics*, a news release (www.bls.gov).

The data are available in the eighth month after the quarter to which they refer. Although the published data are described as "preliminary," revisions are presently not published because they are minor and do not significantly affect the published data.

Content

Job gains and losses data cover private industry jobs and are derived from the federal–state unemployment insurance system. The main categories of workers excluded from the employment gains and losses data are: government workers, self-employed workers, private household workers, railroad industry workers, most agricultural workers on small farms, religious organization workers, and some not-for-profit organization workers. Also excluded are businesses with zero employment in two consecutive quarters.

The job gains and losses data reflect changes in employment for the same group of business establishments from quarter to quarter (see "Methodology" for the definition of a business establishment). These cover job increases in new and existing businesses, including businesses with positive job levels in one quarter, up from previous zero job levels. Similarly, job decreases are covered in existing businesses, business establishments that go out of business, and those with zero job levels in one quarter, down from previous positive levels.

The job gains and losses data are provided for the United States and for broad industry divisions. Separate data for geographic regions are planned in the future.

The job gains and losses data are provided in absolute levels of the number of jobs and the number of establishments, and in relative rates as a percentage of total employment. The absolute and relative data are classified separately for establishments with gross job gains and gross job losses, with further divisions within the gains and losses categories for increases and decreases other than zero (expansions and contractions), and increases and decreases from zero to positive job levels (job openings) and positive to zero job levels (job closings).

The job gains and losses data represent the last month of each calendar quarter (March, June, September, December). The provision of annual data is planned for a later time.

The job gains and losses data are seasonally adjusted.

Methodology

The job gains and losses data are based on jobs in business establishments. A business establishment is an employer's place of business in a particular geographic location that produces the same or complementary commodities and/or services. For a company that has more than one establishment, each establishment is counted separately. This contrasts with "company" data, in which all establishments of the company are consolidated, regardless of the variety of products made in each establishment.

The data are obtained from the universe of employers that report their employment and wages to the State Unemployment Insurance agencies every quarter. This is a mandatory program that is part of funding the Unemployment Insurance system. It is referred to as the ES-202 program.

The jobs data cover all corporation officials, executives, supervisory personnel, clerical workers, wage earners, pieceworkers, and part-time workers who were on the payroll for the pay period of the establishment that includes the twelfth day of the month. Persons on the payroll for more than one establishment are counted for each job, because this is a count of jobs as distinct from a count of persons (see *employment* for this distinction). The employment data exclude workers who earned zero wages during the pay period (e.g., due to strikes or lockouts, temporary layoffs, illness, unpaid vacations, or wages earned during the month but not during the pay period).

Accuracy

There are no sampling errors with the job gains and losses data because they are obtained from the universe of employers.

Relevance

The gross increases and decreases of jobs in the gains and losses data portray a far more dynamic reality of job markets than only the net changes in employment (increases minus decreases) in the traditional *employment* data. The vast amount of job creation and destruction highlights the continuously shifting strengths and weaknesses in job markets.

Assessments of the job gains and losses data together with the *job openings and labor turnover* data would enhance the understanding of job markets. These assessments should be reflected in shaping fiscal and monetary policies and jobs programs.

Recent Trends

From 1995 to 2004, job gains peaked at 9.1 million in 1999, fell to 7.6 million in 2003, and rose to 8.1 million in 2004. Job losses rose from 7.4 million in 1996 to 8.8 million in 2001, and fell to 7.2 million in 2004. The net change of job gains less job losses peaked at 1.1 million in 1999, fell to a negative 871,000 in 2001, declined to a smaller negative of 175,000 in 2002, and then rose to a positive 344,000 in 2003 and

Table 32.1

Job Gains and Losses (October–December quarter)

	Net change[a]	Job gains	Job losses
Thousands of jobs			
1995	407	7,877	7,470
1996	861	8,278	7,417
1997	702	8,731	8,029
1998	759	8,576	7,817
1999	1,105	9,144	8,039
2000	336	8,691	8,354
2001	−871	7,893	8,764
2002	−175	7,702	7,877
2003	344	7,646	7,302
2004	869	8,081	7,212
Percentage of total employment[b]			
1995	0.4	8.1	7.7
1996	0.9	8.3	7.4
1997	0.6	8.4	7.8
1998	0.7	8.1	7.4
1999	1.1	8.5	7.4
2000	0.3	7.9	7.7
2001	−0.8	7.3	8.1
2002	−0.2	7.1	7.3
2003	0.4	7.2	6.8
2004	0.7	7.4	6.7

[a]Job gains minus job losses; [b]Job gains and job losses as a percentage of the average of the previous and current employment levels.

869,000 in 2004. The percentages of total employment for job gains and losses and the net change in jobs showed a similar pattern as the above absolute movements (see Table 32.1).

Job gains exceeded job losses in the 1995 to 2000 period and in 2003–04. Job losses exceeded job gains in 2001 and 2002.

Reference from Primary Data Source

Bureau of Labor Statistics, U.S. Department of Labor. *Business Employment Dynamics*. Quarterly.

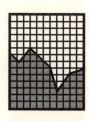

33
Job Openings and Labor Turnover

The job openings and labor turnover survey (JOLTS) data represent the extent to which business establishments and government agencies actively recruit for specific job openings, the extent of job hires, and the extent of job separations.

The JOLTS data cover private nonfarm industries, federal government civilian agencies (excluding uniformed armed forces), state government agencies, and local government agencies. JOLTS is a new economic indicator that was first published in 2002.

Where and When Available

The JOLTS data are prepared monthly by the Bureau of Labor Statistics in the U.S. Department of Labor. The data are published in a news release, *Job Openings and Labor Turnover* (www.bls.gov).

The JOLTS data are available five to six weeks after the month to which they refer. The initial data are revised in the subsequent month. Annual revisions are made in the spring of the following year.

Content

The JOLTS data cover employees on employer payrolls for the pay period that includes the twelfth day of the month. All employees are covered, except proprietors and/or partners of unincorporated businesses and unpaid family workers. Employees of temporary help agencies, employee leasing companies, outside contractors, and consultants are counted as employed by the employer that records them on its payroll, which may not be the employer where they are working. The JOLTS data are published for the United States, four regions of the country, sixteen broad industry categories, the federal government, and state and local governments.

Job Openings

A job opening is defined as: (a) a specific position for which work is available, where (b) work could start within thirty days, and (c) the employer is actively recruiting from outside the establishment to fill the position. The job openings data exclude jobs to be filled from within the establishment such as transfers, promotions, or recall from layoff. The job openings rate is the percentage that job openings are of total employment plus job openings.

Hires

Hires are employee additions to employer payrolls of both new and rehired workers. The hires data do not include transfers or promotions from within the business establishment or the government agency. The hires rate is the percentage that hires are of total employment.

Separations

Separations are job terminations due to quits, layoffs and discharges, retirement, transfers to other locations, disability, and death. The separation rate is the percentage that separations are of total employment.

The JOLTS data are seasonally adjusted for job openings, hires, quits, total separations, and for selected industries.

Methodology

The JOLTS data are obtained from a probability sample of 16,000 nonfarm business establishments and government agencies in all states and the District of Columbia. Large business establishments and government agencies are always included in the sample; that is, they are not subject to random selection. The JOLTS sample is selected from the same sampling frame as the employer establishment survey covered in *employment.*

Table 33.1

Job Openings and Labor Turnover: 2004 (seasonally adjusted)

| | Level (thousands) | | |
	Job openings	Hires	Separations
January	2,864	4,310	3,994
February	2,961	4,159	4,196
March	3,105	4,838	4,289
April	3,111	4,509	4,334
May	3,181	4,339	4,254
June	3,140	4,492	4,235
July	3,231	4,297	4,190
August	3,206	4,504	4,271
September	3,265	4,406	4,214
October	3,300	4,552	4,215
November	3,277	4,990	4,266
December	3,507	4,639	4,435
	Rate (percent)		
January	2.1	3.3	3.1
February	2.2	3.2	3.2
March	2.3	3.7	3.3
April	2.3	3.4	3.3
May	2.4	3.3	3.2
June	2.3	3.4	3.2
July	2.4	3.3	3.2
August	2.4	3.4	3.2
September	2.4	3.3	3.2
October	2.4	3.4	3.2
November	2.4	3.8	3.2
December	2.6	3.5	3.3

The job openings data are based on the last business day of the month. The hires and separations data are based on the entire month.

Accuracy

The sampling error (for one standard error) for the JOLTS monthly rate data is: job openings—0.051 of a percentage point; hires—0.085 of a percentage point; separations—0.083 of a percentage point. For example, if the monthly hires rate were 2 percent, in two of three cases the "true" rate would be somewhere between 1.949 and 2.051 percent. For further information on the interpretation of sampling and nonsampling errors, see the Appendix.

Relevance

The JOLTS data are an approach at the macroeconomic level to compare available job vacancies with *unemployment*. This is referred to as the Beveridge Curve, which shows an inverse relationship between job vacancies and unemployment. Shifts in the Beveridge Curve indicate whether the efficiency of matching jobs with workers is improving or worsening. Shifts in the efficiency are affected by such factors as occupational skills, geographical location of job openings and unemployed workers, quality of labor, and hiring discrimination.

Ideally, the JOLTS data would match job openings with job skills of unemployed workers. But occupational data are not provided in the JOLTS data nor are the industry or geographic detail sufficient for such usage.

Recent Trends

From January to December 2004, job openings generally rose to a high in December, except for declines in August and November. Hires exceeded separations in all months except February, with the largest differential in November of 700,000. Job opening levels were typically 1.2 to 1.5 million below hires, and around 1.0 million below separations.

As a percentage of total employment, job openings were typically 2.3 to 2.4 percent, with a high of 2.6 percent in December; hires were mostly 3.3 to 3.4 percent, though with noticeably higher rates in March and November; and separations were mostly 3.2 to 3.3 percent. (See Table 33.1.)

Reference from Primary Data Source

Bureau of Labor Statistics, U.S. Department of Labor. *Job Openings and Labor Turnover.* News Release. Monthly.

34
Leading, Coincident, and
Lagging Indexes

The leading, coincident, and lagging (LCLg) indexes are an analytic system for assessing current and future economic trends, particularly cyclical expansions and recessions. The system is based on grouping some key indicators according to their tendency to change direction before, during, or after the general economy turns from a recession to an expansion or from an expansion to a recession. Indicators in the leading index change direction before a cyclical turning point in the general economy; those in the coincident index change direction at the same time as the general economy; and those in the lagging index change direction after the change in the general economy. Substantively, the leading index reflects business commitments and expectations, the coincident index reflects the current pace of economic growth, and the lagging index reflects business production costs.

Where and When Available

The Conference Board prepares monthly measures of the leading, coincident, and lagging indexes. They are published in the monthly report of The Conference Board, *Business Cycle Indicators* (www.conference-board.org).

The data are available one month after the month to which they refer; they are revised in the subsequent five months as new source data become available. Annual revisions of the source data are made every December. Comprehensive revisions in the components and the methodology do not follow a regular schedule. The last revision of this type was made in December 1996.

Content

The leading, coincident, and lagging system reflects the business cycle concept that each phase of the business cycle contains the seeds of the subsequent phase.[1] The phases of the business cycle are widely referred to as recovery, expansion, and recession, and less often with an additional phase of contraction. Recovery is the upturn in economic growth from the low point of the previous recession. Expansion is the upward continuation of economic growth from the recovery above the high point attained in the previous expansion before the economy turned down into recession. Recession is the downturn in economic growth from the high point of the previous expansion. Contraction is the downward continuation of economic growth in the recession below the low point of the previous recession (this is the counterpart of the expansion definition), although a recession typically does not become a contraction.

A complete business cycle includes all upward and downward phases. Average economic growth over each cycle is typically measured from the high point of the previous expansion to the high point of the current expansion, and less often from the low point of the previous recession to the low point of the current recession.

The LCLg system is based on the idea that profits are the prime mover of a private enterprise economy and that the recurring business cycles of expansion and recession are caused by changes in the expectation for profits.[2] When anticipated profits are positive, business expands production and investment, but when they are negative, business retrenches. The outlook for profits is reflected in the LCLg system in the leading index and in the ratio of the coincident index to the lagging index.

The leading index represents business commitments and expectations regarding labor, product, and financial markets, and thus points to future business actions. The coincident index represents current movements of production and sales, and so should coincide with business cycle turning points from recovery to expansion to recession to contraction to recovery. The lagging index represents costs of business production. The ratio of the coincident index to the lagging index suggests whether profits will rise or fall in the future due to the differential movements of sales and costs. If the coincident index increases more than the lagging index, or if the coincident index increases and the lagging index falls, profits are likely to rise. Analogously, if the coincident index increases less or declines more than the lagging index, profits are likely to fall. In this way, the coinci-

Table 34.1

Leading, Coincident, and Lagging Composite Indexes and Components

Leading Composite Index
1. Weekly hours of manufacturing production workers (*average weekly hours*)
2. Weekly initial claims for unemployment insurance, state programs—inverted scale (*unemployment*)
3. Manufacturers' new orders for consumer goods and materials, in price-adjusted dollars (*manufacturers' orders*)
4. Vendor performance (percentage of companies receiving slower deliveries)
5. Manufacturers' new orders for nondefense capital goods industries, in price-adjusted dollars (*manufacturers' orders*)
6. New private-housing units authorized by local building permits (*housing starts*)
7. Prices of 500 common stocks, index (*stock market price aggregates and dividend yields*)
8. Money supply (M2), in price-adjusted dollars
9. Interest rate spread, ten-year Treasury bonds less federal funds (*interest rates*)
10. Consumer expectations, index (*consumer attitude indexes*)

Coincident Composite Index
1. Employees on nonagricultural payrolls (*employment*)
2. Personal income less transfer payments, in price-adjusted dollars (*personal income and saving*)
3. Industrial production, index (*industrial production index*)
4. Manufacturing and trade sales, in price-adjusted dollars

Lagging Composite Index
1. Duration of unemployment, weeks—inverted scale (*unemployment*)
2. Inventories divided by sales for manufacturing and trade, ratio, in price-adjusted dollars (*inventory-sales ratios*)
3. Labor cost per unit of output in manufacturing, monthly percentage change (*unit labor costs*)
4. Prime rate charged by banks, percent (*interest rates*)
5. Commercial and industrial loans outstanding, in price-adjusted dollars (*bank loans: commercial and industrial*)
6. Consumer installment credit outstanding divided by personal income, ratio (*consumer credit* and *personal income and saving*)
7. Consumer price index for services, monthly percentage change (*consumer price index*)

dent–lagging ratio, which is internally generated from the LCLg system and is independent of the leading index, is an alternative leading index.

The LCLg indexes are called composite indexes because they group several component indicators. Table 34.1 lists the component indicators in each of three composite indexes. The *leading index* components reflect: the degree of tightness in labor markets due to employer hiring and layoffs; the effect of new orders for manufactured products on future production; financial conditions associated with short-term and long-term interest rate differentials that indicate the stance of Federal Reserve monetary policy; optimism or pessimism reflected by price movements in the stock market, and consumer psychology that affects household spending plans. The *coincident index* components reflect: employment; real personal income generated from production; output in the cyclically sensitive manufacturing, mining, and electric power industries; and real manufacturing and trade sales that encompass the flow of goods between manufacturers, from manufacturers to wholesalers, from wholesalers to retailers, and from retailers to households and businesses. The *lagging index* components reflect: the effect of the duration of unemployment on business wage pressures; the cost of maintaining inventories; labor costs of production in manufacturing; interest payments as a cost of production; the burden of existing business debt in taking on new loans; and prices of consumer services as an indication of production-cost pressures in labor-intensive industries.

The LCLg indexes are currently based on 1996 = 100.

Most of the component indicators of the LCLg indexes are seasonally adjusted. The three composite indexes are not seasonally adjusted at the overall level.

Methodology

The component indicators of the leading, coincident, and lagging indexes are selected based on tests conducted for the following criteria: theoretical rationale for the leading, coincident, and lagging properties; differences in the timing of their change in direction in relation to the cyclical turning points of the economy; consistency with the general upward and downward direction of the business cycle; clear upward or downward trends as distinct from erratic monthly movements from which it is difficult to discern a trend; the quality of the methodology used in collecting the data; promptness of the availability of monthly data; and the extent of revisions to preliminary data.

Data for the components of the LCLg indexes are based on many of the indicators discussed elsewhere in this book. These indicators are referenced in Table 34.1, although they are not always definitionally identical to the LCLg components.

The components are combined in the three indexes and weighted equally. A statistical procedure is used in calculating the indexes to prevent the components that have sharp monthly movements from dominating the indexes. The long-run trends of the leading and lagging indexes are equated to the long-run trend of the coincident index.

Accuracy

There are no estimates of sampling or revision error for the leading, coincident, and lagging indexes.

Relevance

The leading, coincident, and lagging indexes help in assessing the current momentum and future direction of the economy. Because the coincident index reflects actual economic growth, it indicates whether the economy is currently expanding or in recession (the actual designation of a recession period is determined by the Business Cycle Dating Committee of the non-profit National Bureau of Economic Research). Movements in the leading index and the coincident–lagging ratio suggest whether the existing trend measured by the coincident index will continue. A change in direction in the leading index and the coincident–lagging ratio tends to foreshadow movement in the coincident index. But it is important to note that while the LCLg system is a forecasting tool, it does not provide actual forecasts.

Figure 34.1 shows that the lead time between the change in direction of the leading measures and the coincident index is noticeably longer at the cyclical downturn than at the upturn. It also indicates that the lead times vary considerably from cycle to cycle. And in the 1990–91 and 2001 recessions, the lagging index ran counter to the theory when it showed a lead before the onset of each recession; in fact, the lead was twice as long as the lead of the leading index. Changes in the lagging index follow the coincident index and are thus used to confirm that a directional change has occurred, except as just noted. The above-noted variations in timing from cycle to cycle are examples of the continually changing economic landscape that gives each business cycle unique characteristics.

The LCLg indexes are a useful tool for gauging strengths and weaknesses in the economy. However, they are limited for forecasting future economic trends. First, the preliminary contemporaneous data that are available during the months before a downturn into a recession or an upturn into a recovery do not always provide advance signs of a cyclical turning point. The leading index systematically leads at cyclical turning points only in the recalculated historical measures; these incorporate

Figure 34.1   **Leading, Coincident, and Lagging Composite Indexes**
(1996 = 100)

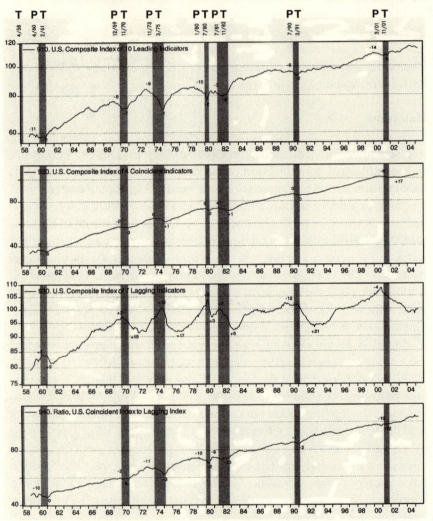

Source: The Conference Board, *Business Cycle Indicators,* June 2005.

Note: Vertical bars are recession periods. Numbers on bars are monthly leads (-) and lags (+) from cyclical turning points. Series numbers are component indicators of the composite index.

P = Peak: High point of expansion.

T = Trough: Low Point of recession

data revisions in the components and changes in the methodology that are made several years later. At the same time, the real time anticipation of changes in economic growth rates has improved as a result of new procedures for incorporating more timely data for selected component indicators of the composite indexes.[3] Second, the LCLg indexes do not forecast quantitative economic growth rates or the timing of future cyclical turning points. Third, the indexes occasionally give false signals of a pending change in the direction of the economy, such as prospective recessions in 1966, 1984, and 1995 that did not materialize.

These complexities make it difficult to develop LCLg system guidelines for forecasting. The Conference Board suggests a nuanced approach for identifying a pending recession.[4] This provides for a decline in the leading index of 1 to 2 percent over a six-month period together with declines in at least half of the components of the leading index.

Recent Trends

From the 1960s to 2004 (Figure 34.1), the leading index led at all cyclical turning points, although by varying numbers of months. The coincident–lagging ratio led at all cyclical turning points except in the recovery in 1960, the recovery in 1975, and the onset of the recession in 1990. The coincident index was exactly at the cyclical turning points, except for divergences of one month in three cases, two months in one case, and three months in one case. The lagging index lagged at all cyclical turning points except at the onset of the 1990–91 and 2001 recessions.

References from Primary Data Source

The Conference Board. *Business Cycle Indicators*. New York, NY. Monthly.
———. *Business Cycles Indicators Handbook*. 2001.

Notes

1. For an insightful explanation of business cycles, including why they are likely to continue into the twenty-first century, see Victor Zarnowitz, "Theory and History Behind Business Cycles: Are the 1990s the Onset of a Golden Age?" *Journal of Economic Perspectives* (Spring 1999).

2. Ibid., p. 241.

3. Robert H. McGuckin, Ataman Ozyildirum, and Victor Zarnowitz, "A More Timely and Useful Index of Leading Indicators" (New York: The Conference Board), October 2004.

4. The Conference Board, *Business Cycle Indicators* (monthly). Inside front cover.

35
Manufacturers' Orders

Manufacturers' orders measure commitments by customers to pay for the subsequent delivery of durable and nondurable goods produced by manufacturers. They include new orders received each month and the backlog of unfilled orders from previous months.

Where and When Available

Manufacturers' new orders and unfilled orders are prepared monthly by the Bureau of the Census in the U.S. Department of Commerce. They are published in a news release and in the monthly report that covers both durable and nondurable goods industries, *Manufacturers' Shipments, Inventories, and Orders* (www.census.gov).

The data are available one month after the month to which they refer. An advance report for durable goods is available three weeks after the month to which the data refer. The monthly data are initially revised in the following month; they are subsequently revised based on annual benchmark information in the following year.

Content

Manufacturers' orders data provide the dollar value of all durable and nondurable industries, industry detail, and market categories of various consumer goods, capital goods, defense products, and materials, plus the delivery, installation, repair, and other services that are associated with the goods in the orders' contract.

Orders are defined to be legally binding documents such as signed contracts, letters of award, or letters of intent, although this definition may not apply in some industries. In the case of letters of intent, the sales value is included if the parties are in substantial agreement on the amount; otherwise, only the funds specifically authorized to be expended are included.

New orders represent the dollar value of orders received each month for delivery during that month or later. They are the net of contract changes, including cancellations, that raise or lower the value of unfilled orders received in previous months.

Unfilled orders represent the dollar value of the backlog of orders that have accumulated from previous months for goods that have not yet been delivered. They are a running total from one month to the next of the backlog at the beginning of the month, plus new orders received during the month, minus shipments of goods to customers and cancellations of existing orders during the month.

The manufacturers' orders data are seasonally adjusted.

Methodology

Manufacturers' orders data are based on monthly surveys of manufacturers. These surveys also obtain information on shipments and inventories (see *inventory–sales ratios*). While respondents are asked about both new and unfilled orders, the survey on new orders is incomplete. Due to a lack of readily accessible records, some survey respondents do not report new orders and others do not report new orders for goods that were shipped from existing inventories in the same month. Consequently, new orders are estimated indirectly from unfilled orders, shipments, and cancellations as follows:

> unfilled orders (end of current month)
> plus: shipments (during month)
> minus: unfilled orders (end of previous month)
> equals: new orders (during month)

The survey sample includes most manufacturing companies with annual shipments of $500 million or more and a limited number of smaller companies. The survey has response problems that prevent it from being a probability sample.[1] The survey sample accounts for about 60 percent of all manufacturing shipments.

Table 35.1

Manufacturers' Orders (billions of dollars)

	New orders (monthly average)	Unfilled orders (end of year)
1995	285.5	447.3
1996	297.3	488.8
1997	315.0	513.2
1998	317.3	496.5
1999	329.8	505.9
2000	346.8	550.0
2001	322.9	517.6
2002	316.7	485.8
2003	329.2	506.3
2004	365.8	552.2

The monthly data are revised every year to reflect more complete information in the *Annual Survey of Manufactures.*

Accuracy

There are no estimates of sampling error for the manufacturers' orders data. Based on annual revisions, monthly new orders are typically revised by plus or minus 0.3 percent, and monthly unfilled orders are typically revised by plus or minus 0.1 percent.

Relevance

Manufacturers' orders indicate current demand, which translates into future production (see *industrial production index*) and *employment* for manufacturing industries. There is a lead time between orders on the one hand and production and employment on the other, although determining when orders result in production is not an exact science. Rising orders are associated with higher current demand and subsequent increased production and employment, while falling orders indicate lower current demand followed by decreased production and employment.

This relationship occurs for both new orders and unfilled orders, with the distinction that new orders reflect current demand and unfilled orders reflect the cumulation of demand from previous periods. The greater the ratio of unfilled orders is to new orders, the more is future production sustained by the backlog of unfilled orders, while the smaller the ratio of unfilled orders is to new orders, the more is future production linked to current new orders. New orders for consumer goods and materials industries in price-adjusted dollars are a component of the leading index of the *leading, coincident, and lagging indexes.*

Recent Trends

From 1995 to 2004, manufacturers' new orders and unfilled orders increased in all years, except for 2001 and 2002 (Table 35.1). After peaking in 2000, new and unfilled orders first exceeded the 2000 levels in 2004. Unfilled orders were consistently 1.5 to 1.6 times as large as new orders.

Reference from Primary Data Source

Bureau of the Census, U.S. Department of Commerce. *Manufacturers' Shipments, Inventories, and Orders.* Monthly.

Note

1. The response problem with this survey is long-standing. While this is a voluntary survey, the response in many other voluntary surveys is adequate to provide a probability sample. If this survey were made mandatory, which would require new legislation, the response would likely increase. For the attributes of probability samples, see the Appendix.

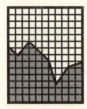

36
Mortgage Loan Applications

Mortgage loan applications indexes represent the number of mortgage applications for single-family houses both for the purchase of a house and for refinancing an existing house mortgage. The data cover conventional, Federal Housing Administration (FHA), and Veterans Administration (VA) mortgages combined, and fixed-rate, adjustable-rate, and balloon mortgages.

Where and When Available

The mortgage loan application indexes are prepared weekly by the Mortgage Bankers Association of America. They are published in the report, *Weekly Mortgage Applications Survey* (www.mortgagebankers.org).

The data are available for the calendar week Monday to Friday on the following Wednesday at 7:00 A.M. The data are not revised.

Content

The mortgage loan applications indexes combine the number of applications for the purchase of a single-family house and for refinancing single-family existing house mortgages, and separate indexes for house purchases and refinancing. Several component indexes are prepared: conventional, FHA, and VA mortgages are combined into "Government" indexes, fixed-rate, adjustable-rate, and indexes for balloon mortgages, and more detailed cross classifications of the above types.

The mortgage applications data comprise mortgages originating with commercial banks, thrift institutions, and mortgage banking companies.

They are estimated to account for approximately 50 percent of all first mortgages of single family houses.

The mortgage applications data give equal weight to each mortgage application. No distinction is made for the different dollar value of the various applications.

The mortgage applications indexes are currently based on March 16, 1990 = 100.

The mortgage applications indexes are seasonally adjusted.

Methodology

The mortgage loan applications data are obtained from a sample of commercial banks, thrift institutions, and mortgage banking companies. The data are not based on a probability sample. In terms of the base-period weights of the indexes, the house purchase index accounts for 85 percent and the refinancing index accounts for 15 percent of total the mortgage applications index.

Accuracy

There are no estimates of sampling or revision error for the mortgage loan applications indexes.

Relevance

Mortgage loan applications indexes provide a partial early indication of *home sales* (house purchase index) and of *retail sales* (mortgage refinance index). Mortgage applications movements should be compared with other determinants of home sales and retail sales to assess the strength of those indicators.

Recent Trends

From 1995 to 2004, there were sharp differences in the movements of the mortgage loan applications indexes between the house purchase index and the refinancing index (Table 36.1). The house purchase index showed a much steadier annual rate of growth, while the refinancing index was volatile with large increases and decreases. The house purchase index did not decline in any year, and except for a nominal increase in 2001, it increased noticeably every other year. In contrast, the

Table 36.1

Mortgage Loan Applications Indexes (March 16, 1990 = 100)

	Total applications	House purchase	Refinancing
1995	190.3	165.2	336.0
1996	222.1	183.3	447.6
1997	252.6	205.6	525.5
1998	482.9	266.0	1,745.2
1999	352.0	275.8	795.3
2000	322.7	302.7	438.8
2001	625.7	304.8	2,492.3
2002	799.7	354.7	3,388.0
2003	1,067.9	395.1	4,981.8
2004	736.1	454.1	2,376.4
	Annual average percentage change		
1995–2000	11.1	12.9	5.5
2000–2004	22.9	10.7	52.6
1995–2004	16.2	11.9	24.3

refinancing index rose sharply in 1998, declined sharply in 1999 and 2000, rose greatly during 2001–03, and declined sharply in 2004.

On an average annual basis, the house purchase index rose more during 1995–2000 than during 2000–04, while the refinancing index rose more during 2000–04 than during 1995–2000. During 1995–2000, the house purchase index rose more than the refinancing index, 12.9 percent compared with 5.5 percent. During 2000–04, the house purchase index rose at an average annual rate of 10.7 percent, but the extraordinarily large average annual increase in the refinancing index of 52.6 percent during 2000–04 resulted in a much greater differential than the differential by which the house purchase index exceeded the refinancing index during 1995–2000. Thus, over the entire 1995–2004 period, the house purchase index rose at an average annual rate of 11.9 percent, while the refinancing index rose at an average annual rate of 24.3 percent.

The total applications index showed movements closer to those of the house purchase index than to those of the refinancing index because the house purchase index has a much greater weight than the refinancing index in the construction of the index (see "Methodology").

Reference from Primary Data Source

Mortgage Bankers Association of America. *Weekly Mortgage Applications Survey.* Washington, DC. Weekly.

37
Mortgage Delinquency and Foreclosure

Mortgage debt delinquency and foreclosure data represent payment difficulties of mortgages on residential properties of one to four housing units for conventional, FHA, and VA fixed-rate and adjustable-rate mortgages. Mortgage delinquency rates are the number of payments on mortgage loans overdue thirty days or more as a percentage of all mortgage loans outstanding. Mortgage foreclosure rates are the number of mortgages in foreclosure as a percentage of all mortgage loans outstanding (foreclosure terminates a mortgagor's right to redeem a mortgaged property).

Where and When Available

The mortgage delinquency and foreclosure data are provided quarterly by the Mortgage Bankers Association of America. They are published in the report, *National Delinquency Survey* (www.mbaa.org).

The data are available approximately ten weeks after the calendar quarters ending March 31, June 30, September 30, and December 31. For example, data for the January–March quarter are published about the second week of June. The delinquency and foreclosure data are occasionally revised.

Content

The mortgage delinquency (MD) data show delinquency rates as of the end of March 31, June 30, September 30, and December 31 for the nation, regions, and states. MD rates are provided separately for payments overdue 30 days, 60 days, and 90 days or more. They show the totals of all loans, prime loans, and subprime loans, and within these categories fixed-rate loans and adjustable-rate loans. Additional MD data are provided for FHA and VA loans.

The national, regional, and state mortgage foreclosure (MF) data show foreclosure rates for foreclosures started during the quarter, and the inventory of all mortgages in the process of foreclosure as of March 31, June 30, September 30, and December 31. Foreclosures started during the quarter include mortgages placed in the process of foreclosure, the voluntary relinquishment of the deed in lieu of proceeding with the foreclosure process, and mortgages assigned to FHA, VA, and other insurers or investors during the quarter. The inventory of all foreclosures at the end of the quarter covers all mortgages in the process of foreclosure. Foreclosures are excluded from the MD data.

The national and regional MD data are seasonally adjusted. The state MD data are not seasonally adjusted.

The national and regional MF data for foreclosures started during the quarter are seasonally adjusted. MF data for the inventory of foreclosures and state MF data are not seasonally adjusted.

Methodology

The mortgage delinquency and mortgage foreclosure data are obtained from a quarterly survey of approximately 38 million mortgage loans from a sample of more than 140 financial institutions that provide mortgage services—mortgage bankers, commercial banks, savings and loan associations, mutual savings banks, life insurance companies, and credit unions. Of these, prime and subprime conventional loans account for approximately 86 percent, FHA loans for 10 percent, and VA loans for 4 percent. The mortgage loans provided by this sample of financial institutions account for approximately 80 percent of all mortgage loans extended. The survey sample is not a probability sample.

The MD and MF data are developed from the sample of outstanding loans. Thus, the sample is updated every quarter for the addition of new loans and the deletion of repaid loans.

Accuracy

There are no estimates of sampling or revision error for the mortgage delinquency and mortgage foreclosure data.

Table 37.1

Mortgage Delinquencies and Foreclosures

	Mortgage delinquencies (percent of loans with installments past due)	Mortgage foreclosures (percentage of loans in foreclosure)
1995	4.24	0.88
1996	4.33	0.99
1997	4.30	1.09
1998	4.45	1.16
1999	4.26	1.17
2000	4.38	1.11
2001	5.11	1.33
2002	5.11	1.48
2003	4.74	1.33
2004	4.35	1.17

Relevance

Analytic interest in the mortgage delinquency and mortgage foreclosure data is associated with their effect on *home sales*, *housing starts*, the *housing affordability index*, the *gross domestic product* (residential investment and consumer expenditure components), and *interest rates* (new home mortgage yields). These effects stem from the behavior of mortgage lenders. When MD and MF rates rise, lenders tend to raise interest rates and eligibility standards for mortgage applicants, if the demand for mortgage loans sustains the higher rates. When MD and MF rates decline, the reverse occurs with lower interest rates and less stringent eligibility standards. The thrust is to balance the generation of interest income revenues with the risk of losses on unpaid loans for their net effect on the profits of mortgage lenders.

Recent Trends

From 1995 to 2004, the mortgage delinquency rate rose from 4.24 percent in 1995 to highs of 5.11 percent in 2001 and 2002, and then fell to 4.35 percent in 2004. The mortgage foreclosure rate rose from 0.88 percent in 1995 to a high of 1.48 percent in 2002, and then fell to 1.17 in 2004. (See Table 37.1.)

Reference from Primary Data Source

Mortgage Bankers Association of America. *National Delinquency Survey.* Washington, DC. Quarterly.

38
Non-Manufacturing Business Activity Index

The non-manufacturing business activity index (NMBAI) represents various aspects of the health of goods and services industries except manufacturing. The business activity index is constructed as a diffusion index, which suggests an indication of the direction of the movement from one period to the next, but not of the size of the movement. The *PMI* is a counterpart diffusion index for manufacturing industries.

Where and When Available

The non-manufacturing business activity index is prepared monthly by the Institute for Supply Management. It is published in a news release and in the *ISM Non-Manufacturing Report on Business* (www.ism.ws).

The data are available the third business day of the month after the month to which they refer. The index is not revised.

Content

The non-manufacturing business activity index represents sales, receipts, or revenues of selected industries within agriculture, mining, construction, trade, transportation, communications, utilities, finance, and services. It is one of several diffusion indexes prepared for non-manufacturing industries. The others are new orders, backlog of orders, inventory change, inventory sentiment, new export orders, imports, prices, supplier deliveries, and employment. Because these indexes were first introduced in 1997, several more years of data are required in order to prepare a composite of some or all of the indexes. The non-manufacturing business activity index is featured here because it is more representative of overall economic activity than the other non-manufacturing indexes. By contrast, the *PMI* for manufacturing is based on several years of data from which a composite index has been developed.

The non-manufacturing business activity index is seasonally adjusted.

Methodology

The non-manufacturing business activity index is prepared from a monthly sample of more than 370 companies in 17 non-manufacturing industries that are members of the Institute for Supply Management. The number of companies reporting for each industry reflects the proportion of the non-manufacturing *gross domestic product* accounted for by the industry.

The survey obtains data on directional movements of each item in comparison with its level in the previous month. Depending on the item surveyed, positive responses are designated "higher," "better," or "faster" than last month; negative responses are designated "lower," "worse," or "slower" than last month; and no-change responses are designated "the same" as last month. Because the responses are supplied by the third week of the month, the survey is based on only partial information for which the entire month is estimated.

The index numbers for the composite and for each component are the proportion of the surveyed companies that report a positive change in activity from the previous month; this includes one-half of the companies reporting "no change." For example, if 56 percent report a positive change, 10 percent report no change, and 34 percent report a negative change, the index is 61 (i.e., 56 plus one-half of 10).

This type of index, which suggests an indication of the direction but not of the size of the movement from one period to the next, is a diffusion index (diffusion indexes are discussed further in the "Content" section of the chapter on *PMI*). In contrast, traditional indexes of economic activity provide the actual direction and magnitude of the movement.

Accuracy

There are no estimates of sampling or revision error for the non-manufacturing business activity index.

Table 38.1

Non-Manufacturing Business Activity Index (seasonally adjusted)

2003		2004	
January	53.4	January	64.2
February	54.3	February	60.8
March	47.9	March	64.0
April	52.6	April	66.9
May	54.7	May	63.3
June	60.3	June	61.1
July	63.1	July	63.4
August	64.9	August	59.3
September	63.4	September	58.7
October	65.0	October	61.5
November	60.2	November	61.9
December	58.9	December	63.9

Relevance

Non-manufacturing business activity accounts for the major part of the economy. But there is insufficient experience with the index to develop relationships between it and the overall economy.

Recent Trends

From 2003 to 2004, the non-manufacturing business activity index rose from lower levels during January–May 2003 to similar higher levels from June 2003 to December 2004 (Table 38.1). There were several monthly changes in direction both from the low of 47.9 in March 2003 to the high of 66.9 in April 2004.

Reference from Primary Data Source

Institute for Supply Management. *ISM Non-Manufacturing Report on Business.* Tempe, AZ. Monthly.

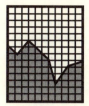

39
PMI

The PMI (formerly the Purchasing Managers' Index) reflects several aspects of the direction of economic activity in manufacturing industries. It is constructed as a diffusion index, which suggests an indication of the direction of the movement from one period to the next, but not of the size of the movement. The *non-manufacturing business activity index* is a counterpart diffusion index for non-manufacturing industries.

Where and When Available

The PMI is prepared by the Institute for Supply Management. It is published in a news release and in the *ISM Manufacturing Report on Business* (www.ism.ws).

The data are available on the first business day of the month after the month to which they refer. The seasonal factors of the index are updated by the U.S. Department of Commerce; they are revised for the previous four years every January. No other revisions are made to the index.

Content

The PMI is a composite of five indexes of manufacturing activity: new orders (*manufacturers' orders*), production (*industrial production index*), employment (*employment*), the promptness of manufacturers' deliveries (the difference between the time a purchased item is scheduled to arrive and the time when it actually arrives), and total purchased inventories. The index numbers for the composite and for each component are the proportion of the surveyed companies that report a positive change in activity from the previous month. This includes one-half of the companies reporting "no change." For example, if 56 percent report a positive change, 10 percent report no change, and 34 percent report a negative change, the index is 61 (i.e., 56 plus one-half of 10).

By showing the proportion of survey respondents that report rising economic activity, a diffusion index suggests that if more respondents follow the dominant upward or downward pattern in successive months, it will lead to similar movements in actual sales, employment, prices, and so on. Thus, as increasing proportions of firms report a rise or decline in economic activity, similar patterns of change would be expected in the percentage rates of growth or decline for the total of all firms.

A diffusion index suggests an indication of the direction, but not of the size of the movement from one period to the next. This contrasts with traditional indexes of economic activity that provide the actual direction and magnitude of the movement.

The index weights all surveyed firms equally regardless of size (or for diffusion indexes of surveyed individuals, all are weighted equally regardless of income). It indicates the pervasiveness of increases and decreases among a surveyed population. Use of a diffusion index assumes that the cyclical movements of small and large firms are similar in terms of their percentage rates of growth and decline, although the timing of the cyclical movements varies among the firms. This implies a direct relationship between the proportion of firms reporting activity moving in a particular direction and changes in the magnitude of the rate of growth or decline.

A diffusion index of 50 occurs when equal numbers of firms have increases and decreases, and therefore the rate of growth from the previous period is approximately zero. When the index is above 50 the rate of growth tends to be positive, and when the index is below 50 the rate of growth tends to be negative. In addition, the farther the index rises above 50, the greater is the magnitude of growth, while the farther the index falls below 50, the greater is the magnitude of decline.

The PMI is seasonally adjusted based on separate seasonal adjustments for each component.

Methodology

The PMI is a composite formed from the five component indexes that reflect various aspects of operations of manufacturing companies. The component weights are assigned judgmentally based on qualitative assessments of their importance. The components and their weights are:

New orders	0.30
Industrial production	0.25
Employment	0.20
Delivery schedules	0.15
Inventories	0.10
Total	1.00

The data for each component are obtained monthly from a survey of a sample of more than 350 manufacturing companies in 20 broad manufacturing industry groups that are members of the Institute for Supply Management. The number of companies included in the sample for each manufacturing industry is based on the proportion of the *gross domestic product* accounted for by each industry. The industries represent food, chemicals, machinery, and other broad manufacturing groups, including finer industry classifications within each broad group such as dairy, meat, and grains within the food group. Each company is weighted equally regardless of the size of the firm.

The survey obtains data on directional movements of each item in comparison to its level in the previous month. Depending on the item surveyed, positive responses are designated "higher," "better," or "faster" than last month; negative responses are designated "lower," "worse," or "slower" than last month; and no-change responses are designated "the same" as last month. Because the responses are supplied by the third week of the month, the survey is based on only partial information for which the entire month is estimated.

Accuracy

There are no estimates of sampling or revision error for the PMI.

Relevance

For the overall economy as measured by the real *gross domestic product* (GDP), the threshold of the PMI is approximately 43. Thus, a PMI above 43 suggests an expanding GDP, while a PMI below 43 suggests a de-

Table 39.1

PMI (seasonally adjusted)

2003		2004	
January	52.8	January	62.8
February	49.9	February	62.1
March	46.4	March	62.3
April	46.1	April	62.3
May	49.8	May	62.6
June	50.4	June	61.2
July	52.5	July	61.6
August	55.6	August	59.6
September	55.1	September	59.1
October	57.7	October	57.5
November	61.3	November	57.6
December	62.1	December	57.3

clining GDP. The figure of 43, rather than 50, reflects the tendency for continued growth in the non-manufacturing part of the economy.

Recent Trends

From 2003 to 2004, the PMI rose from lower levels during January–July 2003 to higher levels during August 2003–July 2004, and then declined to slightly lower levels during August–December 2004 (Table 39.1). There was only one monthly change in direction from the low of 46.1 in April 2003 to the high of 62.8 in January 2004, while a few more occurred from January to December 2004.

Reference from Primary Data Source

Institute for Supply Management. *ISM Manufacturing Report on Business*. Tempe, AZ. Monthly.

40
Personal Income and Saving

Personal income mainly measures the income received by house-holds from employment, self-employment, investments, and transfer payments. It also includes small amounts for expenses of nonprofit organizations and income of certain fiduciary activities. Disposable personal income (DPI) refers to personal income after the payment of income, estate, and certain other taxes and payments to governments. Personal saving is the residual of DPI minus consumer outlays, and the saving rate is saving as a percentage of DPI. The personal income and saving measures are definitionally consistent with those for the *gross domestic product.*

Where and When Available

The personal income and saving measures are prepared monthly by the Bureau of Economic Analysis (BEA) in the U.S. Department of Commerce. The data are published in a monthly news release and in the BEA monthly journal, *Survey of Current Business* (www.bea.gov).

The personal income, disposable personal income, and personal saving data are available during the fourth week of the month after the month to which they refer. The data are revised initially in the subsequent two months. Subsequent revisions are made annually every summer, and in the subsequent benchmark revisions of the national income and product accounts (see the *gross domestic product*). Data on the saving rate are available one month after the above-noted dollar measures.

Content

Personal income (PI) mainly measures income of households. Household income is derived from wages and salaries; fringe benefits; profits from self-employment; rental profits from real property (for persons not primarily engaged in real estate), plus patent, copyright, and natural resource royalties; noncash rent imputed from owner-occupied homes; interest; dividends; Social Security and unemployment insurance benefits, food stamps, and other income maintenance programs. PI also includes operating expenses (excluding depreciation) of nonprofit organizations that primarily serve individuals, and investment income of life insurance companies, private noninsured welfare funds, nonprofit organizations, and private trust funds. PI excludes income changes from capital gains and losses associated with the difference between the purchase and sales price of financial assets, real property, and personal property.

PI reflects income flows before the payment of income, estate, gift, and personal property taxes plus fees, fines, and penalties paid to federal, state, and local governments. Social Security taxes paid by employees and employers are excluded from PI.

Disposable personal income (DPI) is income excluding the tax and nontax payments to governments included in PI. DPI is provided in current and constant dollars.

Personal saving is the income remaining from DPI after deductions for consumer spending for goods and services, interest payments on consumer loans (excluding home mortgage interest), and money sent as gifts abroad (net transfer payments to foreigners). This is part of the national income and product accounts (see *gross domestic product*). The total of consumer spending, interest payments, and foreign gifts is referred to as personal outlays. The saving rate is saving as a percentage of DPI. Saving is not affected by gifts between households (such as when parents give a house to their children) and by sales of homes, cars, and other assets between households (except for payments to intermediaries such as brokers' commissions and used car dealer markups).

The personal income and saving data are seasonally adjusted.

(An alternative measure of saving, referred to as household saving, as distinct from personal saving described above, is provided by the Federal Reserve Board as part of its flow-of-funds accounts. I note the household saving measure to alert the reader to its existence, though it is not included in the book. The household saving measure is based on the change in net worth of financial and tangible assets of households—that is, assets less liabilities. This differs from the personal saving measure that is part of the national income and product accounts, which is obtained as the difference between income and outlays in each period. Other differences between the two saving measures include, but are not limited to, capital gains and losses and changes in the net worth of unincorporated businesses, which are included in the household saving but not in the personal saving measure. Differences in the uses of the two measures include: personal saving seems more relevant for assessing the contribution of personal saving to national saving, while household saving seems more relevant for assessing whether households in the aggregate are preparing adequately for financial needs of retirement.[1])

Methodology

Data for the components of personal income are obtained from several government and nongovernment sources with varying degrees of currency. For example, wages are based on the monthly employment payroll survey, and Social Security and unemployment insurance benefit payments are based on monthly reports from the Social Security Administration and the U.S. Department of Labor. Stock dividend income is derived from the U.S. Census Bureau's *Quarterly Financial Report* and from corporate quarterly reports to stockholders (these quarterly data are interpolated through the three months of the quarter in estimating the monthly figures). Data for other PI components, such as income from fringe benefits, self-employment, rent, interest, and life insurance benefits, typically are available only annually, and the monthly historical and current data are mainly estimated indirectly.

Disposable personal income is calculated by subtracting income, estate, gift, and personal property taxes plus miscellaneous fines, fees, and penalties from PI. Data for these deductions are obtained from two sources. The U.S. Department of the Treasury provides monthly data for the federal component, and the Census Bureau provides a quarterly survey of state and local governments. However, the state and local survey data are used only in the historical quarterly data because they are available too late for the current data every quarter; indirect estimates are made for the current data. DPI in chained dollars is calculated by dividing DPI in current dollars by the chain-type price index for personal consumption expenditures (see *GDP price measures*).

Table 40.1

Personal Income and Saving (billions of dollars)

	Personal income	Disposable personal income	Saving rate (percentage)
1995	6,152.3	5,408.2	4.6
1996	6,520.6	5,688.5	4.0
1997	6,915.1	5,988.8	3.6
1998	7,423.0	6,395.9	4.3
1999	7,802.4	6,695.0	2.4
2000	8,429.7	7,194.0	2.3
2001	8,724.1	7,486.8	1.8
2002	8,881.9	7,830.1	2.4
2003	9,169.1	8,169.2	2.1
2004	9,713.3	8,664.2	1.8

Personal saving represents the difference between DPI and the sum of consumer spending for goods and services, interest payments on consumer loans, and net transfers to foreigners (referred to as personal outlays). The saving rate for each month is calculated as a three-month moving average of saving as a percentage of DPI in order to dampen erratic month-to-month movements.

Accuracy

Revisions to the monthly estimates of personal income indicate that the first three estimates for each month provide the correct indication of the direction of change in 90 percent of the cases.

Relevance

Personal income is the main component of consumer purchasing power, and thus has a prime influence on consumer spending. PI is supplemented by *consumer credit* as a source of financing for consumer spending. Consumer spending accounts for approximately 70 percent of the *gross domestic product* (GDP) and figures prominently in *retail sales.* Consequently, PI has a major effect on overall economic activity and *employment.* Disposable personal income in chained dollars (adjusted for inflation) provides a better analytic measure of consumer purchasing power and its effect on real GDP than current-dollar personal income. Because personal saving indicates consumers' willingness to spend, the saving rate is an element in predicting future spending trends.

Recent Trends

From 1995 to 2004, personal income and disposable personal income increased in all years (Table 40.1). The personal saving rate declined from 4.6 percent in 1995 to 1.8 percent in 2004, with the general level declining from the 4-percent range during 1995–98 to the 2 percent range from 1999 to 2004.

Reference from Primary Data Source

Bureau of Economic Analysis, U.S. Department of Commerce. *Survey of Current Business.* Monthly.

Note

1. Maria G. Perozek and Marshall B. Reinsdorf, "Alternative Measures of Personal Saving," *Survey of Current Business,* April 2002, pp. 13–14.

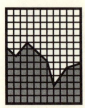

41
Poverty

Measures of poverty count the number of all people (people in families plus unrelated individuals), families, and unrelated individuals with incomes below a specified minimum level. This income threshold defines subsistence living conditions according to societal standards as they existed in the 1960s, adjusted for changes in the cost of living since then. Incomes below the threshold are regarded as subjecting the recipients to living conditions below currently accepted standards of decency. At any point in time, poverty is defined at a specific threshold of income inadequacy ("how much is too little"). The threshold is typically fixed at this level for a period of time. However, what is regarded as poverty also has an evolving dimension over time. Evolving standards typically are raised over time to reflect improved living conditions and higher aspirations afforded by advancements in technology. When the standard is raised, the number of persons defined as living in poverty increases.

There is one official measure of poverty. It counts cash income only, as distinct from noncash benefits such as Medicare; cash income reflects the income before the payment of certain taxes and other items. Sixteen alternative measures now published are based mainly on various treatments of cash and noncash income maintenance payments, taxes, and capital gains.

Where and When Available

The Bureau of the Census in the U.S. Department of Commerce prepares annual measures of poverty. The data are published annually in *Income, Poverty, and Health Insurance Coverage in the United States* (www.census.gov).

The data are available in the fall after the year to which they refer. Revisions for previous years are made in the annual publications.

Content

The poverty data indicate the number of persons and families with money incomes below the poverty threshold based on the number of persons in the family and their ages. The threshold has two components. One is a standard of inadequacy for food, housing, and other living conditions. The other is the income associated with the standard.

The official poverty threshold follows the U.S. Office of Management and Budget's Statistical Policy Directive No. 14. It is based on the poverty standard developed in 1963. Refinements made to the threshold since 1963 have not significantly changed the official count of the poverty population.[1] The threshold measures households' money income before the payment of such items as federal and state income taxes, Social Security taxes, federal employee retirement taxes, property taxes, Medicare deductions, and union dues. Money income is defined as regularly received cash income, such as wages and salaries, profits from self-employment, Social Security, retirement, unemployment insurance, other income maintenance benefits, interest, dividends, rents, royalties, estates and trusts, educational assistance, alimony, child support, and financial assistance from outside the household (excluding gifts and sporadic assistance). Noncash benefits, such as food stamps, Medicare, Medicaid, and rent supplements, as well as income from nonrecurring sources such as capital gains and life insurance settlements, are excluded from money income.

A household consists of all persons who occupy a housing unit. A household may include one or more families and/or one or more unrelated individuals. A family refers to two or more persons related by birth, marriage, or adoption and living together in a house, apartment, a group of rooms, or a single room intended as separate living quarters. An unrelated individual is a person fifteen years and older who does not live with any relatives. A housing unit has direct access from the outside or through a common hall. The occupants of a housing unit do not live or eat with any other people in the structure. The definition of households excludes people living in group quarters (e.g., hotels, dormitories), or institutions (e.g., hospitals, jails, shelters), or having no residence (people living on the street).

The members of a household may or may not share their incomes for personal consumption. Consequently, the household is not a perfect unit for measuring poverty. But the household is a practical device for measuring the incomes of people living in housing units.

The poverty standard used in the first decade of the twenty-first century reflects the same minimum living conditions specified when the standard was developed in 1963. In order to maintain the 1963 income threshold of living conditions, it is routinely updated only for inflation. For example, the annual threshold income before taxes for a four-person family rose from $3,128 in 1963 to $18,810 in 2003. (There was no official poverty standard before the 1960s; as noted below under "Relevance," there was an implied standard in the 1930s.)

Sixteen alternative nonofficial poverty measures that use different definitions of household income are also provided by the Census Bureau. The definitions vary in terms of the treatment of government cash transfer payments, noncash benefits, federal and state income taxes, Social Security payroll taxes, capital gains, and an imputed return on the equity of home ownership. In 2003, under the official measure, 12.5 percent of the population was defined as being in poverty, with the alternative measures ranging from 9.0 to 20.6 percent of the population.

Methodology

The poverty standard is based on estimates made by the U.S. Department of Agriculture in 1961 of the least expensive of four food plans to meet nutritional adequacy standards. The food plan assumed that all meals are prepared at home from foods purchased at retail. This number was multiplied by three to determine total income necessary to meet all living expenses, including housing, health, transportation, and other nonfood items, except medical expenditures. This "multiplier" is based on a 1955 study indicating that food accounts for one-third of the average household budget for families of three or more persons at all income levels, not just low-income families. Other procedures were used to calculate thresholds for one- and two-person units. Thus, the nonfood components are estimated indirectly as a statistical aggregate rather than by estimating each living expense component separately with specific minimum standards for each (e.g., housing, clothing, transportation).

The money income data are based on the Current Population Survey (CPS) conducted by the Census Bureau. The information is collected every March in an income supplement for the previous year. The survey sample is approximately 60,000 households, of whom about 55,500 are interviewed and 4,500 are not available for interviews. For additional detail on the CPS, see *employment.*

Accuracy

The sampling error (for 1.6 standard errors) of the people in poverty as a percentage of the total population is 0.2 of a percentage point. For example, if the estimated poverty population were 13 percent, in nine of ten cases the "true" rate would be somewhere between 12.8 and 13.2 percent. For further information on the interpretation of sampling and nonsampling errors, see the Appendix.

A comparison of the household income estimates of the Census Bureau with the personal income estimates of the U.S. Bureau of Economic Analysis (see *personal income and saving*) for the year 2001, after placing both income estimates on a comparable definitional basis, indicated that total household income was 11 percent below total personal income.[2] The difference is attributed to underreporting by survey respondents on the CPS, which is the source of household income data, as contrasted with administrative records of income tax, unemployment insurance, Social Security, and other income programs that are the source of the personal income data. This overall underreporting is not taken into account in developing the poverty data because determining the variations in underreporting among income groups is difficult.

Relevance

The poverty measure reflects societal concerns about how well the nation is providing for the minimal subsistence needs of the people at the bottom of the income ladder. While it does not reflect the social standards of the 2000s, it focuses attention on the most needy in the population and on the progress made in alleviating their condition. As an absolute number, it quantifies the magnitude of the poverty problem for purposes of political debate regarding appropriate ways to deal with it.

There is extensive American historical evidence that poverty income thresholds are raised over time as absolute poverty lines show a pattern of rising income adjusted for inflation (real income) as the real income of the general population rises. The public's estimate of the amount of real income required for a family to "get along" also rises as the real income of the general population rises. On the basis of that empirical evidence, there is general agreement that poverty is an evolving concept that changes over time to reflect the evolving living conditions and aspirations of society. Thus, the poverty standard adopted in 1964 by President Lyndon Johnson's Council of Economic Advisers was approximately 75 percent higher in real terms than the standard implicit in President Franklin Roosevelt's 1937 statement that one-third of the nation was ill-housed, ill-fed, and ill-clothed. One economist estimated that if the Johnson standard of the 1960s had been used in the 1930s, Roosevelt's "one-third of a nation" would have been close to two-thirds.[3] This illustrates how changing perceptions of what constitutes a minimally acceptable standard of living affect the count of persons in poverty.

These perceptions have also changed between the 1960s and the first decade of the twenty-first century, although the current official poverty measure has remained constant between the two periods. If the poverty measure were raised on the basis of a political consensus of higher minimal subsistence needs in the twenty-first century, the number of persons defined to be in poverty would increase. The federal budget (*government budgets and debt*) is perceived as being a major constraint to reviewing the poverty standard. Many fear that even with some noncash benefits included in the income definition, a new poverty standard would raise the poverty count, and thus increase federal spending for social programs.

Over the years, the president ultimately has decided on the definition of the poverty standard, as the adoption of a poverty standard has been an executive branch function. But this does not preclude that in the future another procedure may be used if a new poverty measure is adopted.

A 1995 report by the National Research Council (NRC, associated with the National Academy of Sciences) recommended a methodology for establishing a new poverty threshold for the United States.[4] While the proposed methodology has several variants, the general approach would result in a poverty threshold that would come close to one-half of the median income after taxes of a four-person family. The methodology incorporates nonmoney income from government programs such as food stamps, housing subsidies, and energy assistance; calculates the income needs threshold using a designated percentage of median household expenditures for food, clothing, shelter, and utilities, augmented by a factor for outlays on additional items such as household supplies

Table 41.1

Poverty Measure (official)

	All people in poverty		Families in poverty	
	Number (millions)	Percentage of population	Number (millions)	Percentage of families
1995	36.4	13.8	7.5	10.8
1996	36.5	13.7	7.7	11.0
1997	35.6	13.3	7.3	10.3
1998	34.5	12.7	7.2	10.0
1999	32.8	11.9	6.8	9.3
2000	31.6	11.3	6.4	8.7
2001	32.9	11.7	6.8	9.2
2002	34.6	12.1	7.2	9.6
2003	35.9	12.5	7.6	10.0
2004	37.0	12.7	7.9	10.2

and personal care, and adjusted for family size and geographic location; supplements the income needs threshold by the value of the Earned Income Tax Credit (EITC); and deducts child care, work-related transportation, and medical out-of-pocket expenses. It also includes a procedure for updating the poverty standard over time based on yearly movements in the income needs threshold, the EITC, and the expense items. A study by the Census Bureau estimates that using the recommended methodology in the NRC report would raise the poverty rate in 2003 from the official level of 12.5 percent to a range of 12.6 to 14.5 percent.[5] Poverty estimates based on the recommended methodology in the NRC report for 2004 were not available at the time of this writing.

Poverty is related to the *distribution of income* and the *distribution of wealth.* Inequality of income stems from many sources, such as the match of workers having particular skills with the job market for those skills, discrimination, inheritance, innate abilities, entrepreneurial spirit, and luck.

Recent Trends

From 1995 to 2004, the count of all people and families living in poverty showed different movements between the entire two intermediate periods within the nine-year span (Table 41.1). The number of people in poverty declined from 1995 to 2000, and rose from 2000 to 2004. This resulted in the poverty population increasing from 36.4 million in 1995 to 37.0 million in 2004. The same pattern occurred for the count of families in poverty.

In 2004, the poverty population rate was 12.7 percent and the families in poverty rate was 10.2 percent. Over the 1995–2004 period, the poverty rates showed the same movements as those for the number in poverty.

Reference from Primary Data Source

Bureau of the Census, U.S. Department of Commerce. *Income, Poverty, and Health Insurance Coverage in the United States.* Annual.

Notes

1. Mollie Orshansky did the seminal work on the 1960s poverty standard that still serves as the official standard. See Mollie Orshansky, "Children of the Poor," *Social Security Bulletin* (July 1963); Orshansky, "Counting the Poor: Another Look at the Poverty Profile," *Social Security Bulletin* (January 1965) (reprinted in the *Bulletin* in October 1988). Gordon Fisher has written the definitive history of the evolution of poverty standards: "From Hunter to Orshansky: An Overview of (Unofficial) Poverty Lines in the United States from 1904 to 1965," mimeo, revised 1997. (For a condensed version, see Fisher, "The Development and History of the Poverty Thresholds," *Social Security Bulletin* [Winter 1992]); Fisher, "The Development of the Orshansky Poverty Thresholds and Their Subsequent History as the Official U.S. Poverty Measure," mimeo, revised 1997; Fisher, "Is There Such a Thing as an Absolute Poverty Line Over Time? Evidence from the United States, Britain, Canada, and Australia on the Income Elasticity of the Poverty Line," mimeo, 1995.) These papers are not official government documents. They can be found on the Internet at www.census.gov/hhes/poverty/povmeas/papers.html, or obtained from Fisher at the Office of the Assistant Secretary for Planning Evaluation, U.S. Department of Health & Human Services. Links to these and other papers on the history of poverty lines can be found at http://aspe.hhs.gov/poverty/contacts.shtml.

2. John Ruser, Adrienne Pilot, and Charles Nelson, "Alternative Measures of Household Income: BEA Personal Income, CPS Money Income, and Beyond," May 2004. Available from the Census Bureau, www.census.gov.

3. Victor Fuchs, "Toward a Theory of Poverty," in *The Concept of Poverty* (Washington, DC: Chamber of Commerce of the United States, 1965), p. 73.

4. Constance F. Citro and Robert T. Michael, eds., National Research Council, *Measuring Poverty: A New Approach* (Washington, DC: National Academy Press, 1995).

5. Bureau of the Census, U.S. Department of Commerce, *Alternative Poverty Estimates in the United States: 2003,* June 2005.

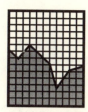

42
Producer Price Indexes

The producer price indexes (PPIs) measure the rate of price change of domestically produced goods in the manufacturing, mining, agriculture, fishing, forestry, and selected services industries. The PPIs exclude prices of construction and imports, although imported goods are indirectly included when they are components of domestically produced items. The PPIs most often used for economic analysis are stage-of-processing indexes for commodities, which are covered in this chapter. Other PPIs are industry net-output indexes and non-stage-of-processing commodity indexes.

Where and When Available

The producer price indexes are prepared monthly by the Bureau of Labor Statistics (BLS) in the U.S. Department of Labor. The data are published in a news release, the *PPI Detailed Report*, and in the BLS monthly journal, *Monthly Labor Review* (www.bls.gov).

The data are prepared around the middle of the month following the month to which they refer. The monthly data are revised for the preceding fourth month—for example, revisions to January data are included with the release of the April data in May.

Content

The producer price indexes (PPIs) are price measures of U.S.-produced commodities that represent three stages of processing in the production of different commodities. The stage-of-processing indexes are: (a) finished goods; (b) intermediate materials, supplies, and components, and (c) crude materials for further processing. In addition, the "all-commodities index" combines the three stage-of-processing indexes into one overall index. The PPIs cover commodities sold in the United States and in foreign markets (exports).

The PPIs reflect the first sale of the goods resulting in net revenue to the producer, and thus exclude price changes associated with resales and markups for the same item through wholesalers, retailers, or other producers, as well as excise taxes. They represent the actual producer transaction price of goods meant for immediate delivery, including premiums and discounts from list prices and changes in the terms of sale such as distinctions for household and business customers and the size of the order. Prices of items with long production lead times are based on the time the item is delivered, not when the order is placed. The price quote is from the site of the producer (f.o.b., free on board), unless the price quote includes transportation charges when the producer provides such services directly and not through an outside transportation company or contractor. Exceptions to this include the use of list prices when transaction prices are not available, and prices quoted at central markets, particularly for farm products.

The PPIs reflect price movements for the same or similar items that are adjusted for enhancement or reduction in the quality or quantity of the item. Prices on futures markets are excluded.

The PPIs are currently based on 1982 = 100.

The producer price indexes are seasonally adjusted.

Stage-of-Processing Components

There are three stage-of-processing components of the commodities PPIs: finished goods; intermediate materials, supplies, and components; and crude materials for further processing.

Finished goods. These are items used by a household, business, government, or foreign buyer in the form in which they were sold, without further fabrication. They include household goods ranging from fresh foods to cars and capital goods such as tractors, trucks, and machine tools.

Intermediate materials, supplies, and components. These are items that have been fabricated but are not ready for independent use. They become part of other products, require further fabrication, or are otherwise used as inputs, such as cotton yarns, chemicals, containers, office supplies, electric power, and internal combustion engines.

Crude materials for further processing. These items are not sold directly to households. They are either sold for the first time in their initial state of production, such as livestock or crude petroleum, or are reused, such as scrap metal.

The three indexes reflect a theoretical typology of goods based on production, moving sequentially from a product's initial state to its end result. Classifying products by end user (household, business, government, or foreigner) and by degree of fabrication is referred to as stage-of-processing classification. Although the stage-of-processing concept theoretically represents a step-by-step flow from crude to intermediate to finished products, in practice this flow does not always occur. For example, there are reverse flows of intermediate containers to crude materials and of finished equipment to both intermediate and crude material groups; there are also products that skip the intermediate stage, such as when crude live poultry becomes finished processed poultry.

Methodology

Monthly price data for the producer price indexes are obtained from a mail survey conducted by the Bureau of Labor Statistics. The survey samples prices for more than 3,200 commodities. These data are supplemented by price information provided by the U.S. Department of Agriculture for farm products. Nearly all price quotes are reported by the sellers rather than the buyers. Prices of most commodities are obtained between the ninth and fifteenth days of the month for which the PPIs are calculated. Examples of exceptions are compact disks and audiotapes, whose prices are obtained one month later.

The weights for the stage-of-processing and the all-commodities PPIs are based on the value of sales of the component commodities and industries. These reflect data in the five-year economic censuses, unless the industry is not covered in the censuses. For example, sales weights for electric power are based on U.S. Department of Energy data. The weights are currently based on 1997 sales volumes. The structuring of commodities in a stage-of-processing chain is based on the commodity ordering in the input–output tables prepared by the Bureau of Economic Analysis in the U.S. Department of Commerce. The weighting structure is updated approximately every five years.

If the reported monthly price includes a change in the quality of the item, an adjustment is made to reflect the improvement or decline. Thus, the PPIs aim at measuring price movements of items having the same functional characteristics over time. For example, if better brakes are included in a car, the price increase attributable to the improved brakes does not appear as a price increase in the PPI, but if an auto bumper is weakened because of relaxed standards and there is no change in market price, the weaker auto bumper is considered a price increase in the PPI. Because product cost data required to make the necessary adjustments are not always available, the PPI contains an unknown amount of price change caused by quality and quantity changes.

One approach for adjusting for quality change in price indexes when product cost data are inadequate or not available is through hedonic price indexes. Hedonic indexes are based on statistical regressions that reflect historical relationships between quality change and price change. Hedonic indexes require vast amounts of data for their calculation. They are currently used for computers and in peripherals in the PPIs. For a brief further description of hedonic price indexes, see the "Methodology" section of the *consumer price index*.

Accuracy

There are no estimates of sampling or revision error for the producer price indexes.

Relevance

Producer price indexes provide a basis for analyzing whether inflation is caused by burgeoning demand or supply bottlenecks. One method is by identifying the stages of processing in which sharp price increases occur.

The PPIs theoretically help predict potential price changes in the sequential development of crude materials to intermediate materials to finished goods. However, the stage-of-processing concept does not establish a complete unidirectional flow of materials in the production process from crude to intermediate to finished goods. While, theoretically, crude prices should predict intermediate prices, and intermediate prices should predict finished prices in the commodities indexes, these lead–lag relationships are not exact because of the failure to maintain a

Table 42.1

Producer Price Indexes
(percentage change)

	Finished goods	Intermediate materials, supplies, and components	Crude materials for further processing	Finished goods less foods and energy
1995	1.9	5.4	0.9	2.1
1996	2.7	0.6	10.8	1.4
1997	0.4	−0.1	−2.4	0.3
1998	−0.8	−2.1	−12.9	0.9
1999	1.8	0.2	1.4	1.7
2000	3.8	4.9	22.8	1.3
2001	2.0	0.4	0.3	1.4
2002	−1.3	−1.5	−10.7	0.1
2003	3.2	4.6	25.2	0.2
2004	3.6	6.6	17.5	1.5
1995–2004 (annual average)	1.7	1.5	5.0	1.2

unidirectional flow in the stage-of-processing groups. More research on the properties of these classifications is needed to realize their analytical potential in the transmission of price change.[1]

The PPIs are also used to determine cost escalation in business contracts and to deflate the *gross domestic product* to constant dollars. Supplementary PPI measures are published that exclude price movements of food and energy products. Because these products sometimes have volatile price movements that are unrelated to underlying inflationary or deflationary forces in the economy, their exclusion provides the "core inflation" rate, which is also referred to as the "underlying rate of inflation."

Recent Trends

From 1995 to 2004, producer price indexes for finished goods and for finished goods less foods and energy showed the least year-to-year volatility of all the PPIs (Table 42.1). And prices of finished goods less foods and energy were less volatile than those of finished goods.

Prices of crude materials were much more volatile and increased far more than those of finished goods and of intermediate materials, supplies, and components. Some of these differences result from fluctuations in oil prices, which have their initial and heaviest impact on crude materials. The effect of price changes of crude oil is successively dampened as an increasing number of nonpetroleum products are incorporated in intermediate products and in finished goods.

Reference from Primary Data Source

Bureau of Labor Statistics, U.S. Department of Labor. *PPI Detailed Report* and *Monthly Labor Review.* Monthly.

Note

1. Tae-Hwy Lee and Stuart Scott, "Investigating Inflation Transmission by Stages of Processing," in *Cointegration, Causality, and Forecasting: A Festschrift in Honor of Clive W.J. Granger,* ed. Ralph Engle and Halbert White (Oxford, UK: Oxford University Press, 1999).

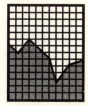

43
Productivity: Business Sector

Productivity represents the nation's efficiency in producing goods and services. There are two economywide productivity measures, labor-hour productivity and multifactor productivity. Labor-hour productivity, which is the traditional measure, encompasses the aggregate effects of employee schooling, experience, and worker skills; equipment, structures, and other capital services used in production; worker effort; technology; and all other factors. Multifactor productivity abstracts from employee schooling, experience, and worker skills and the use of capital services, thus focusing on the aggregate effects of worker effort, technology, and all other factors.

Productivity is calculated as the ratio of output (numerator) to input (denominator), with the quotient being output per unit of input. When output increases more or decreases less than input, productivity rises; and when output increases less or decreases more than input, productivity declines. The two measures covered here, labor-hour productivity and multifactor productivity, have the same output measure, with the small exception of the exclusion of government enterprises for multifactor productivity. Therefore, the different input measures account for practically all of the differences in productivity between the two measures.

Separate measures of labor-hour productivity and multifactor productivity are prepared for the business sector and the nonfarm business sector. The business sectors are derived from the *gross domestic product* (GDP) definitions. Business sectors exclude not-for-profit organizations, household output, rental value of owner-occupied housing, and general government. The nonfarm business sector also excludes farming.

The productivity output definitions for the business sectors are based on the value-added definition of the GDP. This method counts output as the sum of the incomes associated with employee compensation, business profits, interest payments, depreciation allowances, and taxes on production and imports. It excludes purchased materials and services used in production, and thus prevents the duplication that would occur by double counting the value of the purchased materials and services in all stages of production. The productivity measures are expressed as an index.

This chapter covers labor-hour productivity and multifactor productivity separately, except that the categories of Relevance and Recent Trends are discussed jointly at the end of the chapter for both productivity measures.

Labor-Hour Productivity

Where and When Available

Labor-hour productivity data are prepared quarterly by the Bureau of Labor Statistics (BLS) in the U.S. Department of Labor. The data are published in a news release and in the BLS monthly journal, *Monthly Labor Review* (www.bls.gov).

Preliminary data are provided in the second month following the quarter to which the data refer (May for the first quarter, August for the second quarter, and so on). The data are available at the same time as the *unit labor costs* data, and follow soon after publication of the *gross domestic product* measures. The data are initially revised in the subsequent month, and then two months later along with the release of the preliminary data for the following quarter. Annual revisions are made every year as more data become available.

Content

Labor-hour productivity is defined as output per hour of labor expended. Output per hour encompasses the combined influences of all factors affecting the use of labor, such as the services derived from capital equipment and structures, the substitution of capital services for labor, worker skills and effort, executive direction and managerial skills, technology, level of output, capacity utilization, energy consumption, materials quality, public sector infrastructure, and the interactions among them.

Labor-hour productivity includes the quantity of labor hours worked as inputs, and thus eliminates the effect on output of these worker inputs. Labor-hour productivity does not separate the specific contributions to productivity of worker schooling, experience, skills, and effort, capital quantity and quality inputs, and all other inputs contributing to output. Consequently, it reflects the joint effects of all inputs, except the quantity of labor hours worked, including the interactions among them.

The labor-hour productivity indexes are currently based on 1992 = 100.

The labor-hour productivity data are seasonally adjusted.

Methodology

This section concentrates on the inputs of the productivity ratio, because the outputs follow the definitions of the *gross domestic product* business sector, as noted at the beginning of the chapter.

Labor-hour productivity inputs are represented by labor hours worked. Labor hours worked are the product of *employment* multiplied by *average weekly hours,* converted to average annual hours. The employment data are based on the sum of paid jobs counted in the establishment survey and the number of self-employed and unpaid family workers counted in the household survey (see *employment*).

Labor hours obtained from the establishment survey are based on hours at work (called "hours worked"), which is limited to time at the job site, including paid time to travel between job sites, coffee breaks, and machine downtime. It excludes time associated with paid vacation and sick leave. By contrast, the sum of hours worked and of time associated with paid vacation and sick leave is called "hours paid." The data on hours for the self-employed and family workers are less clear, and so their labor input can be described as either hours worked or hours paid. Beginning in 2005, labor hours data for the nonfarm self-employed, nonfarm unpaid family workers, and farm workers were refined to better account for the hours worked by multiple jobholders in their primary as distinct from their secondary jobs.

Mathematically, labor-hour productivity is expressed as follows:

$$\text{Labor-hour} \atop \text{productivity} = \frac{\text{Output}}{\text{Input}} = \frac{\text{Real business GDP*}}{\text{Labor hours†}} = {\text{Real} \atop \text{business} \atop \text{GDP per} \atop \text{labor hour}} \qquad (43.1)$$

Accuracy

In nineteen of twenty cases, labor-hour productivity in the second quarterly revision (four months after the preliminary data) differs from the preliminary index by –1.4 to 1.4 index points.

Multifactor Productivity

Where and When Available

Multifactor productivity data are prepared annually by the Bureau of Labor Statistics in the U.S. Department of Labor. The data are published in a news release, *Multifactor Productivity Trends* (www.bls.gov).

The data are available about six months after the end of the year to which they refer.[1] Revisions are made with each annual release, based on new data or improved methodology for all earlier years and thus provide a consistent long-term time series.

Content

Multifactor productivity is defined as output per unit of labor and capital combined. It excludes the inputs of labor hours worked; and labor-hour inputs adjusted for worker schooling, experience, and skills, and for the capital services inputs of equipment, structures, land, and inventories. Therefore, the resultant productivity measure centers on worker skills and effort, executive direction and managerial skills, technology, level of output, capacity utilization, energy

---

*Gross domestic product, excluding households, not-for-profit organizations, rental value of owner-occupied housing, and general government (adjusted for price change).

†Hours worked by paid employees, the self-employed, and unpaid family workers.

consumption, materials quality, public sector infrastructure, all other factors, and the interactions among them. By excluding the labor-hour and capital services inputs, multifactor productivity also excludes the effect on output of the substitution of capital services for labor.

The multifactor productivity indexes are currently based on 1996 = 100.

Methodology

This section on multifactor productivity concentrates on the inputs of the productivity ratio, because the outputs follow the definitions of the *gross domestic product* business sector, as noted at the beginning of the chapter. The one divergence of the output measure of multifactor productivity from that in labor-hour productivity is that multifactor productivity excludes government enterprises (government enterprises are financed with user fees, in contrast to general government, which is financed with taxes). Thus, multifactor productivity is referred to as the "private business sector," as distinct from labor hour productivity, which is referred to as the "business sector."

Multifactor productivity inputs are the weighted average of the dollar value of labor hours and of capital services. The labor-hour inputs begin with those for labor-hour productivity described above. These are modified by giving greater weight to workers with more schooling, experience, and skills to reflect differences in the capabilities between workers. The assumption is that as the workforce is composed of an increasing proportion of workers with a greater amount of schooling, experience, and skills, the workforce itself becomes more productive.

The capital inputs represent the services that flow from the stocks of capital. They include the rental value of the services of the capital facilities used in the production of goods and services, adjusted for price change—equipment, structures, land, and inventories. Modifications for the composition of equipment and structures facilities give more weight to short-lived equipment items than to long-lived ones, because per dollar short-lived assets provide more services per year than long-lived assets.

Mathematically, multifactor productivity is expressed as follows:

$$\text{Multifactor productivity} = \frac{\text{Output}}{\text{Input}} = \frac{\text{Real business GDP*}}{\text{Weighted labor hours†}\text{ and capital services‡}} \qquad (43.2)$$

$$= \text{Real business GDP per unit of labor and capital services}$$

Accuracy

There are no estimates of sampling or revision error for multifactor productivity.

Relevance

Productivity is important because greater efficiency increases the quantity of goods and services available for civilian and defense needs, and over time is a key ingredient for raising the material living conditions and the security of the population. The relationship of productivity to price change (*consumer price index, producer price indexes, GDP price measures*), *average weekly earnings,* and *employment* is also important. When productivity increases by relatively large amounts, production costs fall, and more goods and services tend to be available at lower or smaller increases in prices than in the absence of the large productivity increases. Analogously, rising productivity permits higher wages by limiting increases in production costs, without lowering profit margins.

But productivity increases can cause employment dislocation, because the introduction of new technology changes or eliminates some jobs. Displaced workers with outmoded skills may not be able to find new jobs or may find work only at lower rates of pay. While some individuals may therefore be adversely affected by productivity growth, rising productivity does not lead to unemployment or lower wages at the economywide level.

Because quarterly movements in productivity are heavily influenced

---

*Same as output in labor-hour productivity above, except that government enterprises are excluded.

†Hours worked by paid employees, the self-employed, and unpaid family workers, modified for schooling, experience, and skills of different groups of workers.

‡Rental value of equipment, structures, land, and inventories adjusted for price change. Depreciated value of equipment and structures modified for short-lived and long-lived items.

Table 43.1

Productivity: Business Sector*
(annual percentage change)

	Labor-hour productivity	Multifactor productivity
1995	0.2	−0.2
1996	3.0	1.7
1997	1.9	0.9
1998	2.8	1.1
1999	3.0	1.3
2000	2.8	1.4
2001	2.5	0.1
2002	4.0	1.9
2003	3.9	3.1P
2004	3.4	3.3P
1995–2004 (annual average)	3.0	1.6P

*Labor-hour productivity is referred to as the "business sector," and multifactor productivity is referred to as the "private business sector."
  P = Preliminary.

by cyclical changes in output, short-term changes in labor-hour productivity mainly reflect cyclical changes in economic growth rather than basic changes in efficiency. Such basic changes are discerned by examining trends over at least several quarters that have relatively steady rates of economic growth as reflected in the *gross domestic product*. Over the long run, basic changes in productivity are seen more directly in the annual movements of multifactor productivity noted below.

Multifactor productivity suggests the extent to which labor, capital, materials, and other aspects of production are improving, in terms of both technology and efficient usage. Changes in multifactor productivity indicate the extent of fundamental changes in the aggregate that impact productivity. However, because multifactor productivity encompasses all of the causal factors, further analysis is necessary to identify which elements are changing significantly.

The productivity measures are prepared from many different data sources that are inconsistent and also have known data problems. The statistical estimation is also based on indirect procedures, which are used in the absence of direct measures. The most serious problems appear in the service industries because of the difficulty of calculating the output of some services. Because of these problems, there is an unknown amount of error in the productivity numbers.

Recent Trends

From 1995 to 2004, productivity in the business sector showed divergent movements between labor-hour productivity and multifactor productivity (Table 43.1). Labor-hour productivity increased significantly more than multifactor productivity in all years. After increasing by only 0.2 percent in 1995, labor-hour productivity increased in the 2 to 3 percent range from 1996 to 2001, rose to increases of 4 percent in 2002–03, and dropped to an increase of 3.4 percent in 2004. Multifactor productivity growth declined from 1.7 percent in 1996 to 0.1 percent in 2001, though with interruptions in this downward trend in the intervening years, and increased to 2 percent in 2002 and 3 percent in 2003–04. The only decline in multifactor productivity occurred in 1995. Over the entire nine-year period, labor-hour productivity increased at an average annual rate of 3 percent, and multifactor productivity increased at an average annual rate of 1.6 percent.

References from Primary Data Source

Bureau of Labor Statistics, U.S. Department of Labor. *Monthly Labor Review.* Monthly.
————. *Multifactor Productivity Trends.* Annual.
Peter B. Meyer, and Michael J. Harper, "Preliminary estimates of multifactor productivity growth," *Monthly Labor Review,* June 2005.

Note

1. The six-month schedule, which provides preliminary estimates, began in 2005 and is a speedup from the previous lag of one to two years. See Meyer and Harper under "References from Primary Data Source."

44
Retail Sales

Retail sales represent the dollar receipts of retail establishments primarily from selling merchandise, and secondarily from services incidental to the sale of goods. Retailers sell to the public, which, in addition to households, includes businesses and governments. Retail establishments cover stores, mail-order houses, vending machines, and house-to-house canvass. Retailing includes a wide range of businesses, such as food, drug, liquor, department, variety, apparel, building material, hardware, furniture, sporting goods, book, jewelry, camera, and optical goods stores; automotive dealers, gasoline stations, restaurants, bars, and florists.

Where and When Available

Retail sales data are prepared monthly by the Bureau of the Census in the U.S. Department of Commerce. They are published in news releases, in the *Monthly Retail Trade and Food Services Survey,* and in the *Annual Benchmark Report for Retail Trade and Food Services* (www.census.gov).

Advance data are available about nine working days after the month to which they refer. Preliminary monthly data, showing additional kinds of business detail, are available six weeks after the reference month; these are accompanied by revised data for the previous two months. Annual revisions are made in March for the previous year.

Content

Retailers mainly resell merchandise purchased from manufacturers and wholesalers, with markups from the purchase price. Their receipts are

221

also derived from delivery, installation, repair, and other services associated with the merchandise. In addition, retailers make goods on their own premises, such as a retail bakery, but such baking is subordinate to selling to the public.[1] Merchandise is composed of nondurable goods such as food and clothing, which last less than three years, and durable goods such as cars and furniture, which last more than three years.

Retail sales are the dollar value of receipts of retail establishments after deductions for refunds, allowances for merchandise returned by customers, and rebates by the retailer. Sales reflect the full price of the item whether sold for cash or on credit, but they exclude receipts from interest and other credit charges to the customer.

Receipts exclude sales and excise taxes collected directly from the customer, but include gasoline, liquor, tobacco, and other excise taxes collected by the manufacturer or wholesaler and passed along to the customer. Merchandise sold at retail by manufacturers, wholesalers, and service establishments is not included in the retail sales data.

The retail sales data are available both seasonally adjusted and not seasonally adjusted.

Methodology

The retail sales data are obtained from a monthly sample survey of retailers. The survey sample is updated quarterly to account for new firms that start in business and existing firms that go out of business. New firms starting in business are added to the survey sample nine months or more after starting in operation, due to lags in obtaining notification of the startup and data on the new firm.

The survey sample includes all firms defined as large based on sales volume. Other firms are selected for the sample randomly based on their kind of business and sales volume. The approximate response rate is 80 percent for the monthly retail sales survey and 89 percent for the annual retail sales survey.

Accuracy

The sampling error (for one standard error) in the monthly percentage range in the retail sales data is 0.5 of a percentage point. For example, if the estimated increase in retail sales from one month to the next were 1 percent, in two of three cases the "true" increase would be somewhere

Table 44.1

Retail Sales

	Billions of dollars (monthly average)	Annual percentage change
1995	189.0	5.2
1996	201.1	6.4
1997	210.0	4.5
1998	220.4	4.9
1999	239.9	8.9
2000	255.8	6.6
2001	263.1	2.8
2002	269.2	2.3
2003	283.3	5.2
2004	305.4	7.8

between 0.5 and 1.5 percent. For further information on the interpretation of sampling and nonsampling errors, see the Appendix. Revisions between the monthly advance and revised monthly data in two of three cases range from –0.3 to 0.6 percent, and between the monthly preliminary and the monthly revised data from –0.2 to 0.2 percent.

Relevance

Retail sales are a key indicator of the strength of consumer spending. Consumer spending typically accounts for 70 percent of the *gross domestic product,* and consumer spending for durable and nondurable goods (the items covered in the retail sales data) accounts for approximately 43 percent of total consumer spending (the remainder of 57 percent represents consumer spending for services). Because the ultimate purpose of economic production is to provide for the well-being of people, consumer spending is a bedrock of the economy. Through its impact on economic growth, consumer spending is also an underlying factor affecting capital investment in equipment and structures. In addition to being an economic indicator in their own right, retail sales are a major data source used in preparing the consumer expenditures component of the *gross domestic product.*

Recent Trends

From 1995 to 2004, retail sales rose continuously to a monthly average of $305 billion in 2004 (Table 44.1). The annual increases peaked at 8.9

percent in 1999 and bottomed at 2.3 percent in 2002. The most typical increases were in the 5 to 7 percent range.

References from Primary Data Source

Bureau of the Census, U.S. Department of Commerce. *Monthly Retail Trade and Food Services Survey,* and *Annual Benchmark Report for Retail Trade and Food Services.*

Note

1. For example, a bakery that makes bread and sells it to stores for resale to the public is classified as a manufacturer, while a bakery that makes bread on the same premises as the store that sells it to the public is classified as a retailer.

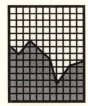

45
Selected Services Revenue

The data on selected services revenue represent private industry operating revenues for three broad service industry categories: (a) information services, (b) professional, scientific, and technical services, (c) administrative and support, waste management, and remediation services, and (d) hospitals and nursing and residential care facilities. These industries sell their services to households, businesses, and governments. The selected services revenue data are a new economic indicator that was first published in 2004.

Where and When Available

The selected services revenue data are prepared quarterly by the Bureau of the Census in the U.S. Department of Commerce. The data are published in a news release, *Quarterly Revenue for Selected Services* (www.census.gov).

The services revenue data are available seventy-five days after the quarter to which they refer. The initial data are revised in the subsequent quarter. Annual revisions are made in the following year.

Content

The selected services private industry operating revenue data cover many component industries within the broad categories of information services; professional, scientific, and technical services; and administrative and support, waste management, and remediation services. Revenues are the charges or billings for the services rendered by a firm's operations, though payment may be received at a later date. Revenues exclude income from nonoperating activities such as interest, investments, sales of securities and real estate, loans, grants, sale of merchandise from retail establishments, and sales and other taxes collected from customers and submitted to government tax agencies.

Industry revenue data are also shown separately for sales to three types of customers: households, businesses, and governments. As this new indicator is developed, expanded industry coverage is planned for transportation and warehousing; finance and insurance; real estate and rental leasing; arts, entertainment, and recreation services; and others.

The services data are provided in current dollars (not adjusted for price change) and as a percentage change from quarter to quarter.

The selected services data are not yet seasonally adjusted. However, there are plans to provide seasonally adjusted data after 16 to 20 quarters of data have been obtained.

Methodology

The selected services data are obtained from a probability sample of approximately 6,000 private industry firms and in some cases from aggregations of several establishments within a firm. An establishment is a single physical location of an employer's operations where payroll and employment records are kept, with firms operating in more than one location having several establishments. The sample covers establishments of all sizes and is updated quarterly for new firms starting in business, for existing firms going out of business, and for other changes to the universe of firms, such as from mergers and acquisitions.

Imputations are made for the firms that do not respond to the survey based on reported revenues for firms of a similar size and in the same industry. Imputations account for the following approximate shares of total revenues: information services (9 percent); professional, scientific, and technical services (26 percent); administrative and support, waste management, and remediation services (30 percent), and hospitals and nursing and residential care facilities (21 percent).

The selected services data are revised annually based on data from the more comprehensive Service Annual Survey.

Accuracy

The reliability of the selected services revenue data for the dollar levels is based on the coefficient of variation. The coefficient of variation is the percentage that the sampling error is of the total dollar level. The coefficient of variation (for 1.65 standard errors) is: information services (0.5 percent); professional, scientific, and technical services (1.4 percent); administrative and support, waste management, and remediation services (2.6 percent), and hospitals and nursing and residential care facilities (1.1 percent). For example, if the estimated quarterly revenue for information services were $230,000 million, in nine of ten cases the "true" level would be somewhere between $228,850 million and $231,150 million.

The sampling error (for one standard error) for the quarter-to-quarter change in the services revenue data is: information services (0.3 of a percentage point); professional, scientific, and technical services (0.9 of a percentage point); administrative and support, waste management, and remediation services (0.9 of a percentage point, and hospitals and nursing and residential care facilities (0.4 of a percentage point). For example, if the estimated increase in information services from one quarter to the next were 5 percent, in two of three cases the "true" increase would be somewhere between 4.7 and 5.3 percent. For further information on the interpretation of sampling and nonsampling errors, see the Appendix.

Relevance

Services are the largest industrial component of the U.S. economy as well as having the greatest growth over time. They are composed of both labor-intensive and high-technology production operations, and run the gamut from low-wage to high-wage employment. The initial coverage of the new quarterly selected services revenue data accounts for about 15 percent of the *gross domestic product*. This coverage will increase considerably as the selected services data are expanded to include many more industries, as noted above under "Content."

Recent Trends

From the fourth quarter of 2004 to the first quarter of 2005, total selected services revenues decreased 1.5 percent; information services decreased 0.5 percent; professional, scientific, and technical services decreased 0.5 percent; administrative and support, waste management, and remediation services decreased 4.3 percent, and hospitals and nursing and residential care facilities increased 2.4 percent. Total selected services revenue was $792 billion in the first quarter of 2005. Among

Table 45.1

Selected Services Revenue, Billions of Dollars
(not seasonally adjusted)

	2004: 4Q	2005: 1Q	Percentage change, 2004: 4Q to 2005: 1Q
Information services	237.0	227.4	−4.1
Professional, scientific, and technical services	251.5	250.2	−0.5
Administrative and support, waste management, and remediation services	129.6	124.0	−4.3
Hospitals and nursing and residential care facilities	185.6	190.1	2.4
Total	803.7	791.7	−1.5

the components, professional, scientific, and technical services was the largest, followed in order by information services, hospitals and nursing and residential care facilities, and administrative and support, waste management, and remediation services (Table 45.1).

Reference from Primary Data Source

Bureau of the Census, U.S. Department of Commerce. *Quarterly Revenue for Selected Services.* Quarterly.

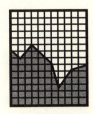

46
Stock Market Price Aggregates and Dividend Yields

Stock market aggregate price measures represent the overall price movements of common stocks and certain other securities such as investment funds and real estate investment trusts of corporations traded on U.S. stock markets. The price performance and dividend yields of four different composite price measures are covered here.

Corporate stockholders are owners who have shares of stock in the company. Stockholders share in company profits through dividends, and in the case of common stocks, also have the right to vote on company policies. Rising and falling stock prices affect capital gains and losses to investors.

The stock market price aggregates and the dividend yields are covered separately, first the price aggregates and then the dividend yields.

Stock Market Price Aggregates

Where and When Available

The selected four stock market price aggregates are prepared daily by the New York Stock Exchange Inc., Nasdaq (National Association of Securities Dealers Automated Quotations), Standard & Poor's Corporation, and Dow Jones & Co. Inc. They are published in daily newspapers and electronically. General Web sites include: Bloomberg Financial (www.bloomberg.com), Wall Street Journal Interactive Edition (www.wsj.com), Barron's (www.barrons.com), MarketWatch (www.marketwatch.com), MoneyCentral (www.moneycentral.msn.com), and Finance Yahoo (www.finance.yahoo.com).

The stock market price aggregates are disseminated continuously during the trading day.

Content

The four stock market price aggregates covered here are: the New York Stock Exchange composite index, Nasdaq composite index, Standard & Poor's 500 composite index, and the Dow Jones industrial average. The first three aggregates, which are referred to as indexes, are referenced to a base period. By contrast, the Dow Jones industrial average is not referenced to a base period. The four stock price aggregates represent different groups of companies in which price movements of each company are combined into a single number. Of the four aggregates, the New York Stock Exchange index and the Nasdaq index are derived from the buying and selling transactions of company shares that are listed on their exchanges. The Standard & Poor's index and the Dow Jones industrial average are based on stock prices of particular companies that are especially selected for inclusion in each price measure.

The stock market price aggregates exclude the effect of changes in the capitalized financial structure of companies such as corporate restructuring, stock splits, mergers, and spinoffs, so that price movements are not distorted by changes in the underlying value of a share of stock following a new capitalization of the company. Therefore, the price aggregates cannot be compared with an average of actual current market prices for the same companies because the latter would reflect the effect of new capitalizations on the price per share without adjusting for changes in the underlying value of each share.

The four stock price aggregates differ in the coverage of companies that are priced and in the methodology used in calculating the aggregates.

The stock market price aggregates are not seasonally adjusted.

New York Stock Exchange Composite Index

The New York Stock Exchange composite index covers prices of approximately 2,100 company issues of common stocks, open-end funds, real estate investment trusts, American depositary receipts, and tracking stocks listed on the New York Stock Exchange. The composite index excludes preferred stocks, closed-end funds, and certain other securities. Component price indexes of the composite are provided for companies in a technology, media, telecom aggregate, and energy, finance, and healthcare groupings.

Nasdaq Composite Index

The Nasdaq composite index covers the prices of over 3,000 company stock issues traded on the Nasdaq: common stocks, real estate investment trusts, American depositary receipts, tracking stocks, and certain other securities. The composite index excludes preferred stocks, closed-end funds, and certain other securities. Component indexes of the composite are provided for companies in industrial, insurance, bank, other finance, transportation, computer, biotechnology, telecommunications, and social groupings.

Standard & Poor's 500 Composite Price Index

The Standard & Poor's 500 composite price index covers prices of 500 companies on the New York Stock Exchange, Nasdaq, and AMEX (American Stock Exchange). As a proportion of the market value of the total index, companies on the New York Stock Exchange accounted for 85.1 percent, the Nasdaq for 14.8 percent, and the AMEX for 0.1 percent as of January 2005. Component indexes of the 500 composite are provided for companies in industrial, transportation, utilities, and financial groupings.

Dow Jones Industrial Average

The Dow Jones industrial average covers prices of thirty U.S. companies. They are widely held large companies in manufacturing, mining, communications, finance, services, and retail industries. Dow Jones indexes are also provided for companies in transportation and utilities groupings.

Methodology

As noted above, the four stock price aggregates are adjusted to eliminate the price effect of changes in the capitalized financial structure of companies, such as corporate restructuring, stock splits, mergers, and spinoffs.

This maintains the capitalized structure of each company as it was when the company was first included in the price measure. The New York Stock Exchange, Nasdaq, and Standard & Poor's 500 price indexes are weighted using the market value of the companies as the weights. The market value of a company is the number of its common stock shares outstanding multiplied by its market price per share. By contrast, the Dow Jones industrial average gives each company equal weight.

New York Stock Exchange Composite Price Index

The New York Stock Exchange composite price index reflects the market value of the securities issues in the index. The stocks are averaged in proportion to the market value of each company, which gives price movements of firms with large market values more weight than those with small market values. The market values are adjusted to reflect the number of shares actually available to investors. New companies are added and old companies are deleted from the index as the companies are listed and delisted on the New York Stock Exchange.

The New York Stock Exchange composite index currently is based on December 31, 2002 = 5,000.

Nasdaq Composite Price Index

The Nasdaq composite price index reflects the market value of the securities issues in the index. The stocks are averaged in proportion to the market values of each company, which gives price movements of firms with large market values more weight than those with small market values. New companies are added and old companies are deleted from the index as the companies are listed and deleted on the Nasdaq.

The Nasdaq composite index currently is based on February 5, 1971 = 100.

Standard & Poor's 500 Composite Price Index

The Standard & Poor's 500 composite index reflects the market value of stocks in the index. Examples of the criteria used for including companies in the index are: they are U.S. operating companies, have adequate liquidity, a reasonable per-share price, market capitalization of $4 billion or more, public float of at least 50 percent of the stock, and are not a closed-end fund. The stocks are averaged in proportion to the market values of each company, which gives price movements of firms with large market values more weight than those with small market values. New companies are substituted for old companies because of mergers, bankruptcies, and capital restructuring, and to update the representation of stocks to more closely represent important industries in the U.S. economy.

The Standard & Poor's 500 composite index currently is based on 1941–43 = 100.

Dow Jones Industrial Average

The Dow Jones industrial average reflects the average price per share of thirty stocks. The index gives each stock an equal base weight of 3.33 percent. This results in more weight to price movements of companies with high prices per share than those with low prices per share. New companies are substituted for old companies because of mergers and to update the index to better represent large, widely held companies.

Accuracy

There are no estimates of sampling or revision error for the stock market price aggregates.

Dividend Yields

Dividend yields represent cash dividend payments to stockholders as a percentage of the market price of each company's stock; stock dividends are excluded from the dividend yield measures. The dividend yield includes all companies in the stock market price aggregates—those companies that pay dividends and those that do not. The annual dividend yield is calculated as the dividends paid for the entire twelve months of the calendar year divided by the stock market price aggregates at the year-end December 31 level.

Company payouts of regular cash dividends and special cash dividends (dividends paid from time to time with no set schedule) are reflected in the three price aggregates based on whatever the dividend effects are on the market price of the company's stock. This differs from total return stock price measures, which add the dividend payments to the change in the stock prices for a given time period.

Dividend yields are provided for the Nasdaq composite price index (the Nasdaq estimate first became available in 2002), Standard & Poor's 500 composite price index, and the Dow Jones industrial average. Dividend yields are not provided for the New York Stock Exchange composite price index.

The dividend yield for the Nasdaq composite price index and the Dow Jones industrial average includes both regular and special cash dividends. The dividend yield for the Standard & Poor's 500 composite index includes regular cash dividends only.

Company buybacks of corporate stock are an implicit dividend yield that supplements the above cash dividend yield. The buyback yield is calculated as the percentage that the value of the repurchased stock is of the company's balance sheet equity value. The buyback yield is a net cash company outflow of the repurchases minus the exercise of employee stock options. A buyback yield is available only for a sample of the largest companies in the Standard & Poor's 500 composite index.[1]

Stock Market Price Aggregates and Dividend Yields

Relevance

Stock market prices influence the course of future economic growth through their effect on perceptions of the health of the economy and the wealth of stockholders. High or rising stock prices encourage consumer and investment spending because they reflect and/or promote optimism about the economy and additions to the wealth of stockholders either as paper capital gains or actual (realized) capital gains when the stocks are sold. Low or falling stock prices discourage such spending because of the pessimistic outlook they foster and a diminished wealth of stockholders either as a paper capital loss or actual (realized) capital loss when the stocks are sold. The Standard & Poor's 500 composite price index is a component of the leading index of the *leading, coincident, and lagging indexes.*

Stock price movements affect consumer spending through their "wealth effect" on households (see *distribution of wealth*). Households feel richer and more willing to spend when the value of their paper stock holdings is high or when they sell the stock to obtain the actual capital gains. The opposite occurs when the value of their stock holdings is low. Stock prices also influence investment spending because high stock prices make it easier for businesses to finance new investment by selling new equity stock or by obtaining loans through new bond sales or other debt financing. The choice of equity (stock) or debt (bond) financing is determined by differences in the cost of raising funds (equity versus debt) and by the effect of selling new stock on the choice of the capital structure of the company. Generally, it is easier to sell new stock when stock prices are high or rising than when they are weak.

Dividend yields affect investor perceptions of future trends in stock prices. Low yields suggest expectations of large or long-term price increases, and high yields indicate anticipated small price increases or long-term price declines. Dividend yields also affect patterns of investment. Thus, low yields may lead investors out of stocks and into bonds, real estate, or other investments that have an expected higher return, leading to a fall in stock prices. By contrast, high yields may entice investors into stocks, both because of the high return and the anticipation that the high yields will stimulate higher stock prices (the latter is counter to the above notion that high yields indicate weak future stock prices).

Recent Trends

From 1995 to 2004, price movements of the four stock market price aggregates were similar over the entire period, but varied during the 1995–2000 and 2000–04 intermediate periods (Table 46.1). The average annual increase over the 1995–2004 period ranged from 8.5 to 9.7 percent in the four aggregates. The New York Stock Exchange composite index and the Dow Jones industrial average showed the closest annual movements during the 1995–2000 and 2000–04 intermediate periods. The Nasdaq composite index showed the most volatile movements and the Standard & Poor's 500 composite index showed the next most volatile movements during 1995–2000 and 2000–04.

From 1995 to 2004, dividend yields typically were around the 1.5 to 2.0 percent range. The Standard & Poor's 500 yield dropped from 2.56 percent in 1995 to a low of 1.15 percent in 2000, and then rose to a high of 1.77 percent in 2003. The Dow Jones industrial average yield dropped from 2.27 percent in 1995 to a low of 1.47 percent in 1999 and then rose to 2.27 percent in 2002 (the same high as in 1995). The Nasdaq yield was 0.48 percent in 2002 and 2003 and rose to 1.5 percent in 2004.

Table 46.1

Stock Market Price Aggregates and Dividend Yields

	New York Stock Exchange Index (12/31/02 = 5,000)	Nasdaq Market Index (2/5/71 = 100)	Standard & Poor's 500 Index (1941–43 = 10)	Dow Jones Industrial Average
1995	3,079	925	542	4,494
1996	3,787	1,165	671	5,743
1997	4,827	1,469	873	7,441
1998	5,818	1,795	1,086	8,626
1999	6,547	2,728	1,327	10,465
2000	6,806	3,784	1,427	10,735
2001	6,398	2,035	1,194	10,189
2002	5,579	1,540	994	9,226
2003	5,447	1,647	965	8,994
2004	6,613	1,987	1,131	10,317
Annual percentage change				
1995–2000	17.2	32.5	21.4	19.0
2000–2004	−0.7	−14.9	−5.6	−1.0
1995–2004	8.9	8.9	8.5	9.7

	Cash dividend yield (percent)				Buyback dividend yield (percent)
	Cash dividend	Cash dividend	Cash dividend	Cash dividend	
1995	NA	NA	2.56	2.27	2.41
1996	NA	NA	2.19	2.03	2.06
1997	NA	NA	1.77	1.72	1.69
1998	NA	NA	1.49	1.65	1.48
1999	NA	NA	1.25	1.47	1.19
2000	NA	NA	1.15	1.60	1.07
2001	NA	NA	1.32	1.81	1.26
2002	NA	0.48	1.61	2.27	NA
2003	NA	0.48	1.77	2.00	NA
2004	NA	1.50	1.72	2.22	NA

NA = Not available.

The buyback dividend yield, when added to the above cash dividend yield, gives an implicit total yield. A buyback yield, which is available only for a sample of the largest companies in the Standard & Poor's 500, declined from 2.41 percent in 1995 to 1.07 percent in 2000, and then rose to 1.26 percent in 2001. Data for 2002 to 2004 are not available.

Note

1. Estimates of the buyback yield in Table 46.1 are based on an analysis of company reports to the Securities and Exchange Commission (10-K reports) of a sample of the largest companies in the Standard & Poor's 500 composite index. See J. Nellie Liang and Steven A. Sharpe, "Share Repurchases and Employee Stock Options and Their Implications for S & P 500 Share Retirements and Expected Returns," *Finance and Economics Discussion Series* no. 59, Federal Reserve Board, 1999. The buyback yields in Table 46.1 reflect revised and updated data since the above paper was published.

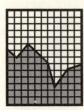

47
Unemployment

Unemployment represents the number of persons without jobs who are available for and actively seeking work. There are two measures of unemployment. One is confined to unemployed workers who collect unemployment insurance benefit payments through the federal-state unemployment insurance system. The other is a more comprehensive definition of unemployment and thus covers many more persons other than those who collect unemployment insurance benefit payments

This chapter covers both unemployment measures. The comprehensive measure is the total rate of unemployment and is referred to here as "total unemployment." It is the familiar one that is used in economic analysis and in developing fiscal and monetary policies for the macro economy. The insured unemployment measure is referred to here as "insured unemployment." It focuses on insurance benefit payments for the unemployed.

Recent trends are covered at the end of the chapter for both total unemployment and insured unemployment.

Total Unemployment

Total unemployment covers all persons sixteen years and older who are available for and actively seeking work who lost or quit previous jobs, and others with no work experience or who have re-entered the workplace. It includes but is not limited to workers who qualify for unemployment insurance benefit payments. The unemployment rate is equal to the number of unemployed persons as a percentage of the sum of the employed and the unemployed. As a measure of additional workers available for *employment,* the unemployment rate reflects the slack or tightness in labor markets.

Where and When Available

Total unemployment measures are prepared monthly by the Bureau of Labor Statistics (BLS) in the U.S. Department of Labor. The data are published in a news release and in two BLS monthly journals, *Monthly Labor Review* and *Employment and Earnings* (www.bls.gov).

The data are available on the third Friday after the week containing the twelfth of the month. Thus, the information is released on the first or second Friday of the month following the month in question. On the day the data are released, the commissioner of labor statistics reports on recent unemployment and employment trends to the Joint Economic Committee of Congress. The monthly data are revised every January for the previous five years, based on updated seasonal factors.

Content

The labor force is defined as the sum of employed and unemployed persons living in the United States. Both citizens and foreigners are included.

Unemployment data measure the number of persons sixteen years and older who do not have jobs and are available for and actively seeking work. The unemployment rate is the percentage of persons in the labor force who are unemployed and is calculated by the formula below. This calculation is done separately for several demographic groups and weighted together to arrive at the overall rate. The demographic groups represent distinctions by age, gender, race, and ethnicity.

$$\text{Unemployment rate} = \frac{\text{Unemployed persons}}{\text{Employed} + \text{unemployed persons (labor force)}} \times 100 \tag{47.1}$$

Employed persons are defined as nonfarm and farm workers aged sixteen years and older who are not institutionalized and who are not residents of homes for the aged.[1] The definition includes full-time and part-time wage and salary employees at paid jobs who work at least one hour a week, self-employed persons working in their own business, and unpaid workers in family businesses who work at least fifteen hours a week (family workers are assumed to share in the profits of the business).[2] Because the employment measures count persons rather than jobs, individuals holding two or more jobs are counted only once—in the job they work the most hours during a week. Persons temporarily absent from their jobs because of illness, vacation, strike, or lockout are included as employed whether or not they are paid while they are absent from work. (This definition of "employment" conforms to the "household" measure of employment discussed in the *employment* chapter.)

Unemployed persons are defined as those who actively sought a job at least once in the previous four weeks through such actions as having a job interview; contacting an employer for a job interview; answering a job advertisement; sending out resumes; contacting an employment agency, a friend, or a relative; placing an advertisement in a newspaper; checking with a union or professional register; obtaining assistance from a community organization, or waiting at a designated labor pickup point. By contrast, looking at job advertisements or attending training programs or courses is defined as a passive search for work and does not meet the criterion of being unemployed. The unemployed include individuals who collect unemployment insurance as well as those who are not eligible for unemployment insurance (for example, formerly employed workers who have exhausted their unemployment insurance or unemployed persons who did not work long enough to qualify for unemployment benefits). Students are counted as unemployed if they sought work and are available at least for part-time jobs.

"Discouraged workers" are not in the labor force and so are not counted as unemployed. These are workers who say they want a job, but are not seeking work because they think there are no jobs available in the local labor market or believe they do not qualify for the existing job vacancies due to lack of schooling or training, employers' thinking they are too young or too old, or other types of discrimination. Persons are classified as discouraged only if they looked for a job at least once during the past twelve months, or since the end of their last job if they held one within the past twelve months.

Discouraged workers, a subset of the category of marginally attached workers, are outside the labor force for the *economic reasons* noted above. Like discouraged workers, "marginally attached" workers other than discouraged workers have looked for a job at least once during the past twelve months, or since the end of their last job if they held one within the past

Table 47.1

Alternative Measures of Labor Underutilization
(seasonally adjusted)

	February 2005 (percent)
U-1. Persons unemployed 15 weeks or longer, as a percentage of the civilian labor force	1.9
U-2. Job losers[a] and persons who completed temporary jobs, as a percentage of the civilian labor force	2.7
U-3. Total unemployed, as a percentage of the civilian labor force (official unemployment rate)	5.4
U-4. U-3 plus discouraged workers, as a percentage of the civilian labor force plus discouraged workers	5.7
U-5. U-4 plus all other marginally attached workers, as a percentage of the civilian labor force plus all marginally attached workers[b]	6.4
U-6. U-5 plus total employed part-time because full-time jobs are not available	9.3

[a]Job losers are unemployed because they were laid off or fired; [b]For the distinction between discouraged and other marginally attached workers, see text.

twelve months. The only difference is that marginally attached workers other than discouraged workers are not currently looking for work because of *noneconomic* reasons, such as illness or medical limitations, child-care problems or other family or personal obligations, school, or training.

Unemployment rates are also calculated by length of time out of work, by demographic components of the workforce such as age, race, gender, and marital status of adults in the household, and for large states and metropolitan areas.

The unemployment data are seasonally adjusted.

Table 47.1 shows the total unemployment rate, plus five alternative measures of labor underutilization. The official number is referred to as U-3. The five alternative measures calculate rates based on the duration of unemployment; number of workers who have lost their jobs; number of temporary jobs that ended; and number of discouraged workers, other marginally attached workers, and part-time workers. These measures provide a range of labor underutilization rates significantly below and above the official rate (discussed further under "Relevance").

The alternative measures of labor underutilization under "Total Unemployment" show a range of 7.4 percentage points in February 2005

(Table 47.1). The lowest rate of U-1, which consists of persons unemployed for fifteen weeks or longer, was 1.9 percent. The highest rate of U-6, which consists of all unemployed workers, plus all marginally attached workers, plus part-time workers who want a full-time job, was 9.3 percent. The official rate, U-3, was 5.4 percent.

Impact of Labor Force Participation on Unemployment

As noted above, the labor force is the sum of employed and unemployed persons. The labor force as a percentage of the civilian noninstitutionalized population (see note 1 for noninstitutionalized persons) is referred to as the labor force participation rate (LFPR). Thus, the LFPR is not used in calculating the unemployment rate. However, trends in the LFPR are important in understanding trends in the unemployment rate.

In 2004, the unemployment rate was 5.5 percent and the LFPR was 66.0 percent. This compares with the unemployment rate of 4.0 percent and the LFPR of 67.1 percent in 2000. Thus, from 2000 to 2004, the unemployment rate rose and the LFPR fell—the unemployment rate rose from 2001 to 2003 and declined in 2004, while the LFPR declined each year during 2001–04. Ordinarily, it would be expected that a falling LFPR over several years would be associated with lower unemployment. This reflects the fact that a falling LFPR would lessen the increase in the number of noninstitutionalized persons not in the labor force (the noninstitutionalized population increased in all years since the end of World War II), and consequently lessen the number of unemployed persons looking for work.

Moreover, during 2001–04, trends in the LFPR reversed or sharply accentuated movements in previous years (Table 47.2). The overall LFPR rose continuously in the decades from the 1960s up to the year 2000, and then declined continuously during 2001–04. The overall increase in the LFPR up to the year 2000 was the net effect of divergent trends in the demographic components of the labor force, with the LFPR for men twenty years and older declining, the LFPR for women twenty years and older rising, and the LFPR for teens rising in the 1960s and 1970s and declining in the 1980s and 1990s up to 2000. Then, from 2001–04, the long-run rate of decline in the LFPR for men increased, the long-run increase in the LFPR for women reversed to a decline, and the decline in the LFPR for teens that began in the 1980s intensified.

Table 47.2

Labor Force Participation Rates (percent)

	Men	Women	Teens	Total
1979	79.8	50.6	57.9	63.7
1980	79.4	51.3	56.7	63.8
1989	78.1	57.7	55.9	66.5
1990	78.2	58.0	53.7	66.5
2000	76.7	60.6	52.0	67.1
2001	76.5	60.6	49.6	66.8
2004	75.8	60.3	43.9	66.0

Notes: Cyclical expansion peaks: 1979, 1989, 2000; Cyclical recession lows: 1980, 1990, 2001; Cyclical expansion: 2004.

I have re-estimated the LFPR in 2004 assuming that trends from 1989 to 2000 (years of cyclical expansion peaks) continued at the same rate during 2001–04, both for the demographic components of men, women, and teens, and in the aggregate. These calculations result in total unemployment rates in 2004 from 7.5 to 7.7 percent. Using the same procedure with the LFPR trends from 1990 to 2001 (years of cyclical recession lows), the resultant unemployment rates in 2004 are 7.4 to 7.9 percent. Thus, at a minimum, if the LFPRs had continued at their long-run trend from 2001 to 2004, the unemployment rate in 2004 would have been at least two percentage points higher than the actual unemployment rate of 5.5 percent.

The focus on the LFPR highlights the discouraged worker effect in the long run. As noted above, the term "discouraged workers," as measured in the alternative measures of labor underutilization, refers to workers who have not looked for work in the past twelve months, the short run, due to economic reasons (Table 47.1). The use of the LFPR in my analysis over several years relates to what the behavior of prospective workers would have been if the job situation had been stronger during 2001–04.

While there are anecdotal reports of mothers with young children who have decided to be at home with their children and thus are not in the labor force, which would tend to lower the LFPR for women, these do not appear to have been great enough to have changed the LFPR for women as sharply as shown in Table 47.2. At the other end of the spectrum, there are anecdotal reports of retired men and women who continue to work at other jobs after retirement, which would tend to raise the LFPR for men and women. but these too do not appear to have caused the sharp changes in Table 47.2.

Methodology

Unemployment data are obtained from a monthly survey of households called the Current Population Survey (CPS). The CPS is a sample of about 60,000 households, which the U.S. Bureau of the Census conducts for the Bureau of Labor Statistics.[3] Responses are actually obtained from about 55,500 households; no responses are obtained from the remaining 4,500 households due to absence, impassable roads, refusals, or for other reasons. The sample is representative of the distribution of households in small and large metropolitan areas and in rural areas. It undergoes a major revision every ten years to be consistent with the most recent decennial population census. The sample currently is based on the 2000 census of population. The sample is also updated annually on a limited basis to reflect current changes in residential locations due to new construction based on *housing starts* data prepared by the Census Bureau.

In order to reduce the reporting burden on any group of households, the CPS is divided into eight subsamples (panels) that are rotated over a sixteen-month period. Each subsample is surveyed for four consecutive months, then dropped from the survey for eight months, and subsequently resurveyed for the following four months. At the end of the sixteen months, the subsample is eliminated from the sample and is replaced with a new panel of households. The result of this procedure is that every month 25 percent of the households in the sample are either new to the survey or are returning after an eight-month hiatus. Correspondingly, 25 percent of the sample households drop out of the survey every month.

The survey refers to the individual's employment status during the calendar week that includes the twelfth of the month. The survey is conducted mainly by telephone interviews, supplemented by personal interviews as necessary.

Accuracy

Assuming an unemployment rate of 5.4 percent, in nine of ten cases (1.6 standard errors), a monthly change in the unemployment rate of at least plus or minus 0.23 of a percentage point is regarded as statistically significant. Although a change of zero or plus or minus 0.10 of a percentage point is not statistically significant for one month, cumulative changes of 0.12 of a percentage point in the same direction for two or more consecutive months are statistically significant. The only difference in these estimates if the unemployment rate is 6.0 percent is that a monthly change in the unemployment rate of at least plus or minus 0.24 is regarded as statistically significant (compared with 0.23 of a percentage point at a 5.4 percent unemployment rate). For further information on the interpretation of sampling and nonsampling errors, see the Appendix.

Relevance

The unemployment rate is a major indicator of the degree to which the economy provides jobs for those seeking work. It is a key consideration when the president, Congress, and Federal Reserve determine whether economic growth should be stimulated or restrained through fiscal and monetary policies (see *government budgets and debt* for fiscal policy and *interest rates* for monetary policy).

In general, there is an inverse relationship between unemployment and the *gross domestic product* (GDP), which is referred to as Okun's Law. In the early 2000s, this relationship functioned roughly as follows: the yearly unemployment rate remains the same if the annual real GDP increases by 2.0 percent, with every 1 percentage point growth in real GDP above 2.0 percent lowering the unemployment rate by 0.5 percentage point, and every 1 percentage point growth in real GDP below 2.0 percent raising unemployment by 0.5 percentage point. These estimates reflect the relationship that averages out over the years, but they do not hold in every year. The formulation of Okun's Law takes price movements into account not only by the utilization of real GDP, but also by limiting the concept to a nonaccelerating inflation rate of unemployment (referred to as NAIRU).

The unemployment rate is also used to analyze the tradeoff between unemployment and inflation (e.g., the *consumer price index*), which is referred to as the Phillips Curve. In theory, there is an inverse relationship between unemployment and inflation: when unemployment declines, inflation rises, and when unemployment rises, inflation declines. But this is not a one-to-one relationship, nor is it equally applicable when the economy is functioning at high and low unemployment. In general, the Phillips Curve is most consistent with the theory at low rates of unemployment and inflation.

Perhaps more significant than the year-to-year movements are long-term shifts in the improvement or worsening of the tradeoff shown in the Phillips Curve. An improvement in the tradeoff means that over time, the same rate of unemployment generates a lower rate of inflation than it had in the past, while a worsening of the tradeoff means that the same rate of unemployment generates more inflation than it had in the past. Current formulations of the Phillips Curve include the effects of inflation expectations on the movement of the curve. This kind of analysis is used to assess goals for minimum unemployment and inflation rates such as are included in the Full Employment and Balanced Growth Act of 1978 (Humphrey-Hawkins Act).

Alternative measures of labor underutilization indicate a range of estimated slackness in the economy, from the lowest rate at the U-1 end of the spectrum to the highest rate at the U-6 end. Depending on the social and political perspectives of those characterizing the extent of unemployment, persons highlighting the economy's strength would point to the U-1 end, while persons highlighting the economy's weakness would point to the U-6 end. Total unemployment (defined as the official rate) is U-3.

In addition, the unemployment rate determines when federally financed supplementary unemployment benefits go into effect for particular localities when unemployment is persistently high. These benefits supplement regular state-provided unemployment benefits that have been exhausted, and are triggered by a formula that includes both the national unemployment rate and state and metropolitan area unemployment rates (see "Insured Unemployment" below).

Insured Unemployment

Insured unemployment represents unemployed workers who are available for and are actively seeking work, provided they are receiving unemployment insurance benefit payments under the federal-state unemployment insurance system. Unemployment insurance benefit payments provide some income subsistence for unemployed workers and also function as automatic stabilizers during cyclical expansions and recessions in the macro economy.

Where and When Available

Insured unemployment data are prepared weekly by the Employment and Training Administration in the U.S. Department of Labor. The data are published in a news release, *Unemployment Insurance Weekly Claims Report* (www.ows.doleta.gov).

The data are available each Thursday following the week to which they refer. The data are revised in the subsequent three weeks.

Content

Insured unemployment applies solely to unemployed workers who are eligible for and apply for unemployment benefit payments through the federal-state unemployment insurance system. The federal-state system allows states to pay benefits up to a maximum of twenty-six weeks of unemployment, though individual states vary in determining the eligibility of unemployed persons to obtain benefit payments. The unemployment insurance program also triggers additional benefit payments when state unemployment is persistently high during recessions. These extended benefit payments go beyond the first twenty-six weeks to an additional thirteen to twenty weeks among individual states.

The benefit payments are financed by a federally mandated tax that employers in each state must pay into a state trust fund. In addition, three states (Alaska, New Jersey, and Pennsylvania) require employees to pay into the state trust fund. State governments administer the unemployment insurance program under general federal guidelines that give the states complete discretion in determining who is eligible for benefit payments, the dollar amount of the benefits, and how long the benefits are paid while the recipient is unemployed. There is considerable variation among the states in applying these aspects of the program. Eligibility for unemployment insurance, benefit amounts, and the length of time benefits are available are determined by each state's law under which unemployment insurance claims are established.

In order to qualify for unemployment insurance benefit payments, the person must have worked a specified period of time for a private employer (in a place of business or as a household worker) or for a state or local government. The unemployment insurance data exclude other unemployment insurance programs that cover federal workers or railroad workers. There is no federal-state unemployment insurance coverage for employees of religious organizations or for self-employed workers.

As an incentive to unemployed workers to create their own jobs by starting their own businesses, Self-Employment Assistance programs allow states to pay a self-employed allowance to help these workers while they are establishing businesses and becoming self-employed. Participants receive weekly allowances while they are getting their businesses off the ground. This is a voluntary program, and in 2004 fewer than ten states had Self-Employment Assistance programs.

Insured unemployment data are prepared for the United States, the fifty states and the District of Columbia, Puerto Rico, and the Virgin Islands. The insured unemployment rate, which is calculated weekly, is the number of persons that receive unemployment insurance benefit payments as a percentage of all persons covered under the unemployment insurance program. The unemployment rate for the week that includes the twelfth of the month represents the monthly unemployment rate. In addition, weekly data are provided on the number of persons filing initial claims for unemployment insurance benefit payments.

The nationwide insured unemployment data are seasonally adjusted. Insured unemployment data for individual states are not seasonally adjusted.

Methodology

The data on insured unemployment are obtained by the Employment and Training Administration in the U.S. Department of Labor from the universe of records of the state employment agencies that administer the Unemployment Insurance program.

Accuracy

There are no sampling errors in the insured unemployment data because the data are collected from the universe of insured workers.

Relevance

In addition to providing some subsistence income for unemployed workers, unemployment insurance benefit payments function as automatic stabilizers for the macro economy. During economic recessions, benefit payments maintain some income for unemployed workers, which in turn contributes to household expenditures and economic growth. And when unemployment declines during economic expansions, benefit payments decline and thus reduce the stimulus to household spending. In eco-

Table 47.3

Unemployment Rate: Total and Insured Measures of Unemployment (percent)

	Total unemployment	Insured unemployment
1995	5.6	2.3
1996	5.4	2.2
1997	4.9	1.9
1998	4.5	1.8
1999	4.2	1.7
2000	4.0	1.6
2001	4.7	2.3
2002	5.8	2.8
2003	6.0	2.8
2004	5.5	2.3

Notes: Cyclical expansion peaks: 1979, 1989, 2000; Cyclical recession lows: 1980, 1990, 2001; Cyclical expansion: 2004.

nomic analysis, the number of persons filing initial claims for unemployment insurance benefit payments when they first become unemployed is a component of the leading index (see *leading, coincident, and lagging indexes*).

Recent Trends

From 1995 to 2004, the total measure of unemployment was typically 2.5 times the level of insured unemployment during 1995–2000 and in 2004, and 2.0 times that of insured unemployment during 2001–03 (Table 47.3). The two measures moved in the same upward and downward yearly direction over the 1995–2002 period and in 2004. In 2003, the total measure rose, while the insured measure did not change.

References from Primary Data Source

Bureau of Labor Statistics, U.S. Department of Labor. *Monthly Labor Review* and *Employment and Earnings.* Monthly.
Employment and Training Administration, U.S. Department of Labor. *Unemployment Insurance Weekly Claims Report.* News Release. Weekly.

Notes

1. Institutionalized persons include those confined to penal or mental facilities.

2. Self-employed persons whose businesses are unincorporated are classified as self-employed, but the self-employed whose businesses are incorporated are classified as wage and salary workers, because technically they are paid employees of a corporation.

3. A household consists of all persons—related family members and unrelated individuals—who occupy a housing unit and have no other usual address. A housing unit is intended as separate living quarters, and encompasses single-family houses, townhouses, condominiums, apartments, mobile homes, single rooms, and group quarters where residents share common facilities or receive formal or authorized care or custody. There were 112 million households in the United States in 2003.

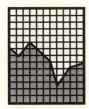

48
Unit Labor Costs:
Business Sector

Unit labor costs (ULC) represent the relationship of labor costs per hour to productivity. When compensation per hour increases more (or declines less) than productivity, ULC increase. Similarly, when compensation increases less (or declines more) than productivity, ULC decline. ULC may also be considered as compensation per unit of output, or the share that compensation is of output. The level and movements of ULC reflect one aspect of cost pressures on prices.

Where and When Available

The measure of unit labor costs is prepared on a quarterly basis by the Bureau of Labor Statistics (BLS) in the U.S. Department of Labor. The data are published in a monthly news release and in the BLS monthly journal, *Monthly Labor Review* (www.bls.gov).

Preliminary data are prepared in the second month following the quarter to which the data refer (May for the first quarter, August for the second quarter, November for the third quarter, and February for the fourth quarter). The data are available at the same time as the *productivity* data and follow soon after publication of the *gross domestic product* measures. The data are initially revised in the subsequent month, and then two months later along with the release of the preliminary data for the following quarter. Annual revisions are made every year as more data become available.

Content

Unit labor costs are defined as the ratio of compensation per hour to *productivity*. This is equivalent to the ratio of compensation to output (real business *gross domestic product*), because the labor hours terms in the numerator and denominator cancel out algebraically, as shown in the following formula:

$$(48.1)$$

$$\text{ULC} = \frac{\dfrac{\text{Compensation*}}{\text{Labor hours}^\dagger}}{\left(\dfrac{\text{Productivity}}{\dfrac{\text{Real GDP}^{\#}}{\text{Labor Hours}^\dagger}}\right)} = \frac{\text{Compensation*}}{\text{Real GDP}^{\#}} = \frac{\text{Compensation per}}{\text{unit of real GDP}}$$

Compensation for work covers the wage, salary, and fringe benefit income of employees, plus the income of self-employed persons, part of which is attributable to wages as distinct from profits.

The business sectors are derived from the *gross domestic product* (GDP) definitions. The GDP value-added concept counts output as the sum of the incomes associated with employee compensation, business profits, interest payments, depreciation allowances, and indirect business taxes. It excludes purchased materials and services used in production. Business sectors exclude not-for-profit organizations, household output, rental value of owner-occupied housing, and general government. The nonfarm business sector also excludes farming. The ULC measures are expressed as an index.

The ULC indexes are currently based on 1992 = 100.

The ULC data are seasonally adjusted.

Methodology

Compensation data for unit labor costs are obtained from the income side of the *gross domestic product,* which is based on *employment* from the establishment and household surveys, *average weekly hours,* and average hourly earnings. An additional estimate is made for the wage component of self-employment income based on data on hours worked by proprietors from the household survey of employment; the estimate assumes that proprietors

---

*Wages, salaries, and fringe benefits and the wage component of income from self employment.

†Hours worked by paid employees, the self-employed, and unpaid family workers.

#Gross domestic product, excluding households, not-for-profit organizations, rental value of owner-occupied housing, and general government (adjusted for price change).

Table 48.1

Unit Labor Costs: Business Sector (annual percentage change)

1995	1.9
1996	0.5
1997	1.3
1998	3.2
1999	1.8
2000	4.0
2001	1.6
2002	−1.1
2003	−0.3
2004	1.0
1995–2004 (annual average)	1.3

work for the same hourly earnings as employees in the industry. Productivity is based on data for the *gross domestic product, employment,* and *average weekly hours* as described in labor-hour *productivity.*

Accuracy

There are no estimates of sampling or revision error for the unit labor cost (ULC) data. However, because ULC are closely linked to *productivity* measures, ULC revision error is assumed to mirror that of productivity. In 19 of 20 cases, the second quarterly revision (four months after the preliminary data) of labor hour productivity differs from the preliminary index by −1.4 to 1.4 index points.

Relevance

Unit labor costs data indicate cost–price pressures. When ULC increase significantly, businesses may raise prices to maintain profit margins. Analogously, when ULC increase slightly or decline, profit margins can be maintained with little or no price increases or even price declines. There is a two-way street between ULC and prices, however, because ULC are affected by cost-of-living wage increases made to compensate for price increases. Moreover, in addition to ULC, prices reflect the demand for goods and services, production costs other than ULC, such as purchased-materials prices (see *producer price indexes*), *interest rates,* the impact of weather on food, and the effect on energy prices of actions taken by the Organization of Petroleum Exporting Countries to control oil production. Thus, ULC are an important, but not necessarily a determining factor of price movements. As in the case of labor-hour *productivity*, quarterly changes in ULC reflect short-term movements in output associated with changes in economic activity over the business cycle. Consequently, ULC movements over several quarters should be observed to determine more basic trends.

Recent Trends

From 1995 to 2004, unit labor costs fluctuated within a range of –1.1 to 4.0 percent (Table 48.1). ULC changes were negative in 2002 and 2003. Over the entire nine-year period, ULC increased at an average annual rate of 1.3 percent.

Reference from Primary Data Source

Bureau of Labor Statistics, U.S. Department of Labor. *Monthly Labor Review.* Monthly.

49
Value of the Dollar

The value of the dollar represents the foreign exchange price of the U.S. dollar in relation to other nations' currencies. It affects the competitive position of U.S. goods in world markets. If the dollar rises in value, and offsetting changes in the prices of exported and imported goods and services are not made, U.S. exports become more expensive to foreigners and imports become less expensive to Americans. If the dollar falls in value and offsetting changes in the price of exported and imported goods and services are not made, U.S. exports become less expensive to foreigners and imports become more expensive to Americans. Measures of the value of the dollar differ according to choices of groups of currencies, weights, and weighting methodologies. The data are provided in nominal values of market exchange rates and in real values of exchange rates adjusted for price change.

Where and When Available

Three nominal and three real value-of-the-dollar indexes are prepared by the Federal Reserve Board (FRB). The six indexes are published in a statistical release (H.10) and in the monthly statistical supplement to the quarterly FRB journal, *Federal Reserve Bulletin* (www.federalreserve.gov).

The indexes are provided daily (Web site only), weekly, and monthly. The weekly data are published on Monday for the previous week. The monthly data are published the first business day of the month for the previous month. The monthly data for the real indexes are revised as more accurate information becomes available.

Content

The six value-of-the-dollar indexes represent the average foreign exchange price of the dollar in relation to the currencies of a group of nations. The nominal indexes are based on exchange rates used in actual market transactions. Real exchange rates are nominal exchange rates adjusted for price movements in the United States and abroad. Different groups of countries are covered by the three nominal indexes: the broad index, the major currencies index, and the other important trading partner (OITP) index (Table 49.1).[1] The list of countries included in these indexes is re-evaluated annually.

The *broad index* is the most comprehensive of the three indexes. The index is composed of the currencies of 25 countries, plus the euro currency area of 12 countries. These countries represent the major trading partners of the United States. Individually, they were selected if they accounted for at least 0.5 percent of U.S. nonoil merchandise imports or U.S. nonagricultural merchandise exports in 1997 (merchandise refers to goods as distinct from services). Collectively, these countries accounted for 93 percent of U.S. nonoil merchandise imports and 91 percent of U.S. nongold/nonmilitary merchandise exports in 2003. The base period of the broad index is currently January 1997 = 100.

The *major currencies index* covers the subset of broad-index currencies that circulate widely outside the country of issue. The index is composed of seven currencies, including the euro. Its movements suggest shifts in the competitiveness of U.S. goods versus goods produced by other industrial countries. It is also an indicator of financial market pressures on the dollar. It accounted for 50 percent of U.S. nonoil merchandise imports and 54 percent of nongold/nonmilitary merchandise exports in 2003. The base period of the major currency index is currently March 1973 = 100.

The *other important trading partner (OITP) index* covers a subset of the broad-index currencies that generally do not circulate or trade widely outside the country of issue. The index is composed of nineteen currencies from Latin America, Asia, the Middle East, and Eastern Europe. Its movements suggest shifts in U.S. competitiveness in its trade with those regions. It accounted for 43 percent of U.S. nonoil merchandise imports and 37 percent of U.S. nongold/nonmilitary merchandise exports in 2003. The base period of the OITP index is currently January 1997 = 100.

The value-of-the-dollar indexes are not seasonally adjusted.

Table 49.1

Value-of-the-Dollar Indexes: Country Coverage
(in order of U.S. trade importance in 2003, largest first)

Broad index (26 countries including Euro area)	Major currencies index (7 countries)	OUTP (19 countries)
Canada	Canada	—
Euro area*	Euro area*	—
China	—	China
Japan	Japan	
Mexico	—	Mexico
United Kingdom	United Kingdom	—
Korea	—	Korea
Taiwan	—	Taiwan
Hong Kong	—	Hong Kong
Malaysia	—	Malaysia
Singapore	—	Singapore
Brazil	—	Brazil
Switzerland	Switzerland	—
Thailand	—	Thailand
Australia	Australia	—
Sweden	—	—
India	—	India
Philippines	—	Philippines
Israel	—	Israel
Indonesia	Sweden	Indonesia
Russia	—	Russia
Saudi Arabia	—	Saudi Arabia
Chile	—	Chile
Argentina	—	Argentina
Columbia	—	Columbia
Venezuela	—	Venezuela

*The Euro-area countries in order of U.S. trade importance, largest first, are: Germany, France, Italy, Ireland, Netherlands, Belgium/Luxembourg, Spain, Austria, Finland, Portugal, Greece.

Methodology

The weights used to combine the individual currencies in the value-of-the-dollar indexes are calculated from the dollar value of internationally traded manufactured, mineral, and agricultural goods. The weights are revised annually based on new trade data.

The value-of-the-dollar indexes use geometric averaging of the individual exchange rates. Geometric averaging, in contrast to arithmetic averaging, treats relative exchange rate currency increases and decreases symmetrically.[2]

The weights are designed to reflect the international trade competitiveness of U.S.-produced goods. They are based on each country's bilateral share of trade with the United States, as well as trade shares in third countries where both the United States and a foreign country compete for sales. For U.S. imports, a country's weight is its share of U.S. merchandise imports, excluding oil imports. For U.S. exports, two weights are calculated. One weight represents each country's share of U.S. nongold/nonmilitary merchandise exports, and measures the competition between U.S. goods and the country's goods in the country's home market. The other export weight reflects competition in a third country between imports of U.S. goods and goods from a competing country. It is defined, formally, as the sum of the shares of U.S. exports to third-market countries multiplied by the shares of the competing country's exports to the third countries in those countries' imports. The overall weights are weighted averages of these three weights.

The bilateral export weights exclude trade in military goods and gold, and the bilateral import weights exclude oil. Military goods are not considered to be heavily influenced by trade competitiveness, because political and strategic factors dominate price differentials between U.S.- and foreign-produced goods. Oil and gold are largely homogeneous products that are priced in world auction markets, which reflect global supply and demand rather than U.S. bilateral trade alone.

The weights are revised every year, based on updated data. For the current calendar year, the weights reflect the trade flows of the year before the immediately preceding year. Because trade data become available with a lag and are also subsequently revised, weights for the current calendar year are subject to at least two revisions. The weights used initially are based on trade data of two years earlier; they are revised later when the data for the immediately preceding year become available, and they are revised again when the data for the calendar year become available. For example, weights for the index calculations for January 2006 will first be based on 2004 trade data; later in 2006, they will be revised to reflect 2005 trade volumes; and in late 2007, they will be revised to reflect 2006 trade flows. Weights may also be affected by occasional revisions of past trade data.

Indexes of the real value of the dollar are based on differential movements of *consumer price indexes* (CPI) in the United States and other countries to convert nominal to real exchange rates. In order to compensate for the late availability of the CPI for some countries, initial estimates of the CPI values for the current month and recent months are based on extrapolations of the most recent twelve-month in which data are available for each country.

Accuracy

There are no estimates of sampling or revision error for the value-of-the-dollar indexes.

Relevance

The value of the dollar affects the U.S. economy in several ways. It influences the competitive position of U.S. goods and services in export and domestic markets, inflation, Federal Reserve monetary policies on *interest rates,* and stock prices (*stock market price aggregates and divided yields*).

When the dollar is perceived to have become low in relation to its intrinsic value compared with other currencies, the effect is thought to raise U.S. production and prices, while when the dollar is considered to have become relatively high, the effect is thought to lower U.S. production and prices. For production measures, see *industrial production index* and *gross domestic product;* for price change measures, see the *consumer price index, producer price indexes,* and *GDP price measures.*

But changes in the dollar are not transmitted to prices in a one-to-one relationship. Part or all of the dollar changes may be offset by opposing changes in export and import prices, as American and foreign exporters try to maintain market shares rather than profit margins. Thus, a fall in the dollar may be followed by a partial, but not fully compensating, increase in U.S. export prices and a decline in import prices, while a rise in the dollar may be followed by a partial decrease in export prices and increase in import prices. The extent of these "pass-throughs" of price changes that partly or fully offset changes in the value of the dollar can be calculated in relation to *import and export price indexes* through the preparation of supplementary trade-weighted exchange rates.

This is further complicated because income increases in the United States generate more of an increase in U.S. imports than comparable income increases in foreign countries generate in U.S. exports. This pattern suggests that in order to maintain a stable surplus or deficit in the *balance of payments* in the long run, continual devaluations of the U.S.

dollar would be required when the rest of the world grows at least as fast (on a trade-weighted basis) as the United States.[3]

The value of the dollar also affects monetary policies by which the Federal Reserve influences the economy. For example, large deficits in the U.S. *balance of trade* are financed by foreigners who invest funds in the United States. If the dollar declines or is expected to decline in the future, this funding may be cut back, potentially leading to rising *interest rates,* declining asset prices, and further downward pressure on the U.S. dollar. In this situation, the Federal Reserve is faced with the prospect of allowing greater increases in interest rates, which may raise the likelihood of a recession. For the Federal Reserve, this international dimension complicates the development of appropriate policies.

In addition, the value of the dollar affects *stock market price aggregates and dividend yields* through foreign investment in equities of U.S. corporations. Expectations of a rising value of the dollar may induce foreigners to buy U.S. stocks, which in turn tends to raise stock prices, while expectations of a declining value of the dollar lessen the incentive for foreigners to buy U.S. stocks (or heighten the incentive to sell U.S. stocks), which tends to lower stock prices.

Because consumer price movements in the United States and other industrialized countries are often in the same general range, the nominal dollar indexes that are based on currencies of industrialized countries, notably the major currencies index, are similar to the real dollar indexes. By contrast, because industrializing countries typically have greater price increases and sometimes encounter hyperinflation rates that no longer occur in industrialized countries, the nominal and real indexes that contain higher proportions of industrializing countries have increasingly divergent movements. Generally, when the nominal and real indexes have large differential movements, the real index is relevant for assessing the long-term impacts of currency fluctuations on trade patterns.

Recent Trends

The three value-of-the-dollar indexes increased in nominal and in real values with occasional interruptions from 1995 until 2002, and then typically declined in both nominal and real values during 2003–04 (Table 49.2). For the entire 1995–2004 period, in nominal values the OITP index increased the most, the broad index showed the next largest increase, and the major currencies index showed virtually no change. Also

Table 49.2

Value-of-the-dollar Indexes: Nominal and Real

	Broad index (January 1997 = 100)	Major currencies index (March 1973 = 100	OITP (January 1997 = 100)
Nominal			
1995	92.7	83.4	92.5
1996	97.5	87.2	98.2
1997	104.4	93.9	104.6
1998	115.9	98.4	125.9
1999	116.0	96.9	129.2
2000	119.4	101.6	129.8
2001	125.9	107.7	135.9
2002	126.8	106.0	140.6
2003	119.3	93.0	144.0
2004	113.8	85.4	144.0
Real			
1995	86.9	81.0	104.1
1996	89.0	85.9	101.1
1997	93.7	93.2	102.1
1998	101.7	98.2	115.5
1999	101.1	98.0	114.2
2000	105.0	104.7	114.3
2001	111.1	112.2	119.0
2002	111.3	110.6	121.6
2003	104.6	97.7	123.3
2004	100.0	90.7	122.1

for the entire 1995–2004 period, the most striking difference between the nominal and real values of the indexes occurred in the major currencies index, in which the nominal index showed little change while the real index increased, in contrast to the OITP index, in which the nominal values increased much more than the real values.

Reference from Primary Data Source

Board of Governors of the Federal Reserve System. *Statistical Supplement to the Federal Reserve Bulletin.* The *Statistical Supplement* is monthly, and the *Federal Reserve Bulletin* is quarterly.

Notes

1. The three indexes were introduced in 1998. See Michael Leahy, "New Summary Measures of the Foreign Exchange Value of the Dollar," *Federal Reserve Bulletin* (October 1998). This was updated in Mico Loretan, "Indexes of the Foreign Exchange Value of the Dollar," *Federal Reserve Bulletin* (Winter 2005).

2. For example, consider an exchange rate index that contains only two currencies, with the two currency weights equal to one-half each. Suppose that one currency's exchange value against the dollar doubles (i.e., appreciates by 100 percent), while the other exchange value is cut in half (i.e., depreciates by 50 percent). A geometric average of two exchange rates—$2^{1/2} \times 0.5^{1/2} = 1$—implies no change in the exchange rate index, while taking an arithmetic average—$(1/2 \times 2) + (1/2 \times 1/2) = 1.25$—implies an appreciation of the dollar.

3. C. Fred Bergsten and John Williamson, "Overview: Designing a Dollar Policy," and Michael Mussa, "Exchange Rate Adjustments Needed to Reduce Global Payments Imbalances," both in *Dollar Adjustment: How Far? Against What?* ed. C. Fred Bergsten and John Williamson (Washington, DC: Institute for International Economics, 2004), pp. 23 and 120.

Appendix:
Note on Sampling and
Nonsampling Errors in
Statistical Surveys

This description of sampling and nonsampling errors in statistical surveys draws largely on explanations by the U.S. Bureau of the Census, to which I have made certain additions. For example, see U.S. Census Bureau, "Housing Vacancy Survey: Source and Accuracy of Estimates," Second Quarter 2004, p. 5, www.census.gov. I have also benefited considerably from discussions with Thomas Jabine.

Sampling Error

Sampling error in statistical surveys (e.g., of households, businesses, or governments) occurs because of variations in the estimated data obtained from any one sample that was surveyed rather than from the entire population. A sampling error can be calculated only for a survey sample that is a probability sample (sampling errors cannot be calculated for nonprobability samples). In a probability sample, the survey respondents are fully representative of the entire population being surveyed, such as of its demographic, economic, and geographic characteristics. A probability sample requires that each member of the entire population has a known chance of being selected as a survey respondent (referred to as random selection). The calculation of a sampling error assumes that estimates of the different samples conform to a statistical normal distribution (bell-shaped curve) that has no biases or skewness.

The measure of sampling variability is referred to as the standard error, which gives the probable error associated with the data estimate that is based on a single sample. The sample estimate and its standard error enable the preparation of confidence intervals, which are ranges that would include the average results of all possible samples with a known probability. For example, if all possible samples were selected, each of the samples being surveyed were under essentially the same general conditions and use the same sample design, and an estimate and its standard error were calculated for each sample, then the approximate confidence intervals are:

•For one standard error, which is a confidence interval of approximately 67 percent, with a likely chance of occurring in two of three cases, 67 percent of the intervals from one standard error below the data estimate to one standard error above the data estimate would include the average of all possible samples.

•For 1.6 standard errors, the confidence interval is approximately 90 percent, with a likely chance of occurring in nine of ten cases.

•For two standard errors, the confidence interval is approximately 95 percent, with a likely chance of occurring in 19 of 20 cases.

•For three standard errors, the confidence interval is approximately 99 percent, with a likely chance of occurring in 99 of 100 cases.

Of course, as the confidence interval increases from one to three standard errors, the size of the probable error in the data estimate also increases. Also, the average data estimate derived from all possible samples may not be contained in any particular computed interval. However, for a particular sample, one can say with specified confidence that the average data estimate derived from all possible samples is included within the confidence interval.

Nonsampling Error

In contrast to sampling errors, nonsampling errors in statistical surveys cannot be calculated from the sample itself. Examples of nonsampling errors are definitional difficulties in the survey questions, differences in the interpretation of questions, inability or unwillingness of respondents to provide correct information, inability to recall information, errors made in the collection or coding the data, errors made in processing the data, errors made in estimating missing data, and failure to represent all units of the entire population in the sample.

While nonsampling errors are more difficult to measure than sampling errors, there are ways of assessing certain aspects of nonsampling errors. For example: Sometimes special studies are undertaken to measure nonsampling errors, such as post-numeration surveys, and by checking the sample survey data against comparable data such as from administrative records of government programs. Another technique in assessing nonsampling error is to analyze the nonresponse rate in a survey to evaluate the characteristics of the nonrespondents. And in the case of coding classifications such as of industries or occupations, an independent verification of the sample is a check to see that the coding was done correctly.

References

Administrative Office of the United States Courts, Statistics Division. *Statistical Tables for the Federal Judiciary.* Quarterly.

Aizcorbe, Ana M., Arthur B. Kennickell, and Kevin B. Moore. 2003. "Recent Changes in U.S. Family Finances: Evidence from the 1998 and 2001 Survey of Consumer Finances." *Federal Reserve Bulletin.* January.

American Bankers Association. *Consumer Credit Delinquency Bulletin.* Washington, DC. Quarterly.

Aten, Bettina H. 2005. "Report on Interarea Price Levels." Bureau of Economic Analysis, U.S. Department of Commerce. April 25. Available from the Bureau of Economic Analyses, www.bea.gov.

Bergsten, C. Fred, and John Williamson. 2004. "Overview: Designing a Dollar Policy." In *Dollar Adjustment: How Far? Against What?* ed. C. Fred Bergsten and John Williamson. Washington, DC: Institute for International Economics.

Board of Governors of the Federal Reserve System. *Federal Reserve Bulletin.* Quarterly.

———. *Statistical Supplement to the Federal Reserve Bulletin.* Monthly.

Broda, Christian, and David Weinstein. 2005. "Are We Underestimating the Gains from Globalization for the United States?" *Current Issues in Economics and Finance,* Federal Reserve Bank of New York. April; idem. 2004. "Globalization and the Gains from Variety." NBER Working Paper 10314. National Bureau of Economic Research. Cambridge, MA.

Bureau of the Census, U.S. Department of Commerce. *FT 900 Supplement.* Monthly.

———. *Housing Starts.* Monthly.

———. *Housing Vacancy Survey.* Quarterly.

———. *Income, Poverty, and Health Insurance Coverage in the United States.* Annual.

———. 2005. *Alternative Poverty Estimates in the United States: 2003.* June.

———. *Manufacturers' Shipments, Inventories, and Orders.* Monthly.

———. *Monthly Retail Trade and Food Services Survey,* and *Annual Benchmark Report for Retail Trade and Food Services.* Monthly and Annual.

———. *Price Index of New One-Family Houses Sold.* Quarterly.

———. *Quarterly Revenue for Selected Services.* Quarterly.

Bureau of the Census, U.S. Department of Commerce, and U.S. Department of Housing and Urban Development. *New Residential Sales.* Monthly.

Bureau of Economic Analysis, U.S. Department of Commerce. *Survey of Current Business.* Monthly.

Bureau of Economic Analysis and Bureau of the Census, U.S. Department of Commerce. *U.S. International Trade in Goods and Services.* Monthly.

Bureau of Labor Statistics, U.S. Department of Labor. *CPI Detailed Report.* Monthly.

———. *Business Employment Dynamics.* Quarterly.

———. *Employment and Earnings.* Monthly.

———. *Job Openings and Labor Turnover.* News Release. Monthly.

———. *Monthly Labor Review.* Monthly.

———. *Multifactor Productivity Trends.* Annual.

———. *PPI Detailed Report.* Monthly

The Conference Board. *Business Cycle Indicators.* New York, NY. Monthly.

———. 2001. *Business Cycles Indicators Handbook.*

———. *Consumer Confidence Survey.* Monthly.

Employment and Training Administration, U.S. Department of Labor. *Unemployment Insurance Weekly Claims Report.* Weekly.

Executive Office of the President, Office of Management and Budget. 2004. *Statistical Programs of the United States Government: Fiscal Year 2005.*

Fisher, Gordon. 1997 (revised). "From Hunter to Orshansky: An Overview of (Unofficial) Poverty Lines in the United States from 1904 to 1965." Mimeo. This and the following two papers can be obtained from Fisher at the Office of the Assistant Secretary for Planning Evaluation, U.S. Department of Health & Human Services.

———. 1997 (revised). "The Development of the Orshansky Poverty Thresholds and Their Subsequent History as the Official U.S. Poverty Measure." Mimeo.

———. 1995. "Is There Such a Thing as an Absolute Poverty Line over Time? Evidence from the United States, Britain, Canada, and Australia on the Income Elasticity of the Poverty Line." Mimeo.

———. 1992. "The Development and History of the Poverty Thresholds." *Social Security Bulletin.* Winter.

Fixler, Dennis J., and Bruce T. Grimm. 2005. "Reliability of the NIPA Estimates of U.S. Economic Activity." *Survey of Current Business.* February.

Frumkin, Norman. 2004. *Tracking America's Economy.* 4th ed. Armonk, NY: M.E. Sharpe.

Fuchs, Victor. 1965. "Toward a Theory of Poverty." *The Concept of Poverty.* Washington, DC: Chamber of Commerce of the United States.

Garner, C. Alan. 1998. "A Closer Look at the Employment Cost Index." *Economic Review.* Federal Reserve Bank of Kansas City. Third Quarter.

Groshen, Erica L., and Simon Potter. 2003. "Has Structural Change Contributed to a Jobless Recovery?" *Current Issues in Economics and Finance.* Federal Reserve Bank of New York. August.

Institute for Supply Management. *ISM Manufacturing Report on Business.* Tempe, AZ. Monthly.

———. *ISM Non-Manufacturing Report on Business.* Tempe, AZ. Monthly.

Kennickell, Arthur B. 2003. *A Rolling Tide: Changes in the Distribution of Wealth in the U.S., 1989–2001.* Federal Reserve Board. September.

Kowalewski, Kim. 2000. "Personal Bankruptcy: A Literature Review." CBO Paper. Congressional Budget Office. September.

Leahy, Michael. 1998. "New Summary Measures of the Foreign Exchange Value of the Dollar." *Federal Reserve Bulletin.* October.

Lee, Tae-Hwy, and Stuart Scott. 1999. "Investigating Inflation Transmission by Stages of Processing." *Cointegration, Causality, and Forecasting: A Festschrift in Honor of Clive W.J. Granger,* ed. Ralph Engle and Halbert White. Oxford, UK: Oxford University Press.

Liang J. Nellie, and Steven A. Sharpe. 1999. "Share Repurchases and Employee Stock Options and Their Implications for S & P 500 Share Retirements and Expected Returns." *Finance and Economics Discussion Series* no. 59. Federal Reserve Board.

Loretan, Mico. 2005. "Indexes of the Foreign Exchange Value of the Dollar." *Federal Reserve Bulletin.* Winter.

McGuckin, Robert H., Ataman Ozyildirum, and Victor Zarnowitz. 2004. "A More Timely and Useful Index of Leading Indicators." The Conference Board. October.

Meyer, Peter B., and Michael J. Harper. 2005. "Preliminary estimates of multifactor productivity growth." *Monthly Labor Review.* June.

Modigliani, Franco, and Richard Sutch. 1996. "Innovations in Interest Rate Policy." *American Economic Review.* March.

Mortgage Bankers Association of America. *National Delinquency Survey.* Quarterly.

———. *Weekly Mortgage Applications Survey.* Weekly.

Mussa, Michael. 2004. "Exchange Rate Adjustments Needed to Reduce Global Payments Imbalances." In *Dollar Adjustment: How Far? Against What?* ed. C. Fred Bergsten and John Williamson. Washington, DC: Institute for International Economics.

National Agricultural Statistics Service, U.S. Department of Agriculture. *Agricultural Prices.* Monthly.

National Association of Realtors. *Real Estate Outlook: Market Trends and Insights.* Monthly.

National Research Council. 1995. *Measuring Poverty: A New Approach,* ed. Constance F. Citro and Robert T. Michael. Washington, DC: National Academy Press.

Office of Federal Housing Enterprise Oversight, U.S. Department of Housing and Urban Development. *House Price Index.* Quarterly.

Orshansky, Mollie. 1963. "Children of the Poor." *Social Security Bulletin.* July.

———. 1965. "Counting the Poor: Another Look at the Poverty Profile." *Social Security Bulletin.* January. Reprinted in the *Social Security Bulletin* in October 1988.

Paquin, Paul, and Melissa Squire Weiss. 1997. *An Analysis of the Determinants of Personal Bankruptcies.* Fall Church, VA: Capital One Financial Corporation. October.

Perozek, Maria G., and Marshall B. Reinsdorf. 2002. "Alternative Measures of Personal Saving." *Survey of Current Business.* April.

Ruser, John, Adrienne Pilot, and Charles Nelson. 2004. "Alternative Measures of Household Income: BEA Personal Income, CPS Money Income, and Beyond." Available from the Census Bureau, www.census.gov.

Ryscavage, Paul. 1999. *Income Inequality in America.* Armonk, NY: M.E. Sharpe.

Schreft, Stacey L., and Aarti Singh. 2003. "A Closer Look at Jobless Recoveries." *Economic Review.* Federal Reserve Bank of Kansas City. Second Quarter.

University of Michigan, Survey Research Center. *Surveys of Consumers.* Ann Arbor. Monthly.

Visa U.S.A. Inc. 1996. *Consumer Bankruptcy: Causes and Implications.* July.

WEFA Group, Resource Planning Service. 1998. *The Financial Costs of Personal Bankruptcy.* Burlington, MA. February.

Zarnowitz, Victor. 1999. "Theory and History Behind Business Cycles: Are the 1990s the Onset of a Golden Age?" *Journal of Economic Perspectives.* Spring.

Index

About the Author

Norman Frumkin, an economics writer in Washington, D.C., has a long-standing interest in macroeconomic analysis, forecasting, and policies, and in improving the quality of economic statistics. He has worked in the U.S. government, industry, as an independent consultant, and has taught courses on the use of economic indicators. He is also the author of *Tracking America's Economy,* 4th ed. (M.E. Sharpe, 2004).